MASTERING

HOLD'EM
&
OMAHA

POKER

D0916772

This book is dedicated to Howard Schwartz of Gambler's Book Club—a man who has helped in uncountable ways to bring reliable gambling literature out of the dark ages of homespun wisdom and into the modern age of reason.

MASTERING

HOLD'EM
&
OMAHA

POKER

MIKE CAPPELLETTI
with exclusive contributions from
MIKE CARO

CARDOZA PUBLISHING

Cardoza Publishing is the foremost gaming publisher in the world, with a library of over 200 up-to-date and easy-to-read books and strategies. These authoritative works are written by the top experts in their fields and with more than 9,500,000 books in print, represent the best-selling and most popular gaming books anywhere.

FIRST CARDOZA EDITION

Copyright © 2003, 2007 by Mike Caro & Mike Cappelletti
- All Rights Reserved -

An earlier version of this book was released under the title *Poker at the Millennium.* This version has been *completely* updated and revised.

Library of Congress Control Number: 2004101411
ISBN: 1-58042-139-3

Visit our web site—www.cardozapub.com—or write for a full list of books and computer strategies.

CARDOZA PUBLISHING
P.O. Box 1500, Cooper Station, New York, NY 10276
Phone (800) 577-WINS
email: cardozapub@aol.com
www.cardozapub.com

ABOUT THE AUTHORS

MIKE CAPPELLETTI
The Leading Authority on Omaha

Mike Cappelletti, renowned for his poker expertise, was formerly a lawyer for the U.S. Department of Justice and is also a well known bridge player who has represented the United States in international competition. He has authored many bridge books, articles and bidding conventions including *100 Bridge Problems* and *"Cappelletti Over No Trump."* In the 1980s, the *New York Times* referred to Mike and his wife as the best husband-and-wife bridge partnership in the world.

Mike wrote the bestselling textbook on teaching players how to win at Omaha poker, *Cappelletti on Omaha*, and has been writing columns for poker publications for almost two decades. In addition to *Mastering Hold'em and Omaha*, his poker books include *The Best of Cappelletti on Omaha* and *How to Win at Omaha High-Low Poker*. Mike Cappelletti is often referred to as the leading authority on Omaha.

MIKE CARO
The Legendary "Mad Genius of Poker"

Mike Caro is the world's foremost authority on poker theory and he is the founder of Mike Caro University of Poker, Gaming, and Life Strategy. His expertise and accomplishments have been cited in publications from *Newsweek* to *Playboy* and in over fifty books.

Caro is the author of more than a dozen best-selling poker and gambling books, videos and DVDs including *Caro's Book of Poker Tells, Caro's Most Profitable Hold'em Advice,* and *Caro's Fundamental Secrets of Poker*. Additionally, he was an expert collaborator and the key contributor for Doyle Brunson's *Super System* and *Super System 2*.

The Mad Genius has devoted much of his life to analyzing poker and making his research available to the public through his standing-room-only seminars, advanced reports and poker books. For more than 30 years, Caro has used mathematical analysis and his own revolutionary computer programs to pioneer the powerful modern poker strategies that thousands of world-class and serious professionals plus millions of player use today.

TABLE OF CONTENTS

Mike Caro and Mike Cappelletti

When Mike Cappelletti asked me to collaborate with him on this book over 12 years ago, I recognized immediately that his concept was very powerful. Why not devote a poker book to the two most significant modern forms of the game? Fine. But, there was a slight problem with his plan. Apparently, Mike hadn't heard about the long delays between the time I traditionally announce a project and the time I actually complete it. Soon, he couldn't wait for me any longer and was asking to incorporate my research and material, and to write the hold'em sections himself—along with his wife Susan. He said, as long as I gave him rights to my research, he would have no problem presenting the material in a way that would allow poker players of all skill levels to understand the book and profit from it.

So, it was agreed. Decided. A done deal. Time passed. About seven years later (and I'm not making this up, folks), along comes a completed manuscript for what he called *Poker in the Nineties*. I mean, I'd forgotten all about it. I got a little worried. Was this Cappelletti fellow trying to steal away my stature as being the poker industry's greatest procrastinator?

I felt challenged. He asked me to do a quick read-through and to suggest changes and additions. He hoped to have the book on the market within a month. Well, here it is, many years later and I'm just adding the final touches. Call it revenge. Who wins? I think you do, because this book teaches powerful winning techniques and tactics for both Omaha (including high-low split) and hold'em.

One thing you should know: The Omaha sections are almost entirely based on Mike Cappelletti's analysis and teachings. While he has demonstrated to me that he has significant professional expertise in all forms of poker, Omaha is his specialty. For that reason, I have not interfered with his chosen method of teaching. And he has decided to present my concepts and advice on hold'em—which he selected—without much intervention. Occasionally, you'll see the lessons interrupted with comments from me, usually enhancing points I wanted to add.

And now you know the reason why we can truthfully say, "Twelve years in the making."

1 INTRODUCTION

In poker, one of the parties can have an *edge*, whether the edge results from skill or from the conditions of the game. The bottom line is simply that the more skillful poker players expect to win in the long run. Although anything can happen in the short run at the poker tables, the knowledgeable players are indeed exploiting the less knowledgeable and making money from their weaker play.

Poker players fall into two broad categories: winning players and losing players. Winning players—and that category includes professional players—know that the key to winning requires knowledge, discipline, and dedication. While gambling may be fun for them, they generally don't play for the sake of gambling or for the thrills. They play to win money. Losing players can be divided into two broad categories: action junkies, and calling stations who like to play lots of hands by calling along. Both groups play too many hands, but the difference is that the action players like to bet and raise while the calling stations like to, well, just call.

Poker is a zero-sum game, which means that for there to be winners, there must be losers. But even though not everyone will become a winning player, there are enough less-than-serious poker players—those who don't try to improve their game—to make it a profitable situation for that other group: the winners.

Anyone can be a winning poker player. If you're not already, you will be after reading this book. And if you already are, you'll win more and more often. If you regularly play medium limits or higher, what you're about to read will bring you many thousands of dollars in profit every year.

Hold'em and Omaha Opportunities

One of the main reasons why hold'em and Omaha appeal to both winning and losing players is because the three-card flop creates lots of winning possibilities. Just as a lottery ticket can produce sudden riches, any two-card hand can make a big winner if it hits the right flop.

Winning players like hold'em because, by following a relatively simple formula—playing sound starting hands in early seats and artfully loosening up their starting requirements in late position—they're virtually guaranteed a long-term profit against average or weaker players. Hold'em strategy is simple in concept (though complex in execution) such that even average-level players have a large advantage over the unknowledgeable. Thus, at hold'em, the unknowledgeable not only lose to the good players but also to the average ones.

Losing players like hold'em because it's exciting and because any random hand can flop into pure gold. Both action players and calling stations play too many hands, ignoring the realities of hand quality and position. They will win occasionally on their "good" nights, but in the long run, they will be consistent losers. And on those good nights, action players will thoroughly enjoy themselves and get lots of action. Because of the good night upside, many action players will convince themselves that they're winners, when in reality, they're not.

It's worse for the calling stations. They're not overall winners, and unless the cards run all over them, that is, break hugely in their favor (or they're in a game in which their opponents just give away money), they have even fewer winning nights.

Losing players love the flop so much that they often go out of their way to see it, even with hands that have little chance of winning. Although the flop can perform miracles, all good players realize that miracles are infrequent. Thus, good players usually pay to see the flop when justified by the percentages. It is often cost effective to see the flop, if possible, for a small additional price. For example, when a player has one of the blinds, he can often see the flop for no extra cost or for less than the other players pay.

One of the biggest differences between winning and losing players is that the former fold much more frequently before and after the flop. Again, it comes down to percentages. When playing further into a hand is no longer profitable in the long run, winning players will fold, while losing players will continue to put more chips into the middle—either unaware that they should fold, or stubbornly pursuing lucky cards.

In the past several years, a large number of losing players have converted from hold'em to Omaha and Omaha high-low because they enjoy better results and get more action for their money. Not only is Omaha fun for them, but even an average-to-bad player will have an occasional good night at the game.

At Omaha, especially on a lucky night, an overall loser can play questionable hands and still do reasonably well. That is probably the main reason why it is getting easier and easier to find a great Omaha game. A quick look at current trends tells us that Omaha, especially Omaha high-low, is really catching on.

> **NOTE**
>
> While much of the information presented in subsequent chapters focuses on limit hold'em, most concepts and principles can be extended to both pot-limit and no-limit hold'em, assuming that the size of the potential bets in relation to the pot size and the blind size is taken into consideration. As in all forms of poker, the larger the established pot in relation to your proposed investment, the more liberally you should play.

2 THE WINNING FORMULA

INTRODUCTION

At the outset of your poker career, you should be aware of these important questions: Is your objective entertainment or to win money? Are some games easier to beat than others? What makes a profitable game?

The answers to these questions determine how you'll approach the game before you even sit down at the table to play. Following are four fundamentals of beating poker games:

---

1. If you're trying to win money, seek out weak opponents!
2. Be aware of the level of your own poker skills. Quoting Clint Eastwood: "A man has to know his own limitations."
3. Once in a game, seek out the best seat, if there is one.
4. A combination of the above: Change tables if the game is not to your liking! Don't get stuck in a rut.

Opponents can be weak players because they don't know how to play well or because they aren't playing up to their capabilities. In either case, you should seek games with weak opponents. If you find yourself playing in a game with mostly good players, don't expect to make much money, or any at all. You may want to play in a "good" game for the challenge or to improve your skills, and either is a valid reason; but if you want to make money, seek out games where your opponents are weaker and the profit opportunities are better.

Remember the old poker paradox, a good game is not a good game; a good game is a bad game!

You'll soon learn how to distinguish the players who are contributing money to the table (those who play too many hands), those who usually make sound decisions (they make good percentage decisions), those who are easy to play against (they merely call as oppose to raise), and those who are dangerously overaggressive (dangerous to their bankroll as well as yours).

As you gain more experience, you'll consciously or unconsciously find yourself **shifting gears** more often; that is, modifying your level of aggressiveness and the number of hands you play, so that you can more optimally adjust your style of play to various situations.

THE MENTAL GAME

It is important to evaluate where you best "fit in" while you're honing your skills. Since you're intelligent enough to be reading this book, you're probably smart enough to start off by playing poker—whether hold'em or Omaha—according to a solid formula of winning principles and strategies. As you gain more experience, you'll consciously or unconsciously find yourself shifting gears more often, keeping your opponents off balance and improving your profit potential.

You must learn what to do in a loose poker game as well as a tight one, and you also must be able to apply your knowledge. You'd be surprised how many intelligent players take the trouble to learn what to do and then *don't* do it. Often, that's because their emotions get the best of them.

In poker, you must always stay emotionally in control, no matter what. If the cards run bad, they run bad. Bad cards aren't your fault and there's nothing you can do to prevent that. But if you let bad cards spoil your good judgment, that's your fault. Never let bad cards cost you more than they should.

STRATEGIC POSITION AT THE TABLE

Your choice of seat has a big influence in the dynamics of how you'll play, and consequently, your results. Sitting **behind**, acting after certain players, as opposed to sitting **in front,** acting before them, can make a big difference in your monetary expectations. Of course, you should strive to maneuver into the best seat for any given game.

Sometimes it takes a lot of maneuvering to get into the most favorable location and situation. How do you know when have you arrived?

In poker, you like to have players who bet and raise frequently on your right, and the nonraisers on your left. This is obviously the case when you're considering loose calls and don't want to get raised. You can take advantage of an overly aggressive bettor on your right by frequently raising his bets. This often eliminates all other competition leaving you heads-up against an opponent who does not always have cards.

You can pick up a lot of small pots when the rest of your competition are on drawing hands and fail to improve, for example, when two suited cards in the flop fail to get a third flush-making card. In no-limit and pot-limit games, it is particularly unfavorable to have a big bettor on your left. When faced with this situation, you have to tighten up on your calls so you don't end up throwing away hands that, if raised, have to be folded. The good news is that you might do some lucrative trapping on good hands, since more players make loose calls against aggressive bettors and end up sucked in for your check-raise.

But all in all, when you're faced with an aggressive player on your left in cash games, try to change seats.

LUCK AND KNOWING WHEN TO QUIT

Picture yourself sitting in front of a large mass of chips in a very comfortable game where you can just sit back and coast. You're playing your best game and continue to stack up more chips as the hours go by. When and if things appear to be changing negatively, then you'll probably wisely consider quitting and harvesting your big win. Hopefully you'll be there many times.

An important part of playing poker is preparing to encounter and handle both extremes of luck. Occasionally, you'll be unable to win a hand for several hours. Remember that all luck is temporary and will even out in the long run.

The following chapters contain much of what you need to know to win at both hold'em and Omaha games in the long run. But no book creates a winner or a loser. They can give you knowledge, but only you can choose to apply or not apply what you learn.

PROFIT POTENTIAL

If there are two or more hold'em games of different stakes, the lower-stakes games are almost always looser and wilder than their higher-stakes counterparts. And generally, the quality of play at the higher-stakes tables is better and more closely resembles correctly played poker. The higher the stakes, the more value players place on what they're playing for and the more important it is for players to win, or to at least not lose their money too quickly.

How much a skilled player actually wins per hour in the long run—usually between one to two double-size bets per hour—is determined by the average quality of the games he plays in and how effectively he plays them.

3 THE BASICS OF PLAY

In hold'em and Omaha, each player has a hand that consists of two parts: a private part, consisting of the cards in his possession, and a public part, consisting of five **community cards**, called the **board**, that are dealt face up in the middle of the table. These community cards are shared by all **active players**, i.e., ones who have not folded and are still in competition for the **pot** (the collection of all bets up for grabs by all active players). Every player's goal is to win that pot, either by having the best hand after the betting is over, or by forcing other players out of action by making bets they won't meet.

THE DEAL

The cards are dealt clockwise starting with the player to the left of the dealer position. Casinos and cardrooms usually have a nonplaying dealer to distribute the cards. The position at which the dealer would be sitting if the players dealt the cards is indicated by a disk known as the **dealer button** (or simply **button**). The term *button* is also used for the player sitting in that position or for the position itself.

The button rotates clockwise around the table after each hand so that each player, in turn, has a chance to enjoy that favorable position.

Prior to receiving cards, the player immediately to the left of the button must put in chips usually equivalent to half a minimum bet with the player to his left (two to the left of the button) putting in chips equivalent to a full bet. These are called **blind bets** or, more commonly, **blinds**. The smaller bet or player making that forced bet is called the **small blind** and the larger forced bet is called the **big blind**.

These forced bets are made before any player receives cards and are made to stimulate action. Without money to contend for, no player would have a reason to enter a pot except with the best of cards. Blinds have the same purpose as antes in stud games. In fact, some variants of hold'em, particularly no-limit hold'em tournaments after a certain number of rounds, have both blinds and antes. Limit games, which is the focus of this book, have only blinds.

THE FOUR BETTING ROUNDS

Now let's describe a hand of play in detail, which is identical for hold'em and Omaha, including the blinds and the four rounds of betting:

Preflop: The First Round of Betting

Each participating player starts out by receiving his private cards, called **downcards** or **holecards**—two in hold'em and four in Omaha. These cards constitute the entire private hand—no more downcards will be dealt. Cards are dealt clockwise starting with the player to the left of the button until each player has received the proper number of downcards.

Hold'em Starting Cards

Omaha Starting Cards

25

On this first round only, the betting starts with the first player to the left of the small blind, and it will proceed clockwise around the table. Each player in turn, after looking at his downcards, has the option of calling the big blind bet, folding, or raising. Of course, at this point, no one knows which five cards will turn up on the board. Every player is betting on potential, on the hopes his eventual five-card hand will end up being the winner. Some starting combinations are better than others, as we shall see.

When the betting is equalized, that is when every active player has put into the pot as much as any other player, and assuming that two or more players remain, additional cards will be dealt. Occasionally everyone folds in response to a raise on the preflop round, in which case the raiser wins the blinds (and any bets that were made) and the hand is over.

Flop: Second Round of Betting

Assuming more than one player remains after the first round of betting, the dealer deals three cards face up on the table. These three board cards, called the **flop**, belong equally to all players. This is followed by a second round of betting.

The Flop

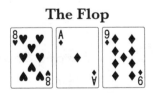

Turn: Third Round of Betting

Assuming that more than one player remains after the second round of betting, the dealer adds a fourth board card face up on the table, next to the three cards of the flop. This is called the **turn**. There is a third round of betting.

The Turn

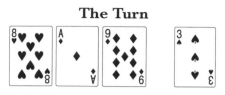

River: Fourth and Last Round of Betting

If more than one player remains in the hand, the dealer adds a fifth board card face up on the table. This is the **river**. At this point, each remaining player has formed his best five-card poker hand. This is followed by a fourth and final round of betting.

The River

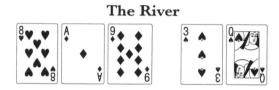

THE SHOWDOWN

If two or more players remain in the pot, there is a **showdown**, and the best five-card poker hand will be the winner. If the best hands are identical, which can happen if players have the same rank of private cards or if the board is being played, the pot is split among the winners. Second-best or worse hands get nothing.

WINNING BY DEFAULT BEFORE THE SHOWDOWN

At any time, if one player makes a bet that no one else is willing to meet, there is no showdown and the bettor wins the pot immediately. That can happen at any point in the hand, not necessarily on the last round of betting. It doesn't even matter how weak a player's hand is. If opponents fold to his betting, the hand is over and the player whose bet went unmatched, wins by default.

An active player does not reveal his private cards until the end of the hand, when all bets have been completed and two or more players remain to contest the pot.

BEST HOLD'EM AND OMAHA HANDS

The cards used to form the final winning hand are handled differently in hold'em than Omaha. Let's look at that now.

Final Hold'em Hand

In hold'em, your *entire* poker hand is drawn from seven cards—the two downcards plus five common board cards. If two or more players remain in the pot for the showdown after the last round of betting, the best five-card poker hand wins by using any five of those seven cards. This hand can be formed by using both of your downcards in combination with three board cards, one downcard in combination with four from the board, or even by using all five board cards.

The last case is called **playing the board**. If more than one player plays the board and no one else can produce a better hand, then those players divide the pot equally. If you play the board, you obviously can do no better than tie with every remaining player.

Final Omaha Hand

In Omaha, the combining rules are different. You start with four downcards. To form your best five-card hand, you *must* use precisely two of your downcards in combination with precisely three of the community cards. You may not use four board cards or all five, as in hold'em, or even just two board cards; in Omaha, your final hand must use exactly three board cards to form your final five-card hand.

Omaha High-Low

Omaha is also played as a high-low game, alternatively called **Omaha high-low**, **Omaha high-low split**, **Omaha high-low 8-or-better**, or some variations of these wordings. Omaha high-low split is usually played **8-or-better** to qualify for low; that is, the lowest hand with five different cards 8 or lower wins half the pot. And the best high hand wins the other half of the pot. If one player holds both the best high and the best qualifying low, he wins the entire pot, called **scooping**. If there are no qualifying low hands at the showdown, the highest hand scoops the whole pot. If there is a tie for either end of the pot, those players with equal high or low hands will split that portion of the pot.

GAME STRUCTURES

The three main betting structures in hold'em and Omaha are *limit*, *pot-limit* and *no-limit*. There are also several hybrid structures, such as "Cavern rules," where high Omaha is played as limit before the flop, pot-limit on the flop, and no-limit after the last two rounds.

In the United States, most hold'em and Omaha games are played as limit, while in Europe, the predominant structure played is pot-limit. Televised hold'em events, including those of the World Poker Tour and many of the events of the annual World Series of Poker in Las Vegas, are typically played as no-limit hold'em.

Let's see what each of these structures mean.

Limit

Limit or **fixed-limit** means that the permissible amount of each bet on any given betting round is pre-established. In American casinos, limit games are described by two numbers, such as $5/$10 or $10/$20. The first number states the fixed amount of all bets and raises during the first two rounds of betting and the second number states the amount of all bets and raises in the last two rounds of betting. Thus, unless a player has less money on the table than required and must go all in, the amount of each bet or raise is set at those amounts.

In a typical 10-handed casino $10/$20 hold'em game, the first two players to the left of the button will have each **post** the blinds—in other words, they will put the forced blind bets into the pot prior to cards being dealt. The small blind in a $10/$20 game will be $5 (also known as a **half-bet**) and is made by the player immediately to the left of the button. The big blind will be $10, and is made by the player two seats to the left of the button.

The first person to voluntarily act in this opening betting round, the preflop, will be the third player to the left of the button—the player immediately to the big blind's left. That player can **call** the $10 unit bet, put an equal amount of money into the pot, **raise** $10, making the total bet $20. Or the player can **fold**, discard his two cards without placing money into the pot, and have no further interest in the hand.

All bets and raises made during the first two rounds of betting are in the lower range of the two-tier structure, in this case, in increments of $10. All bets and raises made during the last two rounds of betting, on the turn and river, the fourth and fifth board cards, respectively, are upper range of the two-tier structure, in increments of $20.

Pot-Limit

In **pot-limit**, the blinds are identical to those in limit. For example, in a $5/$10 game, the blinds would be $5 and $10 for the first two positions, and in a $10/$20 game, they would be $10 and $20 in the same first two positions.

However, in pot-limit, bets are not limited to any fixed amount, but rather may be any amount up to the *present* size of the pot. The minimum bet must be equal to the size of the previous bet or raise, or if none has yet been made, the size of the big blind. A bet can fall anywhere between the upper and lower limit as long as the restriction on the raise is observed. For example, if the pot is $80 and an opponent bets $40, the size of the pot is $120. When it is your turn to play, you have several options:

1. You may fold.
2. You may call the $40.
3. You may raise by calling the $40, making the pot $160, and then raising any amount from $40, the size of the previous bet, to $160, the new size of the pot.

No-Limit

In a **no-limit** game, which usually has a blind structure similar to those described above, any size bet or raise is permissible, with the proviso that any raise must be at least the amount of the previous bet. There is no upper limit other than the amount a player has available on the table (and that his opponents can match).

TABLE STAKES

There is one exception to the minimum bet required in any game. If any player runs out of chips and cannot meet the minimum bet, that player is said to be **all in** and is not forced out of the pot. He can continue to receive cards until the river.

If other active players remain with sufficient chips to continue betting, a **side pot** is created that the all-in player does not participate in and cannot win. No player can lose more than the chips or cash in front of him at the start of a hand; nor can he win more than that amount from any one player. This concept, which is enforced in virtually every cardroom, is called **table stakes**. Players who need or want more chips can buy them whenever they're not actively involved in a hand—but not while a hand is in progress.

No player can bet more than the amount he has on the table. Nor is he liable for more than that amount. If one player bets more than another player can call, that player may put in all the chips he has, but he cannot be forced out of the pot. He can win from any one player only as much as he can call. This forms one or more side pots that players who are all in cannot win. Such betting is called **betting on the side**.

4 HOLD'EM PREFLOP CONCEPTS

The most important single decision you make in hold'em occurs when you receive your two-card private starting hand. That decision is not just whether to play or not to play, but in cases where you decide to play, whether to call or raise. Most of your profit derives from choosing the right preflop options.

Many decisions about the quality of your position will be borderline. You must take into consideration the nature of your opponents, the structure of the game, your image, and all other factors you would normally think about before deciding whether to play aggressively, conservatively, or not at all.

This chapter is devoted entirely to getting you on the right road to profit by making certain you know when to call, when to raise, and when to fold before the flop. Playing the preflop correctly is often enough to win against weak-to-average competition, assuming you have judgment that is at least equal to your unsophisticated opponents on the other betting rounds.

BASIC PREFLOP STRATEGY

Basic strategy presumes playing only good hands to the flop. When good hands compete against inferior hands, the good hands are the favorite and will show a profit in the long run. It is simply a matter of how much. You should be able to win, or at least hold your own simply by playing a conservative basic strategy. Indeed, even an experienced expert uses a similar basic strategy as a point of departure before expanding his play into opportunistic situations as skill and experience dictate.

To sum up, a skilled hold'em player follows basic strategy most of the time, and diverges only to increase profit in certain situations and to provide a diversionary tactic.

A basic strategy for winning at hold'em is so sufficiently objective that even non-experts should be able to play it and show a profit in a typically loose game. Basic strategy is based on the simple concept that you play only good hands with good percentages going for them. This means you should play **tight** (i.e. few hands), but aggressive once you're involved in a pot.

Basic strategy under most conditions constitutes a winning formula of play. As a basic strategy player, you conservatively sit back, expending little or no money, and wait for winning hands. When a high-percentage hand finally comes along before the flop, for example, A-Q or better, you usually want to raise before the flop so that you can build a big pot. Sometimes you'll just call.

However, in poker you should not *always* do the same thing in the same situation. If you become too predictable, you provide opponents with extra opportunities to outplay you. To maximize your profits, you need to vary your play.

Thus, basic strategy allows occasional instances of going against conservative guidelines, for example, aggressively pushing preflop with lesser hands such as **suited connectors** (two cards of adjacent ranks in the same suit, such as the 5 and 6 of diamonds) when you're in last or near-last position. And the emphasis is definitely on *occasional*. These plays won't always show a profit in themselves, but by keeping opponents off balance and guessing, they improve your overall profit expectation.

THE IMPORTANCE OF POSITION

One of the main differences between winning and losing hold'em players is how they play before the flop. And the key to playing before the flop is position. **Position**, a player's relative order of acting compared to opponents particularly with respect to the number of players acting after his turn, is very important on any given round of betting. And although the importance of position is ingrained in the mindset of all experienced hold'em players, new players seldom realize just how important it is.

In hold'em, if you act after an opponent on the first betting round, you act after that opponent on every betting round, except the temporary situation in which the blinds act last on the first betting round. Conversely, if you act before an opponent on the first betting round, you must act before that opponent on every betting round. Unlike stud and some other forms of poker, in hold'em the positional advantage or disadvantage remains constant throughout the hand.

Since position remains the same for all four rounds of betting with the notable exception of the blinds in the preflop round, the player who acts last has the biggest advantage. Why is acting last such a great advantage? Simply stated, it's because you see what players in front of you do before making your decisions. If you find yourself acting first with a weak or marginal hand, you don't have the advantage of seeing what the other players do first. For example, if you are the first of three players to act, you might bet, be raised and then be reraised and have to surrender your bet. If you're last to act, however, and there is a bet and a raise before the action reaches you, you can pass, risking nothing. Over time, that adds up to a lot of bets you'll win, lose, or save.

If you want to be a winning hold'em player, you must learn how to play your position. You must learn that sitting in an early seat is a trap. Even world-class professional players have lost a lot of money by needlessly playing too many hands from early positions. Many hands that are good enough to play in last or middle positions should be folded in early positions. If you want to be a winner, you must discipline yourself to avoid the early-seat trap.

Your positional disadvantage dictates that you'll often have to fold lesser hands because of pressure behind you. You'll frequently get raised after you're in a pot, either before the flop or at some point afterwards. If your hand is mediocre and not worth the extra chips, you'll soon learn that you can often save even more money by avoiding the whole problem before it starts: by anticipating the positional disadvantage and folding weak hands even before the flop. Think of it as "an ounce of prevention" approach.

For the same reasons that you must play conservatively in early positions, you should play much more liberally from the late positions, especially in last position. Because the benefits of acting last are so great in hold'em, some amount of loose and aggressive play from late position is winning poker.

EARLY POSITION

Count the number of players still to act behind you, up to and including the blinds. You might count double for a player who is known to raise frequently. If this number is six or greater, you're in an early position regardless of the number of players in the game.

Most experienced hold'em players instinctively know that they must be conservative in early positions, but few realize just *how* conservative. Even world-class players make the mistake of playing losing hands from early position, because they assume that they must play a representative selection of their better hands. But if they knew the actual expected cost of playing these hands in most games, they would probably fold many of these hands much more frequently.

There is a big difference between which hands you can profitably play in tight-aggressive or normal games and in loose "no-fold 'em hold'em" games. In a very loose game, you might profitably play certain lesser hands from early positions simply because most of the other players are playing much worse hands. But if you seem to be experiencing bad luck with these hands, it might not actually *be* bad luck. When in doubt, play more conservatively and wait for better hands.

If you're at a full-table fixed-limit tight-aggressive or normal (as opposed to loose) hold'em game in early position with several aggressive players still to act, there are strong arguments for playing only the very best hands. It may even be true that under certain rare playing conditions (with very aggressive and very skilled players behind you), playing even some of the very best hands may not be profitable. Always remember though, you have no reason to enter a hand if it is not clearly profitable.

The positional disadvantage of acting early in hold'em is so strong that you should usually play premium hands conservatively before the flop. Even the natural strength of aces can be seriously negated. There are many flops in which aces in first seat are vulnerable. Few players understand this overpowering hold'em concept. Even players who joke and whine about losing big with aces fail to realize how much cheaper it could have been. Otherwise put, when you finally pick up two aces, but you're in first seat, you may be a flop away from going to the bank. And, with many flops, when there are several aggressive players behind you, your aces could develop into an underdog to win the pot.

NOTE FROM CARO

Get it through your head that most hold'em players, even winning hold'em players, including professionals and world champions, lose vast sums of money from early positions over their entire poker-playing careers! I always teach that most hold'em hands thought to be profitable in early positions are clearly losers. But until recent analysis, I did not realize just how important this concept is and how many hands it pertains to. ↓

> While it is hard to make an accurate estimate, I believe that 40 percent of all the early-position hands, with which professional hold'em players enter the pot, lose money for them over their lifetimes! Average players (who don't know what to do when they see the flop) lose money on about 60 percent of all hands they play from early positions over their lifetimes. The reason I'm emphasizing this point now is so that you can make an immediate, very critical, improvement in your play and understand the underlying concepts that make this advice differ from other advice you may have encountered. Keep in mind that hold'em is not a strategically balanced poker game. It is overwhelmingly geared for late position play.

Early Position Hands to Play

Once you understand the vulnerability of early position, you have to mix up your play. Practical poker demands that you play more hands than strict theory advises. For the most part, you do this to disguise the conservatism of your early position play. However, don't use it as an excuse to play too many hands. Now, this may seem counterintuitive and somewhat contradictory, but once you have established an aggressive image and have psychological dominance in your game, you can actually play more hands profitably.

In a game with mostly good players and with a positional disadvantage, you should wait for very good starting cards before voluntarily getting involved. Thus, the operative rule here is that you must be very patient in early positions. Until you learn to employ a more deceptive approach, the starting hands that you can expect to play profitably in good games in first or second seat are A-A, K-K, Q-Q, A-K (suited or unsuited), and A-Q suited.

The odds against being dealt one of those hands are 33.9 to 1. So, using just that power grouping, you're going to expect to throw your cards away almost every time. In a game with tight players, you should not play an ace with anything unsuited less than a king or a queen in this very-early-to-act situation. If you want to extend this conservative recommendation (in slightly looser games), K-Q suited, J-J, and A-Q of mixed suits are the only profitable additions with many tough and sophisticated players still to act. Even with this extended list, it is still 21.1 to 1 against your picking up one of these hands.

Although these early standards may seem ultraconservative, it may even be that these standards are too liberal.

In a normal to tight-aggressive hold'em game, you might adjust the above tight standards a bit by allowing yourself a few more hands, especially if there are few aggressive players behind you and if your image is tight-aggressive—that is, you're "feared" rather than "loved." You might also play a few lesser hands if you would be betting into sophisticated players who tend to be aggressive. There are other reasons why you might make adjustments (or speculative "investments" in lesser hands) so always study your opponents' preflop tendencies.

Early Position: Additional Hands to Play

If your image is tight-aggressive and you're playing against several loose and easy-to-outplay opponents, you can add hands such as J-10 suited, 10-9 suited, and medium-high pairs. Medium pairs and medium-high suited cards of adjacent ranks can be played from early positions if opponents tend to be loose but not aggressive (they call often but seldom raise). However, when you play A-Q, A-J, or A-10 from early positions, you'll frequently be either outgunned or out-positioned (or both), even in loose games in which these hands may be profitable. Even when your opponents in later positions tend to have lesser hands than you, their superior positions may give them an overall advantage.

Why play at a disadvantage? You should not voluntarily enter into situations where you may be an underdog.

As the early positions become less early, you can add a few more hands to your arsenal of playable holdings. Extending the spectrum of hands you're willing to play from an early position is justifiable mainly for image and psychological reasons. Obviously, if your opponents know that you play only super top-notch hands, your playing effectiveness greatly decreases.

However loose the game and however weak the opposition, though, unpaired, unsuited, medium-quality hands should not be played from an early position. And in most normal to tight-aggressive hold'em environments, you should not play the following unsuited hands, or anything worse, from early position: A-10, K-J. Play A-J only in average to weak games.

Early Position: To Raise or Not to Raise

When you're in an early seat before the flop, very few hands actually have enough of an edge over opponents to justify a raise, though you should sometimes raise to protect fragile hands, such as paired tens through kings and K-Q. Many professional-level players raise too often preflop when another player has already called the big blind. A more profitable play is often to just call and see the flop cheaply.

The prime justification for an early raise is that it will greatly enhance your chances of either taking a pot right then or narrowing the field to just one other competitor. Even so, knowledgeable players raise too often before the flop, costing themselves long-run dollars by not simply calling.

In a typical hold'em game, it is often okay to just call as an option instead of raising from an early position. In fact, in a loose game or tournament, it is often a mistake to raise. It depends mostly on the caliber of opponents sitting behind you. It also depends somewhat on your image, more specifically the aspect as to whether you're "loved" (loose) or "feared" (tight).

There are good arguments for early-position raising before the flop. Many of these arguments are well thought out and powerful. But, on balance, extensive analysis shows that for anything less than a high pair or perhaps K-Q, the minuses of early raising can often outweigh the pluses for a typical hold'em game.

If you judge that your typical opponents are likely to call and see an unraised flop with inadequate hands, you should not discourage this practice by raising, since their starting-hand inadequacies will cost them money in the long run. This is money you'll get a share of. The typical opponent wastes a lot of money by continuing to make mistakes on subsequent betting rounds, so it must be wrong to discourage such opponents from entering the pot.

Too many otherwise skilled hold'em players are too aggressive before the flop in early positions. In many games, most hands make more money if you just call the blind bets, rather than raise from an early seat.

Determining whether on not you should raise depends mostly on these three factors:

1. Position
2. Type of game
3. Expected reaction from opponents still to act

If a raise might immediately take the pot or get you heads-up or against, rarely, two players, then the raise is usually justified on many reasonable hands. You either take the pot now or on the next round with the cards you have or a good flop which yields a positive expectancy.

You must never lose sight of your prime objective, which is to maximize the amount of money you can win at minimum risk of losing your own money. Position, type of game, and your image all combine to dictate your playing strategy.

Looking Ahead to the Flop

Your hand's possibilities are greatly defined by the three cards coming simultaneously on the flop. If you analyze millions of hands using a computer simulation, you'll see that most of the time you're going to be disappointed by the flop. Unless you have a hand that can profitably drive most flops, that is, a very high pair, a reasonable strategy is to see the flop cheaply. Then, if you have a staying hand you'll be able to outplay your opponents from that point on and win extra money. If your hand is not worth continuing with, you can abandon it more cheaply.

In aggressive games in which raises seem to induce frequent reraises, it is a bad play to raise in early position with A-10 or less, except as an occasional decoy or bluff. Calls or reraises from those who act later put you in an extremely disadvantageous situation. You're out-positioned and are likely to be outgunned also. The fact is, only a few flops can save you. Fold non-premium hands in first or second seat—unless you're playing with weak players in a very loose game and raises before the flop are infrequent.

PLAYING LATE POSITION

In late positions, you sometimes can play medium-strength hands when a lot of players have entered before the flop. This is because the positional advantage on future rounds is enormous, and you might get lucky on the flop. Nevertheless, it is foolish to get involved with hands that have few prospects of getting a flop that you're happy to pursue, so the medium-strength hands we're talking about must have speculative value—in other words, you have reasonable chances of making a straight or a flush. Lesser hands have more potential for "unlucky" bad beats on the last card.

Playing Suited Connectors

If many players pass before the action reaches you, it is wrong to play medium-strength speculative hands such as 8-7 suited or 10-8 suited. Playing suited connections against small fields is a common and costly mistake. You need high-ranking cards to challenge short-handed or one-on-one situations. If you don't have it, don't play. Never play hands that depend on multiway pots for profit if the opportunity for such a pot has been diminished.

It is occasionally correct to play low suited cards such as 8-7 from an early position in a loose field where you can confidently expect many callers—and not raisers. But this hand and hands like it are financial suicide in games against aggressive opponents where there is an increased likelihood of raises and reraises before the flop.

The smaller your starting ranks, the more important it is that they be suited. Even then, they're usually not worth playing. Small suited cards are not good hands. They have few means of making the nuts other than by making a straight, and they can easily get beat, even when they connect with an early straight or flush—and at great expense!

Knowing which hands play better against many opponents and which ones play best against few opponents is critically important in hold'em. You should raise with suited cards only in exceptional situations. Suited cards cry out for a simple call or a pass if they're not strong enough. You don't want a hand with two lower cards in your suit to fold. A simple but reasonable rule of thumb is this: On all borderline raising hands, those with which you cannot decide whether to call or raise, call if the cards are suited, otherwise raise.

Late Raise

A good play you should occasionally make, is to raise in late positions with medium hands before the flop. This may get players to check to you, giving you a powerful advantage after you see the flop. Let's say two players have called the blind from middle positions. You're in late position with J♦ 9♦.

Now the flop comes J♣ 8♥ 10♠.

You're in a doubly powerful position, because you'll get checked to and you have a profitable hand that is confusing to your opponents. A hand that appears confusing is always more potentially profitable in any form of poker than the same hand when its contents can be guessed by your opponents.

Your opponents now figure you for high cards, so psychologically, you own this hand.

Maneuvering Into Last Position!

If the pot has already been voluntarily entered by a player before the action reaches you, you might sometimes force yourself into a late position by raising and getting one-on-one with the original aggressor, chasing out later-position opponents. Then you'll act behind the original bettor for all future betting rounds. This concept of forcing yourself into good position sometimes works in fixed-limit games. It is even better in pot-limit and no-limit games.

When you're in a moderately late position, study players to your left to see if they're going to fold. If you're observant, you'll often pick up signs whether or not a player has interest in the hand. If they're not going to fold, a raise will sometimes be necessary with medium-strong hands. You're not raising with the intent of numerically limiting the field (although this is the effect); you're raising to ensure that you'll have last position on subsequent rounds. If you're not in last position in hold'em, always ask yourself the question: Can I get in last position for a reasonable price?

Late Position: Playing Speculative Hands

If one player calls early and everyone passes to you in late position, you should normally fold with low ranking speculative hands such as 7-6 suited (which hits about 27 percent[1] good flops) or 10-8 suited. It is tempting to occasionally raise in an attempt to drive the blinds out, take the initiative, and leave the spoils up for grabs to just you and the opener. You might also correctly reason that you should often be able to steal this one-on-one pot on the flop if your opponent checks. However, you should raise only if there is little chance that the caller is slow-playing a quality hand. (Some opponents never slow-play any hands.) And, remember, this is meant to be only an occasional play. If you overdo it, it won't work and will only cost you money.

By the way, the term *speculative hand* usually means suited cards. The occasional exceptions are Q-J, Q-10, J-10, and J-9. Neighboring ranks higher than these are seldom primarily speculative. And lower ranks are seldom playable, unless suited.

Late Position: No One Has Entered the Pot

If you're in the late position and all the players acting before you have folded, you sometimes have opportunities to pick up the blinds with weak hands or try to build the pot with strong ones.

You should evaluate in advance which of the blinds is most likely to fold to preflop raises. They will be the prime

---

[1] Sum of 12.5% (four-flush), 11% (open-ended straight), 3.5% (two pair or trips)

targets for the times you raise with weaker hands. With some hands, particularly big cards, big suited cards, and low pairs, there might be a higher profit expectancy—including less money lost—by simply calling, if doing so causes more loose money to join the action.

PLAYING THE BLINDS

If you're one of the blinds, you're in an early position and should enter pots, and especially call raises, with caution. The fact that it costs you a reduced amount to play when you're in a blind position is often consideration enough to stay for the flop. But you must usually see considerable improvement on the flop to call any bets thereafter.

In any form of hold'em, unless your starting cards are powerful, such as a pair of aces or kings in no-limit, you should see the flop for free as the big blind. You have poor position on all future betting rounds, making a raise less desirable, and it keeps your hand deceptive, especially when you sometimes play strong hands that way. For the same reason, if you're either blind, you should frequently just call a raise, even if your hand seems to suggest a reraise. A lot of money is lost by players, especially by professionals, because of overly aggressive play from a blind position. This does not apply in big-versus-small-blind situations, in which aggressive play is helpful.

If the small blind raises and no one else is involved in the pot, there is no hand you should automatically fold if you're the big blind, although you should usually, but not automatically, fold your weakest holdings like 9-4, 6-3, 8-2, and such. Otherwise, you should almost always call one-on-one and see the flop with any vaguely reasonable hand.

The reason to ever fold anything but pure garbage hands is that it gives you slightly more leverage with the majority of hands you do play, assuming your opponents are observant.

NOTE FROM CARO

Sometimes when I'm playing short-handed, especially heads-up, against an opponent who's much too conservative, I throw away even slightly better hands myself—making sure to show them. This encourages too-tight play and allows me to pick up many more pots by betting. Keep in mind that one key to short-handed play is to enter hands much more liberally and win pots often.

If you feel a raise will chase the big blind out and add that forfeited money to the pot, you should raise as the small blind, even with small connecting cards. Otherwise, you'll make more money just calling. Actually, the best hands to reraise with are big ranks, sometimes even just one big rank against a late raiser. These are precisely the kinds of cards that play best one-on-one.

Example: You're in the small blind. The raise comes from the player immediately to the dealer position's right. Dealer position passes. It's up to you.

With 8♠ 6♠, 10♦ 9♣, or 6♥ 5♥, you usually just call. These hands recover some of the disadvantage of letting the big blind in cheaply because they tend to be most profitable multihanded.

With A♠ J♦, K♦ Q♣, or A♣ 8♠, you usually raise. You want to chase the big blind out, because these hands play best one-on-one, with you and your opponent fighting for the forfeited blind.

With high-ranking suited cards, A- K, A-Q, A-J, K-Q, K-J, it's okay either to raise or call as the small blind against a late raise. Mix it up.

Small Blind

In general, given the chance to enter the pot from the small blind for the minimum amount, you should call.

Except in the situations we just discussed (against a late raiser), you should seldom raise or reraise, even with quality hands. However, if you hold queens, kings, or aces when many players are already involved, you raise to build the pot and thin the field.

Raising with anything but the premium pairs is generally not worthwhile, since you sacrifice excellent pot odds and the chance to see the flop before committing further funds. A raise cannot improve your position, since you'll always act first on future rounds of betting. This is an ideal example of where being able to see the flop cheaply overwhelms any advantage you might have of chasing the big blind out. Only consider raising if you find yourself against just one active opponent who is in a late position.

To sum it up, from the small blind, usually just call; rarely raise; occasionally pass and with fairly hopeless hands against players who have flat-called the blind; and usually pass if it has been raised. Playing the small blind, in this manner will make a big difference in your overall profit.

Big Blind

The hands should you play in the big blind when the small blind raises (and no one else has entered the pot) depends on the type of player who raised, but in general, throw away only the following hand types:

- ♠ Unsuited hands whose high card is a jack or lower and whose low card is a 2. Specifically, hands like 3♠ 2♥ through J♠ 2♥.
- ♠ Unsuited hands whose high card is a 5 through 10 and whose low card is a 3. Specifically, hands like 5♠ 3♥ through 10♠ 3♥.
- ♠ Unsuited hands whose high card is a 7, 8, or 9 and whose low card is a 4. Specifically, hands like 7♠ 4♥ through 9♠ 4♥.

All other hands are roughly worth a call, because the big blind is getting current pot odds of 3 to 1 and will have controlling position throughout the last three betting rounds.

Defending Your Blinds

There is a basic concept you need to understand: Don't defend your blind with a bad hand against only one or two opponents, except in the rare case when by calling you go all in.

When you're the big blind and everyone else, including the small blind, folds to a preflop raise, you're getting 3.5 to 1 odds on the chips if you call. Since even bad hands win more than 22 percent of the time, if you were then all in, any hand would have sufficient odds to call. But most of the time you're not all in and defending your blind makes it possible, and likely, that you'll lose more money.

Let's look at a situation to better understand this. Suppose you hold two low cards against a preflop raiser who usually raises with two high cards or a pocket pair. If you fold 18 times, your total loss for those 18 hands would be 18 betting units. If you call 18 times, planning to fold on the flop unless you hit a pair or better, then you would fold about 12 hands on the flop since you hit a "piece of the flop" about one-third of the time. The total loss from the 12 hands you folded on the flop would be 24 units.

In the other six hands when you hit a pair or better, your opponent hits or has a better hand about one-third of the time—that's two hands in which he either flops or started with a better hand. In the four hands when you're ahead on the flop, he outdraws you once. Normally you'll win three and lose three of these six contested hands. Assuming all hands improved on the flop are played to the river, the amount that you lose on the three hands that don't win is slightly more than the gain on the three that you win when you're defending the blind. Overall, as you see, these bad hands have less secondary potential and you're at a tremendous positional disadvantage by always acting first.

However, in those six contested hands, a number of skill factors might affect and change the outcome. Knowing your opponent's weaknesses and what he tends to do with certain holdings, combined with skillful play and occasional bluffing, will give you a significant edge. If the skill factor is merely sufficient to allow the blind defender to counteract the positional disadvantage and break even or do slightly better on the six hands that are contested, you do better overall by not playing them. The bottom line shows that you lose 24 units on the 12 hands where you fold on the flop compared with the 18 units on the 18 hands if you had simply folded initially.

Since you approximately break even on the other six hands when you don't fold, you lose more money by defending your blind with weak cards, except possibly against weak players.

That six-unit difference is difficult to overcome, especially when players are relatively equal in skill level. However, if your opponent is weak—for example, he bets on the flop only when he hits—then you might well make up the six-unit difference through his mistakes. Thus, if you have a big edge in skill or if you have somewhat better than a bad hand, then it is preferable to defend your blind when practical.

Although it is often correct to defend your big blind in a multihanded pot, defending your blind with a bad hand against only one or two opponents usually has a negative expectation. Generally, the worse your hand, the greater the money odds you need to justify further investment. For bad hands you would like about 10 to 1 when there is no threat of reraise. The following is a brief summary of blind-defending situations in an aggressive but slightly loose hold'em game.

If you're in the small blind (half a bet) in the situation where everyone else folds, it is advantageous to have a "chop" (take back your blinds if everyone else folds) agreement with the big blind on your left if the game you're playing in allows chopping. Otherwise, you should raise frequently whenever you have enough to call—very roughly, two cards 8 or higher—and follow through very aggressively. Whenever there are callers (not raisers), you should usually call the half bet because only the big blind can raise after you and you always get adequate odds if there is no raise.

However, if there is a raise before the flop, you generally concede your half blind (rather than put up another one-and-a-half bets) unless you have a very good hand. Occasionally, you may judge that your situational percentages are sufficient to play one of the better blind defending hands described below.

Big Blind vs. Late Position Raiser

If you're in the big blind and everyone else folds against an early-position or very conservative raiser, what you should do depends on what that raiser usually comes in with. The more likely he is to have a high pair, the more likely you are to fold. Conversely, against an aggressive last-seat raiser who would raise with as little as J-9, you're much more likely to put up one bet for the three-and-a-half bets you can win.

The following chart gives your percentage likelihood of winning with two "good" blind-defending hands, 8-6 suited and Q-6 suited and with two "bad" blind defending hands, 8-6 unsuited and 8-2 unsuited, if you were all in against a typical aggressive last-seat preflop raiser (shown in the left column).

	8♠ 6♠	Q♠ 6♠	Q♣ 6♦	8♣ 2♦
J♣ J♦	21%	32%	28%	11%
5♣ 5♦	49%	47%	45%	29%
K♥ 10♥	38%	37%	33%	30%
A♣ 9♦	41%	41%	36%	32%
J♣ 9♦	39%	59%	56%	30%

(For convenience, we have made all suited hands hearts on the left and spades on the top, and all unsuited hands clubs and diamonds. The results would be slightly different if other suit matchups had been chosen.)

If it were a simple question of going all in or not, you would obviously call with any hand. The real-life problem is that if you're not all in, you'll probably be confronted with one or more postflop bets, which will reduce your winning chances significantly. Also, because the raiser acts last, he has a significant advantage. You can lessen the raiser's positional edge slightly by coming out betting.

UNDERSTANDING TYPES OF RAISES

It is essential that you understand the difference between a raise immediately *behind* an early opener and a raise *after* many players have already called. Let's look at them both.

The immediate raise is designed mostly to keep players out and divide the pot among you and one opponent or take it outright. With this raise, either:

♠ You would rather thin the field;
♠ You know that opponents behind you are so weak that they will call if you raise, so raising with a powerful hand earns extra money.

The raise with many players already committed is generally done with a hand that figures to be stronger than most or all hands already involved. You don't mind if everyone calls, because your chances of winning are well above average. Actually, you earn money whether they call or don't call, but for different reasons. Depending on the strength of your hand compared with theirs, your first choice may be that they pass or that they call or that some of them call and the others pass. In all cases your raise is profitable.

RAISING CONCEPTS

Strategic principle number one: You usually don't want to make weak players fold when you have good cards. But, if there are several weak players already calling in front of you, a raise will increase the likelihood of good players folding behind you. However, beware if they don't fold.

And even when a raise is justified because of tight table conditions—where most raises are folded—you're frequently better off just calling if you have suited cards since more callers make better drawing odds.

Arguments for Raising

Here are some general arguments for raising:

- ♠ You can make other players think you're strong and they will check to you, especially on a threatening flop.
- ♠ You might be able to steal the hand on the flop, or at least limit the field so you can steal on the turn.
- ♠ You increase the likelihood that your "fragile" hands, such as pocket queens and medium-high pairs with a big kicker, will win the pot.
- ♠ You help maintain an aggressive image.
- ♠ You might convince late positions players, especially good players, not to call behind you. Later-acting-players detract from your positional advantage. If your raise tends to make an opponent fold medium-ace holdings, then big-king holdings are promoted.

Arguments Against Raising

The above reasons are all true, but they're often not enough to fully justify the raise. There are usually even better reasons for simply calling when a bet has already been made.

Here are some of the general arguments against raising:

- ♠ You give away less information about your hand.
- ♠ You pressure opponents into correctly folding, when they might have incorrectly called the unraised bet with weaker values.
- ♠ Most players who call on inadequate values also make mistakes in subsequent betting rounds—thus, you like to have them in your pots.
- ♠ You "create a monster." That is, if you manage to get enough money into the pot before the flop, the chances of calling on the flop change. Then, not only might you get yourself sucked in with calls and possibly raises, but also, instead of players coming in incorrectly, they're often calling correctly.
- ♠ If you have less money invested, you lose less when you fold on the flop, which is most of the time.
- ♠ You don't help an early caller with a big hand that he was slow-playing.

RERAISING CONCEPTS

While raising with medium-high quality hands is often wrong, a reraise is often correct! Against just the middle or late-position opener, you should reraise from late position with any pair of 9s through queens or A-K, A-Q, A-J, K-Q, K-J, or Q-J unsuited. You may also consider reraising with the smaller pairs you could not profitably play from early positions.

The object is to use the double raise to chase out the competition, solidify your position so that you'll be acting last against the original raiser on all future betting rounds, and force the blind money to be forfeited to the pot. This reraise is also a powerful psychological weapon. In fact, this reraise is so powerful that you should make it a regular part of your hold'em arsenal. We don't recommend that you use it *every* time, because then some players will see what's happening and adapt. Use it as often as you can without making it obvious.

That a particular profitable hand usually wins *more* against many opponents does not mean you shouldn't try to limit the field. Once there's already money invested by opponents, there is treasure left behind when players leave the pot. This treasure will be shared in some proportions by players who stay in the hand and try to win it. As you see, chasing players out of the pot has big value. The main value is not, as commonly thought, to diminish your chance of losing, though that's a factor. The main value is that you and all remaining players share the forfeited treasure.

Think of it as a political race. If there are three candidates and one withdraws, the other two will share those forfeited votes. The votes must go *somewhere*. In poker, the same is true: The pot must go somewhere. And if you're still in the pot, the money is that much closer to you.

Keep in mind that, if a hand makes more money against many opponents than it makes against few, sometimes the benefit of surrendered money may be outweighed by the benefit of having that opponent stick around at unfavorable odds. In hold'em, the value of attempting to limit the field is less on the first round of betting than on later rounds.

It is also a strong move to reraise with a moderately strong hand if several players have just called and the raise comes from the last active player. Suppose fourth position calls the blind. Then fifth position calls, then seventh and finally eighth position. Now ninth position raises. You hold 10♥ 10♣ or A♦ Q♠. Reraise. You're very likely to chase out the blinds and most of the callers. That is a great deal of forfeited money to split among a few players. And your hand is strong enough to be a major threat, especially if you have position.

Playing Strong Hands

Chasing opponents out who have nothing already invested is not the same as chasing opponents out who leave money behind. Actually, it does not matter who the money in the pot belongs to, only that it is there. When someone folds, he is surrendering his share of that pot.

On the first betting round in hold'em, there is little money already in the pot. The benefit of having opponents come in against your strong hand is much greater than the benefit of having them fold. It is often wrong to raise before the flop with a quality hand with the idea of having players fold. You want them to call. An exception is when you chase the blinds out to solidify your position and end up one-on-one against a raiser.

Against the Blinds

If no one has entered the pot, you should raise aggressively from the dealer position or up to two seats to the right of the dealer position. You should call more than normal if the opponents behind you are aggressive. Otherwise, make it your policy to raise with any non-speculative playable hand. Against just the blinds when you're in the dealer position, it is all right to raise with ace-anything and usually with king-anything or two lesser ranks fairly close in sequence.

For example, you're on the button and everyone has passed. You hold Q♠ 9♥. This hand is primarily non-speculative, because its chances of winning with something other than a straight are relatively great. This hand could win by making a pair of queens or 9s, because it is not apt to face more than one opponent and it is not pitting itself against anyone who has already raised or voluntarily called. The best thing that can happen to this hand is both blinds pass immediately. If there is no chance of that happening, the play is not nearly as profitable and you would be better off just calling. Again, always study your opponents' tendencies and mix up your play.

BIG HAND STRATEGY

In fixed-limit games, you should either call or raise with quality hands, but if you're subsequently raised or reraised, you should call only. You may reraise after just calling with a pair of aces or a pair of kings. With anything else, you usually should not reraise after opening quietly. Wait to see what the flop brings, remembering that your position will be poor relative to your opponents on further betting rounds.

In pot-limit or no-limit games, you should just call with a quality hand; however, if raised when holding a pair of aces or kings, make certain you reraise as much money as possible. In no-limit, this means putting either you or your opponents all in.. In pot-limit, you should reraise the maximum if such an action does not leave an opponent an opportunity to bet a substantial amount on the flop.

Keep in mind that, although you should often move all in with major hands in both pot-limit and no-limit games, if you know your opponents well enough, you might do something quite different. You want to bet the maximum amount that will bring the biggest profit. Usually this is the highest wager above the theoretical point at which it doesn't matter in terms of long-range profit whether you get the call or not. Whatever the highest amount that you can "sell" above that neutral point defines your most-profitable wagering choice.

If, by raising the maximum, you'll leave an opponent with a threatening bet opportunity, you should often only call and wait to see what happens on the flop.

Trapping with Aces

Is it correct to simply call with aces before the flop if you're in an early position? Should you then reraise anyone who raises?

The answer, in limit hold'em, is that it all depends. You may be able to argue convincingly for sometimes just calling early with aces and then, if raised, just calling again. In fact, you should do this occasionally in any kind of hold'em game. However, in fixed-limit games, you should seldom just call in early position before the flop with the intent of trapping players. Not with A-K suited, not with pocket queens or kings, and not even with pocket aces. In fixed limit, you would not routinely want to make it three bets after you just called from early position with aces and were raised. Yes, you'll reraise in this situation often, but not routinely. Sometimes, even with aces, it's better to just call. This increases your potential to mislead opponents. Then you act in accordance with what the luck of the flop brings your way, either checking, usually with the hope of making a successful check-raise, or betting.

In pot-limit, the same concept holds true unless you can bet enough to move all in or close to it, or do the same to your opponents. Remember, when you're in an early position, you'll generally remain in an early position through all four betting rounds. This is a serious disadvantage. It does not make aces an underdog before the flop, of course, but it is a factor to be considered.

Aces are profitable even in the earliest positions. But

at the same time, you'll typically make more money with aces or any quality hand in the long run if you pay as little as possible to see the flop in an early position. Sometimes, though, with queens, kings, and aces, you'll make more money by investing the maximum number of raises before the flop. That's the only major exception to the rule, and this only happens if there are already many opponents who have called the previous raise, meaning that your reraise won't chase them out.

If you raise with aces in early position and expect just as many players to stay in the pot as you would by calling, you do want to raise. In such games, where opponents are weak, loose, and show no respect for a raise, it is a clear decision to raise. All opposing hands are significant losers against aces, even when you're first to act.

But in most games, you're often better off just calling with big hands (even aces) from an early position. This entire concept is not just a marginal aid to your profit; it is an overriding force in winning hold'em. It's so strong that many players who would otherwise beat hold'em for small amounts year in and year out are losing today because they're unaware of it.

BLUFFING PLAYS

There is something to be said for check-raising on the flop against a novice, especially if you're into mind games. If you have the goods, you could wait for the double-size bets of the turn or river to raise. If you plan to invest two more units and give up if he does not fold, then you would have to expect him to fold about 40 percent of the time to justify that investment. You might plan to follow through (if he does not fold) and make two more double-bets. If your opponent would fold more than one out of four times after the turn or river, then with this play you would lose less than by folding to his bet on the flop. This situation is highly dependent on your evaluation of your opponent.

The most believable bluff is raising on the turn, rather then betting the river. Although this play has fair chances of making your opponent fold, unfortunately, because of the large investment required compared to pot size, it would need a success rate greater than 50 percent to show a profit if you never have the best hand. Thus, it is advisable to try this play only when you also have some chance of drawing a winner.

But this is a play that you must occasionally make to protect your real hands. If you get caught, you'll be more likely to get paid off in the future when you do have a good hand.

UNDERSTANDING NON-PROFITABLE HANDS

Many players miss the reason why it is almost always terrible to play hands such as Q-8 offsuit. Understanding that reason can automatically help you with many on-the-spot evaluations.

For example, why is Q-9 offsuit much better than Q-8 offsuit?

Well, you can see two reasons readily:

- ♠ 9 is higher than 8.
- ♠ Q-9 has a narrower span, allowing two sets of ranks to form a straight (K-J-10 or J-10-8), rather than just one (J-10-9 for the Q-8).

But the actual advantage of Q-9 over Q-8 is much greater than you would expect even considering those factors. Here's why.

With Q-9, a flop of J-10-8 means you absolutely have the

best hand. The flop K-J-10, while good, does not guarantee that you hold the nuts (A-Q beats you). But with Q-8, you have *no* chance whatsoever of flopping a nut straight. The flop J-10-9 does not do it, because there is a very reasonable chance it is beaten by someone holding K-Q. And that is not just one less hand you win; that is often a financial disaster.

This is just one example of a long category of hands that are not profitable if you're aiming for a straight that has any reasonable chance, however slight, of being best. Straight tries with no chance of flopping an absolutely guaranteed-best straight should be played cautiously, if at all.

UNDERSTANDING CERTAIN HANDS
Pocket Queens vs. A-K

It has long been held that A-K suited or unsuited is much stronger than a pair of queens as a starting hand. This is simply not true in no-limit, pot-limit, or limit. Queens are usually much more desirable. Against heavy betting, you should be more willing to abandon A-K suited without seeing the flop than a pair of queens.

A pair of queens is much more likely to win a major pot than A-K suited when you analyze actual situations. Why many experts have contended the opposite for the past forty years, is hard to explain. But, without doubt, A-K has been overrated and pocket queens have been underrated—as have all medium to high pairs.

Keep in mind that high pairs other than aces are most profitable with few opponents.

Suited Ace

As a rule, A-9 suited and lower should not be played unless no one has entered the pot and you're doing the raising from a late position, you're calling cheaply, or you're one of the blinds. The enormous big-pot potential of the nut flush makes it correct to call when there are two or more opponents that have entered the pot with calls. If a raise precedes your position, however, fold. And by the same token, don't raise either. This is a call or fold hand.

Unsuited Ace-Small

Many hold'em players don't understand the real reason a hand like A-7 of mixed suits is at a disadvantage. For one thing, they overestimate the chances of finding themselves against another ace, especially against few opponents.

It is not so much that you'll always run into another ace, although you often will and it can be expensive when you do—the main problem is that if a player comes in early, there is a good chance that *both* his cards are higher than your 7. Then, if one of his cards pairs, or he starts with a medium pocket pair, you'll be able to win only by pairing your ace—and your 7 won't be much good at all.

THE CONCEPT OF MOMENTUM

It has often been suggested that momentum is a great force in hold'em. Even world-class players routinely play follow-up hands after winning the previous one. Many games give a psychological advantage to the player who's been winning; however, in hold'em, medium hands have less chance of drawing out and continuing the lucky streak. Playing the next hand automatically, especially in limit hold'em, is a long-range bankroll disaster. Paraphrasing and corrupting an old baseball adage, in hold'em, momentum is only as good as your next starting hand.

NOTE FROM CARO

> When you have the right image, have been winning, and own everyone's attention, ignore all the wait-and-see advice and raise whenever it seems remotely reasonable. Keep raising until your image is tarnished. Then go back to the basic plan. When events reestablish your winning image and you have total control, come out firing again. My advice is simple: Before the flop, use the wait-and-see method most of the time unless your image is outstanding at that moment. If you don't have complete psychological control over your table, tend just to call rather than raise.

TABLE OF MISERY

This "Table of Misery" chart assumes you have a pair of deuces through aces and you want to know how often you won't flop trips and an overcard will hit the board. This is strong information. If you have a pair of jacks, you'd either like to see another jack or all cards smaller than a jack. This table gives the likelihood of that *not* happening.

The following chart shows all possible pairs and gives the chances that you won't catch a third card matching the pair in rank and you'll be overcarded.

Starting Pair	Misery Index After Flop
2-2	88.24%
3-3	88.22%
4-4	87.96%
5-5	87.12%
6-6	85.39%
7-7	82.43%
8-8	77.92%
9-9	71.53%
10-10	62.94%
J-J	51.82%
Q-Q	37.84%
K-K	20.67%
A-A	0.00%

This table shows why some of the advice in this book is radically different from other advice you may have encountered elsewhere. If you don't make three of a kind on the flop, then there are overwhelming advantages to having a pocket pair higher than anything on the board. Among the smallest pairs, deuces through fours, there's scarcely a difference in effectiveness. However, with a pair of eights, you're about as likely to be holding a pocket pair higher than anything on the flop as you are to make trips. In simple language, you're twice as likely to get a favorable flop.

As we move up to bigger pairs, this effect is much more pronounced. Therefore, in any situation in which it might be borderline to play a pair of sixes, you should be in a very profitable situation with a pair of nines. Few players understand the extent of this difference. Beginning with a pair of jacks, you're probably going to like the flop. (Of course, this statement is made for the sake of illustration and we're not dealing with straights or flushes or the possibility of opponents holding higher hands or having made them.) This should help you accept two of the contentions of this book more clearly:

- ♠ Medium pairs if played from a late position, are much more profitable than most players think.
- ♠ A pair of queens is usually much stronger than A-K, suited or not.

5 HOLD'EM FLOP CONCEPTS

The flop hits the table. There is perhaps no more exciting moment in all of poker, when so much happens at one time. These three upcards can easily turn a great two-card starting hand into foldable mush or turn two junk cards into pure gold. You now have five of the seven cards of your eventual hand, all for the price of one round of betting. This is quite a bargain compared with seven-card stud, in which five cards are seen only after three rounds of betting.

For beginners, the most-important consideration is which hands to play before the flop. But, once you've opted to participate in a pot, it's vitally important to know what to do when the flop appears. The flop gives everyone the same three common cards to mesh with. After just one betting round, you have well over half of your hand. How to play these first five cards, your own two downcards plus the three common flop cards, is one of the most demanding skills in hold'em.

With the five board cards common to all players, a good leading hand on the flop is likely to hold up. If three deuces happen to turn up on the board, they belong to you as well as your opponents; the high pair in your hand may well make the best hand. If four clubs turn up on the board, your high club in hand may make the highest flush.

The on-the-flop decisions are clearly some of the most challenging. This is where you decide when to proceed and when to fold—important factors in the maintenance of your bankroll. And, for many experienced players, a great share of their profit comes from correctly making decisions on the flop.

This important chapter explores these considerations.

WATCH YOUR OPPONENTS' REACTIONS

As the flop hits the table, look around at the other players instead of figuring out what it did for your hand. (You can look at the flop later.) At this particular moment, some very useful information is available to those savvy enough to look for it.

Quite often even good players make spontaneous facial expressions or other motions, called **tells**, that indicate whether they particularly like or dislike the flop. If this is one of the many hands that you have chosen not to play, this is a great time to study the active players to check out what kinds of hands they bet, call, or raise with. And you can determine whether they play loose or tight, whether they tend to "chase" or fold when behind, "pay off" at the end, and so on. This is information to store in your memory to help when you make subsequent close decisions.

The flop hits the table. You have scrutinized the

NOTE FROM CARO

Watch the players, not the flop, even when you're not involved in the hand. There's absolutely no reason for you to watch the flop. If you do, you'll miss the most important tells in hold'em. The flop will still be there when you're ready to look. Pick out one opponent and watch that player watch the flop. Either the opponent continues to stare at the flop for several seconds or the opponent looks away uninterested. Which was it? Make a decision each time you see that opponent look at the flop. Usually when opponents scrutinize a flop and then nonchalantly look away, they like the flop. They're simply pretending that it doesn't interest them. Conversely, if they continue to stare as if studying the flop optimistically, it probably didn't help them at all. I will not discuss their motives in depth, but I devoted a book (complete with 179 photographs) to that complex topic. It's called *Caro's Book of Poker Tells: The Body Language and Psychology of Poker.*

opposition. Now it is time to commence firing. What are the main guiding principles? If the flop gives you a hand that is very unlikely to lose, you should probably check in an early seat about two-thirds of the time. If the flop completely misses you, you'll probably check intending to fold at the first bet. (In an early seat, it is rare to bluff with nothing—unless you have some specific knowledge about your opponents.)

Very good and very bad hands are relatively easy to play. But planning your campaign after the flop with in-between hands is probably the most skill-intensive area in hold'em. And your position with respect to the button is an extremely important aspect of your planning.

FUNDAMENTAL THEORUM OF HOLD'EM: AGGRESSION

Aggressiveness is the one trait that you must possess if you are going to be a winner at hold'em. You'll be surprised at how often aggressive betting automatically wins a pot. You see it over and over again in hold'em. A player bets or raises, opponents fold, and the pot is won uncalled.

Although players have their own individual quirks and characteristics, all experts and professionals agree that hold'em—even more than most other poker games—is a game that should be played aggressively. There are times as well, as with all things, that it is best to be conservative. And of course, the true wisdom is to know the difference.

Aggressive play is an integral part of the percentages that determine whether a given action at hold'em is favorable. This concept is so important that it is sometimes referred to as *The Fundamental Theorem of Hold'em*. Hold'em has many situations in which an aggressive bet or raise in a given situation will show a profit in the long run. When you make the aggressive move, you have two ways to win: You can show down the best hand or your opponent can fold. When an opponent misjudges your strength and folds hands that would have beaten you at the showdown, you have achieved a desired result. This adds incentive for you to make those aggressive plays.

Those two possibilities, your hand winning or your opponents folding, often total up to a positive expectation. On the other hand, the more conservative or passive actions in a given situation, such as calling or folding, often show a net loss in the long run. When you just call, you have only one way to win: You must show down the best hand.

PLAYING THE IMAGE

Up-for-grabs situations, those in which no one has good cards, occur more frequently at hold'em than at any other form of poker. And since tight images are more successful at winning these pots, a particular Machiavellian principle applies at hold'em: "It is better to be feared than loved."

Mike Caro has an additional and different method of winning. He conveys an always-friendly, wild, and unpredictable image to take advantage of weak opponents' tendencies to call too often.

AGGRESSIVE POST-FLOP PLAY

In most after-the-flop competitive situations, the more aggressive players jockey around (especially when the pot has been enlarged by preflop raises) to further their own

NOTE FROM CARO

Keep in mind though, that there are exceptions to the prevailing path to profit through reasonable aggression in hold'em. Sometimes, against atypical opponents who bluff too often or try to attack the game with too many bets, it's more profitable to surrender the stage and just call (or check and call), letting these players "hang themselves."

NOTE FROM CARO: CARO'S 65-35 TARGET

Aggressive means to bet when checking (or passing) seems like a reasonable alternative or to raise when calling seems like a reasonable alternative. *Conservative* means the opposite. This assumes you've taken the usual strategic things into consideration, such as position and the habits of opponents, and you still cannot decide how to play a hand for certain.

The best approach is to play aggressively about 65 percent of the time and conservatively 35 percent of the time. These are not frivolous figures, but they're hard to apply since so much depends on your judgment and the situation at hand. It is apparent to me that players who opt for the aggressive choice less than half the time get far from maximum value out of limit hold'em. Players who play aggressively 80 percent or more in borderline situations lose effectiveness. When in doubt, try the aggressive approach less than two out of three times. Keep in mind that you'll play aggressively much more often in late positions, but conservatively before the flop more than most experts advise. Actual game conditions and the habits of your opponents also help you decide how often to play aggressively. But, in general...

65 percent aggressive—35 percent conservative—Aim for it!

prospects by intimidating and eliminating less-tenacious competition. Good players usually understand what they're trying to accomplish. They categorize their actions as "taking the initiative," "narrowing the field," or "grabbing the raiser's edge." But many players act aggressively on instinct or are imitating the actions of good players, and often inappropriately. Or they may be simply reacting to previous events.

You often cannot make reliable inferences from after-the-flop raises, apart from realizing that most often these bets and raises are based on marginal rather than truly good cards.

Last Raiser's Advantage

If no one has a good hand on the flop, the player who bets often wins the pot by default This is a situation that occurs perhaps more than one-third of the time. Whenever there are one or more raises on the flop, it is the last raiser who is most likely to win the pot uncalled. Even though well under half of the pots are stolen—perhaps between 10 and 30 percent, depending on the game—being the bettor when no one has much is an edge worth having and worth fighting for. You might refer to the extra percentages of winning by default as a result of betting or raising as "the bettor's equity" or "the raiser's edge."

A number of other tangible benefits are gained by betting aggressively on the flop. There are positional considerations, as well as image factors.

An example of sound aggressive raising strategy on the flop is in the following situation. A player makes a late preflop raise and gets several callers, creating a big initial pot. The flop comes and one of the early players bet. You have a reasonable but not great call, and you would like to compete because of the pot size. But you suspect that the preflop raiser behind you might raise if you call. And he'll frequently do so with nothing but high cards.

In this situation, sound aggressive hold'em play says that if you're going to compete, your chances improve considerably if *you* take the initiative by raising. Here, you're essentially inverting your normal strategy. You raise with lesser marginal hands and merely call with very good hands. Your raise tends to get rid of marginal hands behind you, sometimes including the original bettor, and it puts you in good position for the remainder of the hand. Sometimes, everyone folds. Occasionally, you get reraised; but more often a really good hand, particularly one in front of you, just calls and waits to check-raise on the later rounds, where the bets are double. If the preflop raiser behind you reluctantly folds, he might well have raised if you had not beat him to it.

If you get reraised by the lead better and it is now one-on-one, there is much to be said for either folding or reraising rather than calling! Such hands quite often end without a showdown. That is, either you or your opponent backs down on the turn when the betting doubles. One of the most common sequences of events is that your raise narrows the field to just the two of you. Then you have to decide whether to compete on the turn. What you do is as much dependent upon what your opponent is likely to do as on what you actually have in your hand. If you suspect your opponent is pushing a draw or two big cards, you might decide to call him down or raise on the turn.

CARO SAYS...

Caro discussed the preceding situation in the now-classic *12 Days to Hold'em Succe$$* (1987, Day Eight):

...anytime you're trapped between the bettor and the previous round raiser with medium power (that is, a borderline calling decision), either raise or pass. Don't just call.

Very little is written about what to do when you're between the bettor and an aggressive player. A good understanding of how to act in such situations is an essential ingredient in any professional poker toolbox. When you really do have an appropriate calling hand, you should raise about one-third of the time; about two-thirds of the time you should pass. Remember, it is seldom correct to just call. You'll find that it is not as frightening to raise as you might have expected. Maybe nothing good will happen the first few times, but over the years, you'll discover that a raise will chase out the threat behind you much of the time! Often, that player will actually throw away the best hand!

The times you decided to pass with these borderline calling hands you didn't sacrifice much. Analysis shows that hands most players consider borderline good calls add very little profit. The bottom line is that a raise now and then, when you're considering calling, will often chase the player out behind you and put you in ⬇

> a commanding position against the bettor. If the bettor just calls
> now, he'll likely check to begin the next betting round (if there is
> one). ... If you do decide to adopt this policy permanently, you
> might be giving your bankroll a break. It works!

The Aggressive Image

Playing aggressive hold'em not only will make money
for you when it works, but sometimes, even when it doesn't
work. If your opponents notice that you sometimes raise on
speculation, it greatly helps you win more money when you
have a good hand. Hold'em has many competitive situations,
such as the preceding one, in which it is correct either to
raise or fold. It is often wrong to merely call, because the
"raiser's edge" lets you play with positive percentages.

When you bet or raise, you have two main ways to get
the best of it: Either you have the best cards or nobody calls
you. There is also another way to win a hand in the early
betting rounds; by not having the best cards, being called,
and then improving to make the winning hand. When you're
the caller, the main way to win is having the best cards. Or
you luck out and later make the best hand if it's not the final
betting round.

On any given hand, you may have some valid reason for
just calling. But if you want to be a winner at hold'em, you
must use aggressive betting and raising to gain these extra
winning percentages and to have your share of default wins.
It is extremely important to understand and employ these
two-way actions. With an aggressive "hold'em mentality,"
you often fight fiercely for the "raiser's edge."

After you play hold'em for a while, hopefully you'll get
into this aggressive hold'em mindset. Sometimes, you can
actually feel it clicking in. This is part of what some call
being *in the zone*. Over the long run, sound playing practices
are rewarded by wins, and unsound practices are penalized
by losses.

FLOP TYPES

You'll be greatly aided by categorizing flop types as *strong*, *weak*, and *medium*, or *normal* (sometimes called *mixed*). Many principles and generalities regarding after-the-flop strategy vary depending on the type of flop.

A **strong flop** is one that makes it likely that a relatively strong hand will win this pot. This includes a high pair, three of a suit, and three high cards. A **weak flop**, such as three scattered low cards, immediately suggests that a relatively weak hand might win this pot and that quite likely this pot is up for grabs. (If most of the players remaining in the hand are playing two high cards, a low pair might well win this pot.)

Strong and weak flops occur less than half of the time. The rest of the time (more than half), you see a **medium flop**, **normal flop** or **mixed flop**, (i.e., neither strong nor weak). A medium flop might have one high card and two cards of the same suit. In all hold'em games, medium flops are the most highly contested and the most frequently chased, making them the most difficult to steal.

Your first preference is to get a strong flop that hits your hand. What you least want to occur is a strong flop that does not hit your hand. Your second preference is for a medium or weak flop with a two-card hit: one in which two cards in the flop hit your hand and give you trips or two pair.

Unfortunately, you don't hit a big flop very often: roughly 1 hand in 20 when you start with suited connectors. Much more frequently, roughly one-third of the time, you flop a one-card hit, in which one of your hole cards matches (makes a pair) with a card in the flop. If you have the high pair on board, especially when you have a high kicker, you should usually bet or raise to lessen your competition. This increases your chances of winning without improving.

If you started with a high pocket pair, you're quite happy

to settle for any medium or weak flop, in which your high pair is higher than any card on the board. In other words, you have an overpair. On the flop, having an overpair—or the highest pair with the best kicker and enough chips to bet and push out competition—often produces a winner.

EARLY POSITION BETTING DYNAMICS
Bad Flop

Even if you start with a very good hand in early position, if the additional three cards of the flop don't help you, that good hand might become not so good. You now have two choices. You can be aggressive and bet the flop, or you can become defensive and check. Let's look at both of these choices.

1. Get Aggressive and Bet

Occasionally, you may try what is essentially a drive bluff bet in an early position with a weaker hand. These early bluffs are most effective if made with a hand that has some potential of improving, even if it's a bit of a long shot. Betting with a holding that is not strong enough to justify a normal call is known as a **semibluff**.

The two possibilities, winning when everyone folds or when you hit the best hand, often combine to a positive long-run expectation. In these situations, semibluffing is profitable and a good play to make. One frequent variation of the semibluff is when you raise before the flop with two high cards and follow through by betting a non-useful flop. Be careful, though. If you make this play too often, a good opponent will raise and counterbluff.

If you make an aggressive bet on the flop, you could also get in trouble. Opponents with good hands or ones that sense weakness can now raise you. Those getting pot odds with drawing hands can call. Those with nothing might just fold. The net result in these cases would be that you either win a small pot or lose a big one.

An aggressive raiser who follows through from his aggressive preflop action might raise you out of the pot. If you call and fail to improve, you'll probably fold for the next bet, which on the turn, is now double the amount of the preflop and flop rounds.

2. Become Defensive and Check

If you check after a not-so-good flop, you're sending out invitations to all opponents acting after you to make a high-percentage bet, against which you'll usually fold. But even if you have enough of a hand to call a bet, you still have to act first again after the fourth card and again after the last card, facing these same positional disadvantages on each of the rounds—and at twice the price. Quite often an aggressive opponent will bet and you'll be confronted with the unhappy choice of folding the best hand or making a questionable call. In either case, it will cost you a double-size bet.

The bottom line is that you're at a great disadvantage when you don't know what your opponents will do. Caro calls this situation a "bankroll destroyer."

Good Flop

Even if you happen to get a reasonable flop, for example, top pair with a good kicker, all you can do is bet and hope to get some callers who are not raisers. Unfortunately, you'll often get one or more raises, especially when the pot was raised before the flop. You may feel you should call because they often have marginal holdings, which means you're at least temporarily ahead. But, unless you improve, you now face the pressure of double-size bets and may find it difficult to call along even though you may still have the best hand.

Sometimes when you go into the last card with the best

hand, your tormentors might still improve and beat you—and often it's expensive to find out if they bet into you or raise.

When you do get a good flop, all you can do from early position is bet it or try for a check-raise. The trouble with not betting is you might let your opponent continue for free if he checks. But with the same hand in last seat, you can bet if checked to, or, if you want, raise if a bet has been made. With an excellent hand in early position, you can bet and hope that someone chooses this occasion for a clever raise. You would very seldom reraise with a great hand; you would instead lie low and await further developments.

Very Good Flops

With very good flops, you should check up to one-third of the time to vary your play. Unfortunately, this necessary tactic is problematic. Not only might it get checked around, costing you money, but you risk losing the pot to someone who would normally fold for a bet on the flop, but who greatly improves on the "free" turn card, making, for example, four to a flush or straight.

If an opponent improves to a draw that can hit on the last card and wins one out of five times, he is probably getting good odds on his money, which costs the leading bettor money in the long run. To prevent opponents from getting free cards, you want to stay aggressive. When you get a good flop and become the leading bettor from an early position, with one or two passive chasers, you should drive all the way. These passive chasers usually have overcards or a smaller pair than yours and they have to guess whether you have anything or not.

MIDDLE POSITION BETTING DYNAMICS

A middle position is somewhere between early and late positions. You have some degree of the early-position disadvantages and some degree of the later-position advantages. The later-position advantages are so important that, in middle position after the flop, one of your foremost objectives is to gain last position by betting or raising.

In a multiway pot, when two or three early position players have checked around to you, a good play is to bet so that the later players might fold under twin pressures—your bet, plus the early positions on your right who might be trapping and planning to check-raise. In middle position, you might employ this strategy with certain marginal hands with which you would otherwise check and wait in early or later positions.

LATE POSITION BETTING DYNAMICS

In contrast to the early position scenario, let's assume that you're in last position and four players, including the two blinds and yourself, have called to see the flop. The three other players all check around to you. Assume the flop has not improved your hand. But, simply because all of the other players have checked around to you, you often bet here with anything. Except in the loosest of games, the other three players will fold more than one out of five times.

That possibility alone yields an adequate return and justifies your bet. And if you get only one weak caller, he might fold after the next round. That win-by-default situation, of course, is one of the prime advantages of last position. And the tighter your image, the more frequently opponents will fold.

However, don't attempt this last position bluff bet too often, because the other players will soon adapt and trap you with good hands. Also, it's advantageous for you to check some hands on the flop since you retain your last-acting position during the last two double-size betting rounds. In last position you have the best opportunity to judge what to do with marginal hands by opportunely betting, or by simply waiting for opponents' opportunistic efforts. One factor that works against automatically betting in this situation is that last-position bets tend to get more callers than those from other positions.

POSITIONAL BETTING DYNAMICS SUMMARY

Hold'em is a game that you prefer to play in late position. And that applies whether the flop gives you a good hand, a medium hand, or nothing. Generally, you want to play in early position only with strong hands or with lesser hands to occasionally mix up your play. And when you find yourself playing a hand in early position, you should fully understand the inherent disadvantages, and adjust your thinking and playing objectives accordingly.

As an early position bettor, you are subject to trappers and aggressive chasers raising after one of the first three betting rounds. This gives you extra chances to go wrong and once again illustrates the disadvantage of coming into the pot early. That's why you always prefer to have opponents acting in front of you. Whether you want to raise or wait with a good hand, just call with a marginal hand, raise on the flop with a good drawing hand to get a free turn card, or simply make an opportunistic bluff bet if no one else seems to want the pot, it gives you a great edge to act last.

Hold'em has frequent up-for-grabs situations where no one gets a good flop, especially when fewer high cards appear and just a couple of players remain. Obviously, it is much easier to identify these "loose pot" situations and to find profitable bluffing situations when you're last to act.

SEMIBLUFFING

One of the most difficult judgment calls in acting last is whether to semibluff with certain come hands. Usually, you're going to fold if raised. Thus, you might not want to reopen the betting when it has been checked around to you, since someone might be trapping and, if you fold for a raise, you lose your drawing equity. When fate presents you with a free draw, you're forced to decide whether it is preferable to try to win the pot early or take your free draw. Making the semibluff risks facing a costly raise. Not betting also gives opponents a free card possibly causing you to lose a pot you could have won.

It's usually correct to fold when check-raised, unless you have a good hand yourself, or are playing against a dangerous opponent. Caro says, "If you're check-raised on the flop, be prepared to pass often. Remember, chasing down a bluff will cost several more bets. You're not getting nearly the pot odds you might think you are."

Generally, in hold'em, you tend to concede semibluffs on the flop, especially to tight players because it costs too much to pursue these hands through the last two double-bet rounds. You're most likely to call what might be a bluff with a hand that has reasonable chances of improving and beating a non-bluff. But it has to be enough of a shot. When you have a low pair with the flop, your hand will improve on the fourth or fifth cards and beat a higher pair only about 20 to 25 percent of the time. That is too much of a long shot.

You should be willing to call a check-raise with a good come hand such as a high four-flush, which might win by pairing in addition to making the flush.

BUYING TWO CARDS FOR A SINGLE BET

A last-position flop bet will most often result in the next round of betting being checked around to you. Even if someone was trapping on the flop or improves greatly on the turn, he will often check in hopes of check-raising you. Thus, even with a long shot in last position, you often get to see both the turn and river for the price of a single bet if you elect to check after the turn when you don't hit. But, of course, if you happen to hit either card, you're optimally positioned to raise or bet.

Even if you don't hit, if everyone checks around to you both times, the pot can be had often enough to justify an attempt to steal it. But don't try to steal in this position too frequently. How frequent is "too frequently" depends mainly on your image; a tight player can steal successfully more often.

PLAYING FOR THE NUTS

You should frequently remind yourself of the importance of having the high possibilities on an open-end straight try, which means the highest possible straight (the nuts). For example, if the flop is-J-10-9, and you have an 8, you worry if a queen hits, because anyone with a single king will beat your queen-high straight. That means half of your connections are dangerous.

Even when you have two parts of an open-end straight draw in your hand and two parts on the board, such as a flop of J-10-2 when you hold 9-8, there is still danger of being stuck with the ignorant the end of the straight.

With the queen landing, you specifically must worry about A-K or K-9, hands opponents might reasonably be holding. If, on the other hand, you hold K-Q, either an ace or a 9 can complete your open end straight without causing you worry. Having the nuts means that you'll win (or, at worst, tie).

THE EARLY POSITION RAISE

How often does the raiser have something like a high pair, or better, on the flop? If he raised on two big cards, he hits a big pair in the flop about one-third of the time. Add to that the times he starts off with a high pair (let's estimate about 10-15 percent for late raises) or flops a big hand. The bottom line is that the preflop raiser will have a "real" hand (high pair or better) on the flop less than half the time. When one-on-one, most aggressive players bet the flop most of the time, so you have to be prepared for that possibility.

Meanwhile, what do you have? You also will flop a pair or better about one-third of the time. If you have a low pair, are in sound calling position (especially against an overly aggressive player who insists on giving you more money) you can still be in a reasonable situation. Your adversary will have your low pair beat less than half of the time, and he will improve only about one fourth of the remaining time (and you might improve also.)

If you don't have a pair, what happens if you bet out or even check-raise on the flop? If you simply bet the flop, your opponent will call or raise with the nearly 40 percent of his hands that have something. Also, he will often call or raise when he has nothing. If you judge that your opponent will fold more than one out of five times, it's sound to bet out on the flop. You should plan in advance what to do if he raises, especially if you're planning to smooth-call with a draw and would like to increase your chances for a free last card.

THE INHIBITORY RAISE

The last-position come bet bears some similarity to the *inhibitory raise*, in which someone else bets on the flop and you have a good come hand in last position. If you raise, and don't get reraised, it is quite likely that the betting on the turn will get checked around to you. Thus, if you don't hit, you can check and see the river for free.

Raising on the flop costs two single bets. If you didn't raise on the flop but merely called the single bet, it is quite likely that the original bettor will bet again on the turn, and the bet after the turn is a double bet. Thus, if you simply call the bets on the flop and turn, it will usually cost you 33 percent more to see the last card than if you had raised and then checked—as long as opponents check it around to you, the raiser.

Of course, if you just happen to hit the turn card, then your raise opportunely increased the size of the pot and also makes it harder for inveterate callers to back off the pot. Your frequent use of this inhibitory raise, which is based on your later positional advantage, sometimes tempts your opponents to counter by betting into you on the next round—but then you might just have a real hand.

Overall, this type of aggressive raise not only makes you money (and saves you money), but also adds to your command and control of the game, which contributes to your dominant image.

CALLING AND CHASING

No good player likes calling or chasing, unless he happens to be "just calling" with a great hand, waiting to spring a trap. But there are other hands with which "just calling" is best; for example, a good drawing hand with very favorable pot odds. Experts who make a typical chasing call might be thinking, "Well, I have reasonable chances of winning this pot, and I have reasons why I shouldn't raise this time, like not wanting to chase out opponents acting after me, so I guess I'll just call." Of course, even in this situation, a player with a "hold'em mentality" frequently considers making an aggressive raise, especially from a later position, as an alternative to a call.

Chasing calls made after the flop fall into three categories:

1. Good drawing hands, usually with a four-flush or two-way straight
2. Bad chasing hands, perhaps justified by hunches or feelings
3. Good chasing hands, fully justified by pot odds and current potential

1. Good Drawing Hands

When you have a good come hand that's likely to hit a third of the time or better, and there's a good size pot—or there are more than three players in the pot—calling to see if you make a winning hand is clearly justified. However, certain caution signs should be considered. Going for flushes when there are already pairs on the board, even in limit poker, should be fully considered in light of the current and likely final pot size. (In no-limit and pot-limit poker, doing so can be very detrimental to your bankroll.) Going for straights when there are two or three cards of the same suit on the board should be reevaluated in light of possible flushes, as well as possible subsequent full houses.

2. Bad Chasing Hands

One of the most common chasing situations is when you have two overcards to the flop and there is a large pot. Let's

NOTE FROM CARO

When you have the right image, have been winning, and own everyone's attention, ignore all the wait-and-see advice and raise whenever it seems remotely reasonable. Keep raising until your image is tarnished. Then go back to the basic plan. When events reestablish your winning image and you have total control, come out firing again. My advice is simple: Before the flop, use the wait-and-see method most of the time unless your image is outstanding at that moment. If you don't have complete psychological control over your table, tend just to call rather than raise.

say that preflop raises by you have built the pot and you suspect that the bettor leading out on the flop has a medium or small pair. You have about a one-in-four chance of pairing one of your two overcards on the turn or river. Of course, if the bettor or any of the other callers already has two pair or trips, you need a two-card miracle. Sometimes it's best to chase just for the one bet on the flop, and to quit on the turn if nothing good happens. You might be **drawing dead**, which means there are no cards that you can draw that will make you a winner.

Also, as Caro points outs, "One problem with playing large overcards when you see a medium flop with 10-high, jack-high or queen-high, and no straight or flush possibilities, is that the bettor is likely to have paired on the flop and hold one of your overcards as a kicker. This means if you catch that card, he'll make two pair at the same time, so your overcards don't help as much as you might think." That is, only one of your large overcards might win if it arrives on the turn or river. And if you're chasing and calling along with several other players, it is quite possible that each of your overcards is duplicated in the hands of other players, and you may actually be drawing dead. Two overcards are also drawing against big odds when chasing two pairs or trips.

Chasing with two big overcards is so dangerous that it's usually correct only when the pot has been raised several times before the flop, and the players you're chasing frequently bet with weaker hands.

Let me sum it up as follows: Don't chase with overcards unless you think you already have the best hand.

3. Good Chasing Hands

A classic chase comes when you find yourself heads-up in a raised pot after a weak flop, one that has no pairs, aces, strong draws, and one high card or less on the board. You have a small pair and are facing a bet made by the preflop raiser who might have a high pair.

What are the considerations?

Much depends on the propensities of the player doing the betting. In hold'em, a lot of your strategy depends on your knowledge of how likely it is that the raiser will push two high cards that don't match the flop. In other words, if he does not have a pair, you want to get a sense if he'll bet representing that he does, or if he is more likely to fold against your bets.

First, let's take note of the underlying mathematics. A high pair tends to beat a low pair about four out of five times, which means the low pair wins about one in five hands, less than 20 percent of the time. We're assuming that neither hand has strong straight or flush draw possibilities. But if you're chasing with a hand that has secondary straight or draw prospects, the high pair might win around three out of four times and your low pair as much as 25 percent of the time.

For example, A♠ Q♠ against 7♥ 6♥ with a flop of Q♣ 7♠ 5♥ will win almost three out of four times. Note that the chasing hand has two-card straight and flush prospects, which improves the hand's winning possibilities by about 4 percent each. Substitute two aces for the A-Q of spades and the chasing hand wins about 28 percent of the time.

So, as you see, most low pair chasing hands beat a higher pair about 20 to 25 percent of the time.

Let's assume that you have a low pair chasing hand with straight and flush draw possibilities against an opponent with two high cards. The flop has one high card and two low cards. Your opponent raised preflop and now bets the flop. Everyone else drops and it is up to you. You now have to consider how much is in the pot and how likely it is that your opponent will bluff all the way without a pair.

If you consider calling on the flop with your low pair, your three main options are:

1. Seeing one more card.
2. Calling all the way to a showdown.
3. Calling here, and then raising after the turn (assuming he leads out again), a play you make when your opponent is likely to be pushing two big cards and might fold right there on the turn.

For example, assume a hold'em situation where you hold the 7♦ 6♦ and there are six units, including two from you, in the pot. You're heads-up with a low pair facing the raiser's bet on the flop. If you played out this identical situation 100 times, calling all the way, your net gain from the 25 hands that you would win is not nearly enough to offset the 75 other hands that you would lose if your opponent always has the high pair. In this situation, where the driver is the type of player who almost always has a high pair, clearly, you should not chase all the way.

In the preceding example, where you had two secondary draws against a "locksmith," you might choose the alternative of calling to see one more card and folding if you don't improve. There are 21 cards out of the remaining 45 that improve you sufficiently to play further, namely two 7s, three 6s, ten diamonds, and six 8s or 4s—not double-counting the 4 and 8 of diamonds. So, if you're going against a player who only bets the flop with at least a high pair, you should plan to fold after the turn when he bets.

Of course, there is some possibility that the driver will back off and check after the fourth card. If you're playing against a player who is likely to make this play, you should also consider calling the bet on the flop with weaker hands so you can see the turn for free.

But what if your opponent is an aggressive player who will bet the turn even without a high pair?

Most aggressive hold'em players raise before the flop holding a high pocket pair well under 20 percent of the time. Even players who only raise on A-Q or better have pocket tens or higher less than one third of the time. Overall, most preflop raisers will have a high pair with a one-high-card flop less than 50 percent of the time. And depending on their position, their inclinations, and which high card is on the flop, the odds of a heads-up opponent having a high pair may be substantially under 50 percent.

Many players who raise before the flop frequently bet a weak flop with one high card, with or without a high pair. And many of these aggressive players will continue to bet high cards all the way, pushing the bluff right to the end.

Let's assume that the preflop raiser will bet the flop without a pair and try to bluff it through on at least some of the other 75 hands. (If an opponent never bluffed, you would soon catch on and never pay off his good hands.) Given the above numbers, it is correct for you to chase if the preflop raiser tends to follow through with a continuation bet and drive bet all the way to the river roughly 15 percent of the time or more.

If you have one of the lesser chase hands that would win only 20 hands out of the 100, it is correct to chase if he bluffs 20 percent or more of the time. Even if the raising hand bets the flop without a pair, he will then outdraw you about 25 percent of the time. In the above example, if he bet on the flop with the A♠ K♠, he would outdraw you about 27 percent of the time, and with the unsuited A-K about 22 percent (if either is one of his diamonds, about 23 percent). Note that overly aggressive players who routinely drive all the way in these situations are sitting ducks against a player holding a low pair.

HOLD'EM PARADOXES

Let's say you call or raise before the flop with two high cards. Two players also call. The flop comes and gives you a high pair with a good kicker. You bet when it is your turn, then someone playing behind you raises.

What does that raise mean?

On the first level of logic, you might infer that the raiser has made a big hand, say trips or two pair—assuming that no straight or flush flopped. Or perhaps the raiser merely has a high pair also, with or without a higher kicker, and is trying both to slow you down and pressure the third player into folding. Or perhaps the raiser has some good come prospects and is trying for a check on the turn.

My point is this: You should never assume that a raiser is weak, even though raising is often tactically better than calling. All of the above possibilities make sense and hence are likely—except one, the "big hand" possibility.

The Big Hand Possibility

If you're playing against reasonably good players, a raise on the flop means it is *unlikely* that the raiser has a big hand. It is paradoxical that the most straightforward meaning of a raise in poker—that the raiser has a big hand—is actually unlikely in this situation. Most of the time a big hand will patiently call and wait, holding his raise until the turn or river, the double size bet rounds. Thus, most of the time, a raise just after the flop does not usually indicate that the raiser has a big hand!

Of course, a good player will occasionally mix up his play and push his big hand, but generally speaking, he wants to lay back and hide his strength so that he can trap opponents for more chips. On the other hand, a novice player will often get excited and give the show away by raising.

Thus, your reactions to a raise and subsequent actions should be adjusted according to the situation. When you have the disadvantage of acting first, value reraises are usually sound. A "tactical" raiser will often fold to your lead bet on the turn—thus, if the board cards make a draw unlikely, you might check with a good hand.

However, beware when a good tight-aggressive player merely calls you on the flop, especially in an unraised pot. Unfortunately, or perhaps fortunately, if you have top set, it is reasonably likely that your opponent is also calling with a big hand. A good tight player is not likely to be chasing. Most likely he has either a big hand, a good come hand, or a hand comparable or better to whatever you're lead betting with. In this situation, you need to look at the flop and try to figure out what two-card hands he would be calling with— and remember the paradoxes, that he might have raised with certain lesser hands. Before betting on the turn, evaluate the likelihood of your being raised versus your reasons for the necessity of driving.

ULTRA-AGGRESSIVE HEAD-TO-HEAD BETTING

At high-level limit hold'em play, there are occasional hands where many of the above mentioned after-the-flop principles seem to be applied to extremes. When many raises and reraises occur, the result is often a head-to-head confrontation between two aggressive players.

These hands typically start off with one or more preflop raises. Because there is a sizable starting pot, there is more to fight for. There is often a lot of action after a medium flop both strong and weak flops tend to have more clearly defined positions). Since the hands in early position are clearly at a disadvantage if they check, the first hand may lead out with a bet if he has enough to compete for the raised pot and reasonably believes that everyone might fold. But if he checks, he has a dubious chase.

The Advantage of First Aggression

But what is actually happening here, at least on the psychological level, is that this lead bet shows strength to the players behind him, especially to the before-the-flop raisers. In this situation, there is an advantage in acting early because the lead bettor gets his bluff in first. However, if you have a hand that is good enough to bet all the way, you would strongly prefer to be in a later position, where you still would have the option to lead bet all the way if no one else bets.

Since somewhere between 20 to 40 percent of hold'em pots are default pots, where no one has much on the flop, the player that bets or raises often wins without a showdown. Since the late position player knows that an early bettor with a really good hand would probably check to trap a preflop raiser, who usually bets, the lead bettor is quite often pushing thin values or perhaps even bluffing on a come hand.

The Dynamics of Aggression vs. Aggression

If a late position player has any interest in competing for the pot, then it is quite reasonable to raise on both good hands and marginal hands. However, the raiser more likely has a marginal hand, since players holding good hands in later seats often wait until after the turn or river, the double size bets, to raise. Keep in mind that most raises preflop are based upon high cards and it is sometimes correct to call a single bet on the flop given the bigger pot.

The raise also tends to pressure out other competition, thus setting up a head-to-head duel for the pot.

In an aggressive hold'em game, when there is a sizable

pot because of preflop activity, it is not unusual for a speculative early bet and a speculative raise to reduce pot attendance down to two players holding medium or weak hands. The ensuing head-to-head battles after the flop are not only interesting and amusing—sometimes they're almost ridiculous!

To illustrate, let's now take some of these typical aggressive antics to the logical extremes. Assume that the lead bettor faces the not-too-unexpected raise. Although you often plan to fold if raised, especially by a rook this situation is not one of those times. Since the raise is quite likely coming from a player holding a medium or weak hand, there is no reason to panic. In fact the lead bettor might even raise back (could he possibly have the top set?) as if he had a real hand, if he is planning to lead bet on the next round of betting. And he might be planning to bet strong all the way, hoping to convince the late position player to fold a medium holding that just might beat his medium holding. If the later player calls this raise and then does not improve, the early lead bettor often prevails by default.

But, the later seated preflop raiser knows that if he calls, he will probably be faced with double-sized bets on the next two rounds, and also that he is a big underdog to improve. His best chance to win this pot is to reraise one more time (maybe he has the top set also?) and try to get the lead bettor to back down or perhaps fold—or he might get a free fourth card. In limit hold'em it is not that unusual for two aggressive players to go through this sort of head-banging ritual and with one of the players either backing down and folding, or meekly calling the rest of the bets to a showdown.

RERAISING INSTEAD OF JUST CALLING THE RAISE*

Chart key: Action reads left to right, top to bottom. Each betting round begins with → and ends with ←. Other markings and symbols: a (ante); b (blind bet); • (check); = (call, including when big blind sees flop free); ↑ (raise); — (fold); ● (dealer position, a.k.a. "the button"). A seat number surrounded by asterisks (for example, * 1 *) is your seat. Any wager not preceded by a symbol is a voluntary first bet. Wagers indicate the total invested on a betting round. The money in the rightmost column indicates total pot size after the betting.

For full explanation of how the MCU charts work, see Appendix B.

*Note: MCU Poker Charts in this book are bonus examples that may illustrate concepts other than those in nearby text.

MCU Poker Chart. *Game*: Hold 'em *Structure:* $25 and $50 blinds, $50 bets on starting hand and flop, $100 thereafter.

1	2	3	4	5	6	7	8	9	10	Pot
Q♣ J♠	•	b25	B50							$75
										Starting hands <<<
				→—	—	—	—	—	↑100	$375
↑150[1]	—	—	—						=150←	
										Flop J♣ 10♦ 6♠ <<<
=50[3]←									→50[2]	$475
										Turn K♦ <<<
✓[5]←									→✓[4]	$475
										River 2♦ <<<
100[6]									→· / —[7]←	$575
Q♣ J♠ WIN	K♥ 6♠ didn't play[8]	J♥ 2♥ didn't play[9]							A♥ 6♦ folded	Two-card hands revealed <<<

93

1. Okay, here's the deal. You should occasionally consider calling seat #10's raise. He is in a late position, just two seats away from the dealer button, and he doesn't always need a powerful hand to attack. Even more often, you should consider folding. Calling is a little risky and usually weak. Folding is safe and the most standard play.

Folding is good practice. So why do you raise here?

You raise, because you have psychological dominance over the table right now. Things have been going conspicuously well for you, and your opponents seem meek and intimidated. Otherwise, you usually wouldn't consider raising. And because you have psychological control, you want to take advantage of it. Good things can happen. For one, you can chase everyone else out and battle one-on-one for an enhanced pot that contains the forfeited blind money. For another, if you succeed in chasing away the player on the button, you're guaranteed last position throughout all future betting rounds. Also, if this raise goes well, you'll get to see what develops on the flop and your opponent will probably check to you. Then you'll have the luxury of either continuing to lead whether you connect or miss, or checking and taking a free card if you don't improve or you're trapping. So, this occasional reraise has powerful psychological and strategic motives.

2. If you look at the bottom of the chart, you'll see that your opponent has flopped a pair of 6s and has an ace kicker that might come in useful to beat another 6.

3. You've flopped top pair and a queen kicker. That's a good thing, so far. But you decide to just call this time, because your opponent might not have much, and you don't mind letting him think he has the best hand for now—and he actually might have it.

Of course, by not raising, you risk letting him stay in the pot with hands that could draw out on you, such as K-9 or A-7 (not much different from the A-6 he actually holds, but sans the pair), or even A-9. Of course, even if you raise, there's no guarantee he'll fold. In fact, with some hands, he'll almost certainly call; while with others, he might call at whim, even though folding is a superior choice.

So, a raise isn't required. The best reason to raise right now is because you have the best hand and want to win more money, not because you want to chase your opponent out. But, your choice has been made. You just called.

4. The king scared your opponent out of the betting.

5. And, unfortunately, it scared you out of betting too, despite the fact that you also have an open-end straight draw. You should often bet in this type of situation. But checking is okay and that's what you did.

6. You decide to bet on the river. You're only slightly worried about the three diamonds on the board, and you believe that your opponent would have bet a pair of kings rather than check twice in a row. Generally, opponents who check what they think is probably the winning hand on the turn and don't get bet into will not check again on the river when a non-threatening card lands. Since there was no bet on the last round, often they'll do their own betting this time. In the absence of that bet, you have a higher confidence that your pair of jacks is good. So, you bet.

7. Your opponent decides that a pair of 6s isn't strong enough to call. But don't be surprised if many opponents do call. It's why it's so easy to make money at hold'em against typical opponents.

8. Just to illustrate, let's imagine that the player in the small blind threw away K♥ 6♠. That two pair would have beat you badly.

9. And the J♥ 2♥ we're imagining for the player in the big blind would have beaten you, too. That's also two pair. I'm not saying it's likely that both blinds would have held cards that could have beat you and then been chased away because you reraised. But it does happen. And in this imaginary example, it did happen.

The Law of Real Cards

In the above scenario, neither of the players has made unusual or risky plays. Both were merely playing their hands aggressively, trying to maximize their chances of winning by getting his opponent to fold. As you become a more experienced hold'em player, you'll find many other scenarios in which the same concepts apply. But never lose sight of the basic truth: Even the world's most convincing raiser will lose to a player with real cards.

One of Mike Caro's most quoted concepts is that, in poker, when the irresistible force meets the immovable object, the immovable object gets jerked around! A logical corollary to this is as follows: if either the irresistible force or the immovable object happens to have a big hand, the other hand could lose a lot of money!

MIKE CARO STRATEGY RECOMMENDATIONS

Here are some of Mike Caro's after-the-flop strategies:

The Flop: Point of Focus

Always think, 'What's the best, second best, and third best possible hand when you see the flop?' You'd be surprised how many good players have related hold'em stories to me about situations they just never would have gotten into had they asked themselves that basic question. Skilled players think the answer is obvious and they don't have to think, 'What's best?' Practice doing it, anyway, and if you're like most players I've forced to try this, you'll soon find it's ludicrous not to ask that one question before every flop you're involved in. It's a rigid routine worth your effort. You'll see.

There are two conceptually different ways to look at a hold'em hand following the flop. Strong players should use both at once in order to get the best possible grasp of the situation. The first method is to think, 'What do I need to see on the board before looking at the flop?' This gives you a clear notion of what flops will make you happy and what flops won't before getting caught up in the emotion of the moment. Your hand becomes the point of focus. The second method is to look at the flop independently of what cards you're holding and think, "Under the circumstances, what cards must I hold to like this flop?' This automatically tells you whether you have a strong hand and gives you an idea what sort of hands your opponents might have if they bet from power. The flop becomes the point of focus.

While such mental exercises invariably seem trivial to experienced players, I'm convinced that almost all errors in evaluation on the flop would be eliminated if players simply took these elementary steps. In fact, it is not only the human mind that benefits from looking at a flop from both these premises.

This turned out to be far superior to any other method in teaching sophisticated hold'em to a computer. Evaluate the flop from both points of view (your hand and the flop itself) and you'll automatically understand the entire situation.

The Big Picture

Caro also describes basic related concepts:

It is not enough to simply consider how likely a hand is to win. You also need to ask yourself these two questions whenever you're faced with a difficult decision:

- ♠ How likely is it that your hand can win without reaching the showdown?
- ♠ How likely is it that your hand can win a big confrontation?

If you're check-raised on the flop, be prepared to pass often. Remember, in order to chase down a bluff it will cost several more bets. You may not be getting quite the pot odds you think you are.

Pair Flops

Anytime you see a pair on the flop, consider it to be negative unless it specifically helps your hand.

You can almost always routinely throw your hand away against a bet in a multiway pot when a pair flops if you don't hold a pocket pair and it hasn't helped a speculative hand. This is not always true in head-to-head situations.

You should be very reluctant to draw for straights or flushes when the flop shows a pair.

Seldom call a bet on the flop with overcards when there's a pair on the board.

Pocket Pair Abandonment

You should almost always fold after an unpaired flop if you hold a hidden pair lower than the second highest board card.

Let's suppose you hold...

and the flop comes...

At this point there is a bet. Whether you're playing no-limit, pot-limit or fixed-limit hold'em, this bet almost surely represents a hand better than yours. Or it's a bluff. This is a very tough situation to call a bluff, since you'll likely be faced with more bets on future rounds. While most pros agree that you cannot call a bet with this hand, in actual practice, many of them occasionally violate their own best judgment and do call in such a situation.

Unless you have a specific reason to stay in the pot, such as exceptional straight or flush possibilities or a good bluffing opportunity now or later in the hand, you should pass without hesitation when you're bet into and you hold a hidden pair smaller than the top two board cards.

This advice even applies when a pair shows on the flop and you have a hidden pair smaller than both the board pair and the non-matching board card. Here's a good example:

You have...

and the flop is...

If you're bet into, this is almost always a passing situation. While most strong players seem to obey this advice at least half the time, they cost themselves a lot of chips when they stray from the obvious and decide to call.

If there's been a bet and a call on the flop, seldom overcall with any private pair lower than the top rank on board. For instance, if you hold a pair of jacks, and the flop contains a king and two low cards, you should usually fold against a bet and a call.

Playing Pocket Pairs When There is an Ace on the Flop

You should seldom bet and should often abandon a pocket pair if an ace is present and an opponent bets. This includes a pocket pair higher than the second rank on board. You don't always need to surrender; but against typical players, you are better off not committing any chips to the pot.

The following common situation leads to trouble:

You have...

The flop is...

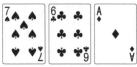

This is not a safe betting situation. Most strong players recognize they're usually in trouble if another player bets, but they're not quite sure whether or not they should bet if they must act first.

The answer is almost always *no*. The ace spells danger. You're likely to get called or raised by a player who has you beaten. And if you're holding the best hand, you're unlikely to win a call. This is rarely a good betting situation if your intention is to win the pot immediately without a fight—it's just too risky.

If you have a hidden pair lower than the highest card on the board, don't bet unless your opponents could reasonably use the weaker board cards. Even then, bet selectively and with caution. You would be more likely to bet if the flop were J-9-A.

Big Pair, Big Kicker

Top pair with an ace kicker is sometimes better for you to hold than an overpair simply because it's easier to get help. Of course, you don't want top pair and an ace if someone else has an overpair. In that situation, you'd rather have an overpair higher than theirs.

For example, with a flop consisting of a 10 and two low cards, you'd rather hold an ace and a 10 than a pair of jacks. Of course, you'd rather not be playing against jacks or a higher pair with a "big 10," as this hand is sometimes called, but the ace kicker gives you a chance to draw better than any opponent who has an overpair, and there are also the 10s which will give you a set. That's five cards that can improve your hand—three aces and two 10s.

On the other hand, the pair of jacks has only two cards (the last two jacks in the deck), that can improve your hand to beat an opponent's higher pair, whether held in the pocket or made in combination with the board.

That doesn't mean their aren't some good reasons you'd rather have the jacks, especially since it leaves more room for opponents to have hands like A-10, that J-J will pulverize. But on balance, expect A-10 frequently to be more profitable.

Big Pair Compared to a Little Ace

Every experienced player knows that a big pair is superior to a little ace (ace plus a small card), but they need to be reminded from time to time. If you hold A-J, you'd usually rather see a flop like J-10-4 than A-10-4. You can get more action from losing hands with the first flop, while with the second, the best hand you could beat would be A-

9. And if you get resistance, you have to be worried about dominating hands like A-Q or A-K or better.

Big Pair Compared to a Little Kicker

If you hold a big **split pair**—half on board, half on hand—of aces, kings, queens or jacks on the flop, you should usually *not* continue to play for one bet if your kicker is small. You cannot gain much and might lose a lot of chips in a bet/call situation, no matter whether you or your opponent does the betting. For this reason, big split pairs with weak kickers are not really playable. While this is a well known hold'em concept, it is often violated both by beginners and strong players who go on tilt. This violation of solid play is extremely costly.

For example, you should be very reluctant to call with or bet a hand in the following two situations.

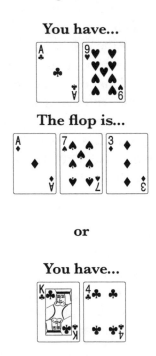

You have...

The flop is...

or

You have...

The flop is...

Of course, the specific suits, the previous action, and your position might influence you to make some plays if you think you can get away with them. However, unless the right situation presents itself, it is usually wrong to invest in a hand with a high split pair when you have a weak kicker.

This principle is especially valid in no-limit and pot-limit. For players making a transition between limit and no-limit, you should automatically pass any such hand if the decision would have been close in a limit game. The penalty is greater for playing big split pairs with weak kickers in the big bet games. This advice seems extremely obvious, even trivial, to experienced players. But their occasional refusal to abide by it is one of the most costly and frequent hold'em errors.

Second Pair Plus

Second best pair simply isn't much good when three unpaired high cards, 10 through A, flop. You have to consider how many reasonable combinations will beat you. Suppose you hold a queen and jack, and the flop is K-J-10.

Many novices fall in love with this hand, but it really is not very good. First, even if you make a straight, which is one reason players admire the hand, you're going to split with an opponent if he also holds a queen. Second, all kinds of hands are out there to beat you. They range from pairs of tens through aces that form either trips or overpairs, to hands like A-Q and Q-9, which form completed straights. There are also pocket cards like K-J, K-10, J-10 that form two pair hands, to simply hands that form top pairs and also have straight possibilities like A-K, K-9 and K-Q (which would be very bad for you).

Note that all of these hands, and A-J, too, are pretty much what you might expect an opponent to have!

The next question to ask is: What can happen to improve my hand and make me feel safe as the aggressor? The answer is: Not much. Even if you hit another jack, you still must worry. If there are two suited cards out there, it's even worse.

The bottom line is that when three cards 10 through ace flop, the second best pair is going to get you into trouble. Don't fall in love with it.

Overcards

When there's a pair on the board, seldom call a bet on the flop with just overcards. One problem with playing big overcards on a medium flop with 10-high, jack-high or queen-high cards and no straight or flush possibilities, is that the bettor is likely to have paired on the flop *and* hold one of your overcards as a kicker. This means if you catch that card, he'll make two pair at the same time you catch your first pair, so your overcards don't help as much as you might think. In fact, it might cost you a lot of chips.

Straight and Flush Draws

Knowing how to play straight and flush draws is very important toward maximizing your wins and minimizing your losses. Following are five principles to keep in mind.

1. You should be very reluctant to draw for straights or flushes when the flop shows a pair.

2. You should almost never draw for a straight when the situation suggests someone is trying for, or might already hold, a flush.

3. In almost all cases, it is wrong to call with even a good straight possibility if there's a reasonable chance that an opponent might make a flush. In other words, if you see two flush cards on the board—and certainly three—and you're on a straight draw, you could be asking for trouble.

For some reason, players have a very tough time abandoning good straight tries. Not doing this can be a disaster. Remember that most straight attempts make only a small theoretical profit when no one can make a flush. That theoretical profit disappears—and a lot more goes with it—when there is a flush try out against you. Pass proudly and quickly. Don't think of this pass as painful. It is a lot more painful to face a big bet after you have made the straight and there is a possible flush (or full house!) out against you. This concept is most valid to no-limit and pot-limit games, but it also applies to limit poker.

4. Unless you have a pair as added incentive, it's generally unprofitable to call in an attempt to make a straight when there are two suited cards on board. Other considerations may make the call worthwhile. If you hold a high card of the flush suit, this helps a little (in the event of two running cards of that suit, and because it diminishes the chances of an opponent making the flush), but usually not enough to cause you to play.

5. Don't bet a flush draw on the flop into one opponent unless you think there's a good enough chance that he will fold. Sometimes 20 percent, or even less, can be a good enough chance. But there usually must be some reasonable chance of capturing the pot outright for you to bet a speculative hand into just one opponent.

The Nut Flush

If you're going for a flush, you want to have the ace in your hand, or if the ace is already on board, or the A-K on board, then the king or queen respectively—in other words, you want to be drawing to the nut flush. This is one of the most important concepts you can add to your hold'em toolbox. There is a tendency among some players to think that K-J suited is almost as good as A-J suited when the flop contains two medium or low cards of that suit. That is not only completely false, it will actually cost a lot of money if you don't recognize the qualitative difference between these two hands.

Some players figure they're a large favorite to win if either flush is made. That's true. But that's also ignoring a serious problem: When you lose on a flush to a hand with that ace, you don't just lose your normal investment. Typically, you lose several bets, or if it's a no-limit or pot-limit game, perhaps a monster bet. This would be a disaster.

Instead, if you'd had the ace, exactly the opposite might have happened—*you'd* win the big confrontation. For this reason, it turns out that starting hands suited without an ace lose money in common situations in which suited hands *with* the ace are hugely profitable. Get it out of your head that the second best flush card is almost as good as the best card.

Three of a Kind

Many players are confused over the relative values of three-of-a-kind hands in different situations. Obviously, the best three of a kind you can have is with a pocket pair that combines with one card of that rank on the board. This makes it impossible that any other player can also hold a three of a kind of that rank. And the lesser three of a kind is made when the pair is on the board and a third card of that rank is held in your hand.

If you have a medium pocket pair and a third card of that rank turns out to be the high board card—say, you hold pocket nines with a flop of 9-7-4—then you're in a very powerful position with the top set.

Contrarily, if you have pocket fours with that same 9-7-4 flop, you're only powerful if you don't run into heavy action. A stronger set of trips than the three 4s in this example would be players holding pocket 7s or 9s, or a pair on the board that is higher in rank than your set which combines with a player's hole cards. If you hold A-Q or even K-Q on a Q-Q-7 flop, there's only a miniscule chance that a player would have seen the flop with Q-7.

The point here is that there are certain flops that provide you with trips that don't figure to have much profit potential, but could easily lose. These are flops in which the hands you'd like your opponents to hold would likely have been discarded before the flop. In such cases, trips that include a hidden pair are frequently overvalued by players.

Two Pair

When you have a two-pair hand on a high flop, it's usually wrong to reraise without the top two pair.

Your two pair on the flop is much stronger if there's no pair on the board. This seems obvious to experienced players, because when one pair is on the board everyone owns it. And it's quite possible that one player may be holding the third card of that rank.

Two pair made with one pair on the board, isn't as rare an event as two pair when there's no pair showing. So, you'd think that players would consider two pair when there's a pair on the board as vastly different from a flop that pairs both cards in their hands. This isn't the case among weak to average players, who don't understand the quality of this distinction.

Although the following list is not frozen and can be rearranged in specific circumstances, when you have two pair on the flop, this is normally the order of strength by category:

It's easy to quarrel with this list and, in fact, it changes according to the speed of the game and the habits of opponents. It is based on the prospects for *profit*, not on the percentage of hands won, which is why category 11 is so poorly regarded by some players.

There are, of course, other considerations that make these broad categories more complex, such as whether the odd cards are high or low for a given situation and whether any other players are apt to have hands that could complement the board. However, even these considerations will not usually cause the value of the listed categories to overlap by much.

You could also subdivide any of the above categories and create a longer list. For instance, in category 11, the example given, K-4 with a flop of J-J-K, is not as strong as the same K-4 with a flop of 7-7-K, because it's less likely an opponent will have three sevens than three jacks.

In general, you should consider the profit potential of your two pair in accordance with the list.

Protected Pair

On the flop, seldom give a free card by checking if you hold top pair or an overpair. There are many higher ranks that could hit the board and beat you, and you don't want to allow that to happen, at least not for free. Routinely bet instead. For example, if you have a pair of jacks and the flop is 10-6-4, bet out—you should not give a free card. Too

---

TWO PAIR ON THE FLOP
Order of Strength

1. Two top pair when there's no pair showing, such as A-10 with a flop of A-10-8.

2. Top and bottom pair when there's no pair showing, such as K-7 with a flop of K-9-7.

3. A big hidden pair of at least jacks, higher than the odd board card when there's a small pair showing, such as K-K with a flop of 5-5-2.

4. Bottom two pair when there's no pair showing, such as 10-9 when the flop is A-10-9.

5. A card pairing the odd board card with a high kicker when there's one pair showing, such as Q-A with a flop of 7-7-Q.

6. A small hidden pair higher than the odd board card when there's a small pair showing, such as 6-6 with an 8-8-5 flop.

7. A hidden pair higher than the odd board card when there's a big pair showing, such as 9-9 with a flop of Q-Q-4.

8. A hidden pair lower than the odd board card when there's a small pair showing, such as 9-9 when the flop is 5-5-A.

9. A hidden pair lower than the odd board card when there's a big pair showing, such as 9-9 when the flop is A-A-K.

10. A card pairing a low odd board card with a low kicker when there's one pair showing, such as 6-4 with a flop of J-J-6.

11. A card pairing a high odd board card with a low kicker when there's one pair showing, such as K-4 with a flop of J-J-K.

---

many big cards could hit on the turn and river, potentially giving opponents the better pair, when instead, they would have folded if there was a cost to play.

Betting When Opponents Check

If you're in last position and take the initiative on the flop, the last round callers will usually check to see what you do on the turn. That's why top players, when they're checked to on the flop, correctly bet many reasonable hands in last position.

Let's say you raise with borderline raising cards, playing your position with cards such as A-10 suited. The flop comes with two high cards that don't connect with your hand, for example, Q-J and a low card.

That's a potentially disastrous bluffing situation. Kings, queens and jacks are the most commonly held ranks by callers when there's been no raise before the flop. A better flop to bluff into is K-9-4. If opponents don't hold a king, you're likely to get away with a bet designed to drive out your opponents.

Pair Plus Draw

Any time you're against one player and you have the high pair plus a nut flush draw or nut straight draw, you should consider betting out. You should also consider raising any bet. The key concept to understand is that you might win the pot right there if your opponent passes. You want that opponent to fold any hand that is better than yours or slightly worse. That's because you'll usually make more money taking the entire pot right then. If you're called, you may have slightly the worst hand, or you may not, but even so, you'll have excellent winning opportunities. Good players use this strategy sometimes—you should use it most of the time.

CONCLUSIONS

Something that you'll learn with experience is that anything goes on the flop! Hold'em is a game that should be played aggressively, and the best time to be push chips into the pot and be creative is when those three cards hit the flop.

But don't forget a very basic truth: When there are a lot of bets and raises made on the flop, ironically, they tend to indicate medium strong or weaker hands—and not the really big hands. Players who are sitting with monsters generally wait for the turn or river to push aggressively, so they can get their bets in at twice the price! That fact should strongly influence your perception of reality.

THE BIG MONEY ROUNDS

Betting on the turn and river in hold'em is like the last two rounds in any other multiple-round poker game. The seeds have already been sown, as indicated by the size of the pot developed by the earlier betting, and now comes harvest time. Hopefully, you're the one doing the harvesting and not your opponents.

In limit hold'em, the betting has indeed become much more serious and expensive because of the double-size bets on the last two rounds of betting. If you were to play a hand of hold'em to completion, in which there was one bet (and no raises) made on each of the four betting rounds, two thirds of the total money that was in the pot would have come from the turn and river bets. This means that the decision made on these last two betting rounds, by strict math, are twice as profitable or costly as those on the preflop and flop.

As the fourth upcard is turned, you should now have a pretty good idea of just where you stand in this hand. If you called a single bet on the flop as a somewhat loose speculation play (you were chasing), now is the time you must shape up or ship out. If you're still behind in this hand, you should know exactly how many of the 46 cards remaining in the deck will give you a winning hand before investing further double-size bets. And your odds of winning should be justified by the pot size.

Perhaps the greatest difference between consistent winners and consistent losers is that the winners play with the percentages and the losers play against them.

On the turn, you need to take a cold, hard objective look at your hand before you put any of those big bets into the pot. Up until now you have been merely dabbling with the potential of how your two cards mesh with the flop. After the fourth card, the possibilities have been considerably narrowed.

With only one more card to come, you have to ask yourself this question: Do the percentages of getting certain last cards, considered together with the percentages of what your opponents are most likely to have, justify your putting double-size bets into this pot? The prospect of actually winning a pot with a miracle last card, which would be a low percentage play, is typically not enough to justify putting in a double-size bet in limit hold'em, especially if raises after a call are possible.

SIZING UP YOUR SITUATION

With just one card to come, you can fairly accurately compute your odds of improving, and if you have a reasonably good idea of the type of hand your opponents have, that will give you a sense of your chances of winning the hand. If your main prospects of winning require that you get a favorable last card or on your opponents not having what they represent based on their previous betting, you may be throwing good money after bad if you commit further chips to the pot—unless your estimates of improving your hand are justified by the pot size.

Of course, if you have a real hand with a reasonable chance of winning, then you belong in the pot, and it is all a matter of what happens on the last card.

One idea you might find helpful on the turn is to categorize your interests in the pot as positive, neutral (medium/borderline hands), or negative. When positive, you generally want to get as much money into the pot as possible, which means that tactically, you do whatever you think best to get as many callers for as many bets as you can. With negative prospects, you hope not to put any more money into this pot, except perhaps to call one bet only so that you can get to the river.

With neutral cards, the medium/borderline hands, it is all relative to what the rest of your opponents are doing. In early seats, you'll often check and hope to see the river for free. You fear bet and raises because they'll often take you out of the hand. Sometimes, in an early seat, you'll do the opposite and make a tactical bet. You hope to grab the initiative in a healthy pot, even though your cards don't justify calling. Opponents may be discouraged from raising, or even calling by an aggressive early position play allowing you to see the last card without further cost of a raise. Or possibly, you'll take down the pot right there. That type of probe bet with a sub-marginal hand is also good to test the waters, If you're indeed raised, you plan to fold or make the very rare all-out bluff reraise.

In later seats, you often bet simply because if no one else has bet. Maybe you do have the best hand and a bet on the turn will drop someone who can draw out and beat you—now or on the last card—or cause a better hand to give up the pot.

Overall, playing the positive and negative hands is relatively straightforward. It is the play of the medium/ borderline hands that separates the good players from the average. In hold'em, as we've stressed over and over again, aggressive play gives you a substantial edge. By aggressive betting, you can inhibit raises and win hands by default against opponents who aren't willing to put chips into the pot on their own medium/borderline hands.

PLAYING LITTLE POTS

In hold'em, there are occasionally hands in which no one raised before the flop and no one bet on the flop, hence there is little money. If you happen to hit a good turn card and you figure you've got the best hand, then by all means bet. Either you'll get more money into the pot, or if everyone folds, you'll win the pot without further play. If you're slightly ahead or if the board suggests straight draws, it is important to pressure the other hands and give them the option of folding. If you judge that the odds of everyone folding compare favorably with the pot size, you might bluff with very little or nothing.

Again, aggressive play wins pots.

One caveat: If you bet with a marginal hand, you have to be aware that a loose player might raise and put a move on you. If you judge that your marginal holding might well be the best hand, then you indeed have enough to call and see another card. But if you have a hand that should be folded against an aggressive raise, then perhaps you should consider not making that bet.

Note that I used the term "loose player" in evaluating your situation in a little-pot raise. A loose player is capable of making moves and his raise does not necessarily suggest strength. A tight player, on the other hand, generally raises only with a hand, so it would be easier to fold a marginal hand when that bet comes from him.

When No One Bets

In many weaker hold'em games, it often appears that no one seems interested enough to bet a small pot. Most often this little pot is up for grabs, and any bet on the turn would pick up the antes. But you have to think about your exposure if you do try to take the pot. On the one hand, you might say that with so little money in the pot, it is hardly worth risking a double size bet. If someone in an early seat is trapping (checking a good hand), or perhaps someone behind you just hit the fourth card, you're out that bet and perhaps more if you continue on with the hand. That the pot may not be worth the strategic risks of bluffing are good arguments for playing passively in these situations.

You also want to consider your "bluffing quota." If you bluff too often, players will give less credit to your bets and call more often. Going after a thin pot with a big bet and being called down on it, is obviously not a profitable play for you. But there could be a further cost to the play. You would rather not have someone call your bluff on a larger pot because they remembered your bluff attempt on this little pot. In other words, maybe you should let some other "genius" steal the pot.

Buying the Pot

On the other hand, one of the most skillful areas in poker is the prudent investment of buying "unwanted" smaller pots. Especially if the fourth card is a **brick**, a card that doesn't appear to help anyone (it doesn't create pairs, flush or straight prospects, and is not an overcard), it is good business to make an occasional fourth round bet to steal more than twice that amount. If your bluff works more than one out of three times, it becomes a profitable play. And if you do it on hands where you get a good last card, you might be the natural winner of the pot. Or if you detect a very weak call, you might try betting again on the river, especially if another brick appears.

Some of the main reasons for engaging in these little pot frays are often more strategic than tactical. Although the few dollars gained from these little endeavors can add up over the long run, a larger consideration is how these plays fit into your overall game plan and image at the table.

If you normally play very tight and can steal one or two hands a session without being noticed (you're "feared"), you may well want to avoid the unfavorable publicity of being caught with your hand in the cookie jar. But if you're a dominant, aggressive player who does a lot of betting and usually gets a lot of callers (you're "loved"), then any unsuccessful bluffs for little pots can easily be chalked off to your advertising budget.

At most hold'em tables, it is better to be feared than loved.

TACTICAL DRIVING ON THE TURN

The turn card has been dealt. You have watched some of the other involved players watch the turn. There are either no players in front of you or they have all checked around to you. It is now your turn to act. You have two options: bet or check.

Following are the three key variables that will influence your tactics: pot size, position and put-ons.

Pot Size

Pot size is always a key factor because your primary objective is to win money. The more money in the pot the more you're willing to invest to win it. Every poker player intuitively understands that concept. Unfortunately, the other players have the same motivations and the more money in the pot the harder it is to win. Since we have already discussed in the preceding section many of the small pot considerations including that maintenance of our strategic image might require that you ignore most small pots, in all of the following discussions, we'll assume that you're dealing with pots that already contain more than a small amount of chips due to preflop raising activity or a bet on the flop with several callers.

After the turn, if no one has opened and it's your turn to bet, you should never lose complete interest in a hand merely because you have bad cards. Remember, you're playing poker! If this is one of the "default" hands where no one has much, there is a good chance that a double-size bet by you would take the pot. If there are around eight units in the pot from previous betting, then a two-unit bet by you is a good investment if all the remaining players fold more than one-fourth of the time—unless there are strategic image considerations involved which would cause you to reevaluate the situation.

If you have some draw prospects, then your total chances of buying the pot plus actually winning with a good last card that completes your hand can add up to a positive expectation.

Position

The position of the remaining players, the number remaining in the pot and where they are seated is another key factor. The fewer players left in the pot, the greater your chances of winning it. And the more players acting in front of you, as opposed to acting behind you, the greater your chances of winning the pot. It is not a joke when someone says, "Well, I did not have a good hand, but I had great position," but a statement underlying a hold'em truth—that position is extremely important.

There is a huge difference between acting first after the turn card with potentially good hands and bettors sitting behind you, and sitting with those same cards with all the remaining players acting *before* you. Of course, if you're sitting last or near last and they have all chosen to check to you, position and a bet may be enough to win the pot.

Put-ons

The third key factor, "put-ons," is who rates to have what, based upon their known tendencies and previous actions. All of the remaining players have either just called or raised before the flop, and have bet, called, or raised on the flop. They have committed chips to the pot and you have to evaluate why. In addition to their betting, they may also have given you extra information with their mannerisms; in other words they may have tells which will help you evaluate the strength of their hands.

In hold'em, an attentive player is often able to spot a potentially profitable situation where a bet or raise will have excellent chances of taking the pot. Although even the greatest experts will not be right all the time, as long as enough of these aggressive plays win pots, the wins will offset the investment losses and show a profit. And the losses are not always so bad. They can be written off to your "advertising budget," which helps get you extra callers on your good hands.

Having reviewed the "three Ps," here you are again after the fourth card and it is your turn to bet or check. What do you tend to do with various bad, medium, and good hands?

PLAYING HAND STRENGTH
Weak Hands

With weak hands you normally fold. After all, in poker, it is the best hand that wins—well, at least if the best hand is around for the showdown. But quite often the best hand is not that good. In these instances, the hand that has the *best position* often wins. If there has been no bet in front of you, you don't have to fold. If you check your weak hand and there is a bet, you might then fold, except in very rare circumstances where you bluff a raise. To simply call in this situation with nothing would be unthinkable.

You might bet and hope that your opponents fold, giving the pot to you uncontested.

And there is a third possibility—an opponent bets out and you consider raising. Bluffing with a check-raise takes twice as much investment and should only be attempted against a player who you have strong reason to believe is bluffing or betting thin cards. Bluffing with a check-raise is a very effective tactic, but of course it depends upon your opponent taking the first step. And it only works if you have read your opponent correctly.

If you think that the remaining players have weak hands, and that bluffing fits into your overall game plan, you might try a simple bet. Of course, there is always the danger that an opponent forgot to bet his good hand, or that a good player preferred the odds of not making a "thin bet," or even that Dangerous Dan might raise with or without a good hand. But in the end, your final thinking is a matter of weighing your possibilities with the likely action of your opponents, and making the best percentage plays.

Good Hands

With most good hands you normally bet. Checking with a good hand in hopes of getting to check-raise is more likely to succeed in hold'em than in Omaha. Hold'em has a larger percentage of "default" pots in which no one has a good hand and later acting players are more likely to be aggressive. It is important to mix up your play. You need to occasionally check a big hand, not only to check-raise, but to vary your style and add intimidation to your checks.

NOTE FROM CARO

When you become sophisticated enough to fool opponents by sometimes betting when you should "obviously" check, checking when you should "obviously" bet, remember that you're making these exceptions for a reason. And they're exceptions.

Don't get into the habit of making "exceptions" so often that you forget that good hands should usually be bet and bad ones should usually be checked.

which normally apply, except for extremely tight players who routinely "pull" instead of "push."

First, when you solicit a check-raise, you should either have the nuts or what you reasonably expect to be the best hand. You should be in a situation where you don't fear a reraise. If someone raises you back, it is highly preferable to be happy rather than sad that you cleverly maneuvered to put in three or more bets rather than just two bets.

A second practical check-raise principle is that it is better to attempt a check-raise when you think you know specifically which opponent is likely to bet. When there are multiple opponents remaining in the pot, check-raising is most effective when you expect that one of the opponents— your "target"— is sitting to your left and will bet.

Medium Hands

With medium hands you normally check. You want to see the last card as cheaply as possible to find out whether your medium hand has become a good hand or a bad hand. However, if you're sitting in a later seat on the turn, and the betting gets checked around to you, should you attempt a bluff and try to win the pot right now?

There is one major consideration worth noting here. If you have a hand that must see the last card to improve, that is, a good come hand such as a four-flush or two-way straight, you should only attempt the bluff if you feel that the odds of a bluff winning the pot are considerably higher than the two negative aspects of betting—one, the odds of running into a raise, which you would have to call; and two, the likelihood of losing action if you hit the last card. In other words, if you complete your draw on the river, you hope that the fifth card improves opponents' hands enough to call or at least doesn't dissuade them enough to fold.

Although bluffing on good draw hands might be

fashionable, it might be less than profitable against very aggressive opponents.

Be aware that many of the bluffs that would have worked on the turn, will still work on the river. Those bluffs that would have worked after the turn and are no longer effective on the river will be somewhat offset by the money you save on ineffective bluffs—and by some new bluffs that will be effective after the last card, but not after the turn when an opponent gets "stuck in." An opponent who called a turn bet is more likely to call on the river than an opponent who had a free turn card.

ATTACKING A WEAK TURN

One opportunity that often occurs after the turn card is "picking up a dropped ball." When the player that bets the flop—a player who may or may not have raised before the flop—checks after the turn card, this creates an opportunity. He is either stating that he did not really like the flop and will go quietly if there is a bet, or that he is trapping and may check-raise, which is less likely. If the player who acts next bets, he puts pressure on the other in-between players, since the original driver is still a threat to raise as well.

If the original driver merely calls this bet, the pressure remains, especially if a brick comes up on the river. The turn bettor probably makes the automatic bet. The players trapped between this bettor and the original driver might be reluctant to call for fear of the raise. The original driver might have overcards only and if the new driver is good enough to know all this, he might well be bluffing.

CHECK-RAISING OR BETTING OUT

Checking into several opponents who have not given any previous information is often unsound unless you know something, such as one or more of the later-position players have a tendency to bet. Absent such knowledge, a check is more likely to cost you money since you can't get more money into the pot. If you check, it might get checked out. And if you check and someone bets, there will be an opponent acting after your position. If you raise an earlier-position opponent who has opened the betting, most other players will fold, and you have accomplished little unless you're a tight player who gets more action as a caller.

If you're hoping to promote a bigger pot, it is often better to start the betting yourself than to check it around to a bettor on your right, unless you have a tight image. Perhaps one of your opponents might even raise.

Although occasional check-raises should be part of your game plan to add more integrity and fear to your usual checks, normally the simple businesslike bet has more going for it and risks less than the check-raise. Contrary to what you would initially think, a free card is often a huge risk! It is usually best to attempt check-raising only with very good hands.

THE RIVER

When the last card hits the table, your hand is no longer a mystery—now you know what you have. Of course, what your opponents have made determines whether you have a good hand or a bad one.

Playing Good Hands for Value

The last card appears and you think you have a winning hand. Absent bets by other players, when it is your turn to act, you bet your good hand. What could be simpler?

The only time you'll check in the hopes of making a check-raise is when you're reasonably sure that a specific opponent is likely to bet, thus getting more money in the pot for you. If your opponent is the driver and you feel he has momentum and will continue to bet, a check on the river might be the best play.

This is particularly true in a multiway pot. If the previous bettor is sitting to your left and cooperates by betting, then the other players have to act before it is your turn and you get a good shot at their action, too. If instead, you had led off with a bet and the player to your left called or raised, they might have dropped and the hand would be less profitable.

There are rare occasions when you trap without a specific target, but on these occasions you're probably trapping because there are several aggressive players behind you. You should be more inclined to check if you have a tight image (you're feared), than if you have a loose image (you're loved).

What happens in the fortuitous situation when you're looking at the nuts or close enough to the nuts that you're willing to raise and some other player bets first? If you're the only other player, or only one of the other players might call, obviously you raise.

But what if, in a multiplayer pot, the first person bets and you're next to act? If there are several other players left, especially if the last card was not a brick, it is usually correct to simply call and hope. Much of the time you'll break even when you get one additional caller, in place of the one or fewer calls from the bettor had you raised. Occasionally, however, you might hit pay dirt with a raise behind you, which can get several more bets in the pot than if you had raised directly.

Bluffing on the River

Let's say that the last card doesn't improve your hand. Your first instinct might be to throw away your cards in disgust or to show your high-percentage failed draws to a neighbor, looking for sympathy. But, wait! All is not lost yet.

Maybe everyone else at the table feels the same way about the river card.

Should you make a random last-card bluff?

There are three types of bluffs to consider: the drive bluff, the random last-card bluff, and the big bluff.

Drive Bluff

Undoubtedly, the most successful form of bluffing at hold'em is the *drive bet*, which is a type of continuation bluff. A **drive bluff** is when a player bets on the flop (he may or may not have raised before the flop), the turn, and the river. Quite often this driver gets several folds each round, and hopefully no callers on the turn or river so the pot is virtually uncontested.

Although everyone knows that most drivers occasionally are driving dubious values, the driving and winning of uncontested pots is very effective in hold'em—and not really considered bluffing unless someone happens to call and catch one. You can often successfully get away with drive bluffing three or four hands in a row.

Another effective continuation bluff is when a player either bets or raises on the turn and then follows through by betting after the last card. This is often a variation of the "big bluff" discussed below, where the bluffer on the turn bets or raises to create an illusion of strength, and then follows through by betting after the last card, especially if the last card is a brick. If no one in the pot has a good hand, which is likely, this two-step bluff is often successful, especially if the player in last calling position is unlikely to call.

The Random Last Card Bluff

A **random last card bluff** is simply a bet made on the river without having bet or raised on the previous round, the turn. The random last card bluff is not as effective as the other types of continued bluffs, which generally have a much higher percentage of success, because it is less believable and has less leverage. An opponent needs to call just one more bet (assuming he is not trapped between players) to win all the bets that have already made it into the middle.

These last card bets can be analyzed into two categories, depending on whether or not the last card was a brick.

When the last card is a brick, then these random last card bluffs are not very effective unless you catch the previous driver with nothing (he might have drive-bluffed) and all other callers with nothing. When there is a weak board, players tend to call you with small pairs, simply because you might be bluffing or thin-betting with a weak hand. In these situations, many players in early seats prefer to check, rather than thin-bet, their high pairs and then "block the plate."

The Big Bluff

If the last card was not a brick but in fact was the third or fourth card to a flush or straight, a bluff bet at this point is called a **big bluff**, because the bettor is representing that this dangerous looking card has just given him a big hand. In this situation, the bluffer might be reasonably successful at causing opponents holding high pairs and sometimes better to fold, even though they have been doing the previous betting. This is especially true if the bluffer has an "honest" image.

You might note that this big bluff does not work very well when someone actually has made a big hand!

PLAYING MARGINAL HANDS

It is relatively easy to play either good hands or bad hands. What to do with marginal hands is usually less clear. If you judge that your marginal hand is probably better than your opponent's hand, you might want to bet to extract one more double size bet from your opponents.

If you have serious doubts as to whether your hand has a reasonable chance to win, you might want to project a strong image and try to check the hand out, that is, get a free last round before the showdown. Occasionally, you might find a situation where a bet, or a raise of a suspected bluffer, increases the likelihood of winning substantially.

If you judge that your hand might be better than opponents acting before you, but perhaps slightly inferior than the player who acts immediately after you, you might want to try betting, which might pressure the player after you into folding a winner. He is in a situation where he not only faces your bet, but there is an opponent acting after him. If your right hand opponent calls your suspected bluff with a lesser hand, then that is pure gravy.

Let's say that the last card hits the table and you have a possible winner, but by no means a great hand. You might have two low pairs (shame on you for playing those bad cards) or perhaps you have high pair on board with a good kicker (much more fashionable). For example, you hold a king and queen, and a queen is the highest card on a board that doesn't look very dangerous.

Should you bet or check?

The answer depends on your position, your evaluation of the remaining players and previous betting, and whether or not the last card was a brick. Once again position is a key factor in how you play. Most often you'll check in first seat and plan to **block the plate**, that is, call if someone bets. One of the advantages in checking is that you might even induce a bluff. However, you would not dream of raising even if you consider yourself to be a slight favorite to have the best hand.

In last seat, if everyone checks around to you, you

might consider risking the thin bet. If everyone folds, you have risked something, and gained nothing—except the right not to show your cards. If someone just calls, you'll probably have the winner a fair percentage of the time. But if someone raises, you'll be beat a large percentage of the time, unless he is bluffing.

So do you call or fold? Wouldn't you rather turn back the clock and have checked instead?

The Brick Rule

The above uncomfortable situation can be avoided a large percentage of the time by using what I call Cappelletti's "Thin Betting Brick Rule." When you get check-raised, most often the trapper has a flush, straight, or trips that were made on the last card. If the last card did not make three suited cards on the board, four to a straight or three straight cards (you assume that your opponents are not playing two unusual cards) or did not pair the board, then betting is safer. The only remaining danger is that the last card brick matched a pocket pair, which again is quite unlikely. If the last card brick gave someone two pairs, he might bet or simply call.

Overall, betting after the last card in a late position is clearly most advantageous when the last card is a brick or if you know your opponents very well.

The "brick rule" also applies in certain strong flop situations. For example, suppose you call in late position with the J♥ and 9♥. The flop hits with the 10♥, 6♥ and 4♥! There is a bet and two calls to you, so you raise, and all three opponents call. The fourth card is the 3♠, everyone checks to you, you bet, and everyone calls. The last card is the 6♣, pairing the board, and everyone checks to you.

Here is what the situation looks like:

You Hold

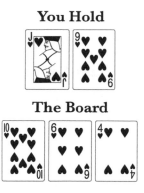

The Board

Although you're happy that no fourth heart appeared, when the last card paired, it seriously hurt your chances. The fact that three players called against a likely flush—especially if your opponents are reasonable players—greatly diminishes the likelihood that betting a non-brick last card will have a positive expectation.

If you bet and have the best hand, you would probably get one or fewer callers. If you bet and are beat—well over a third of the time, you'll either be beat from the start or by a full house on the last card—you'll probably get raised. You should check and be happy to win the present pot or at least not to lose two more big bets. If the last card had been a brick, then you would probably bet, call a raise if one is made, and then hope that your hand holds up.

CONCLUSIONS

We observed at the start of this chapter that most of the creative moves in hold'em take place on the preflop or flop. Not coincidentally, these betting rounds just happen to be the smaller money rounds. On the turn and river, as the stakes increase, play becomes more straightforward. When you have good hands, you bet, raise, or sometimes merely call and "block the plate." When you have inadequate cards you usually fold or occasionally bluff.

On the other hand, quite often there are times when hands that are hotly contested on the flop get checked out on the turn. You might prefer to see the last card free and then check it out if you have some chance of winning with a marginal hand.

After-the-flop raises sometimes muffle the action on hands in which no one improves. Sometimes, when a large starting pot has been narrowed to two or three players, neither player can afford to drop at the showdown, for example, when two players each have the high pair with less than top kicker. Each player might prefer to check and minimize possible losses, since, if one of the players has less than what he's thought to have, a desperation bluff seldom works and a payoff call is almost automatic.

When no one bets on the turn, if you would have called because you believed you might have the best hand (not a drawing hand), you should strongly consider calling a bet on the river. If you would have called a bet on the turn, the river bet might well be an attempt to steal. If an opponent bets and you're not convinced that he has you beat, it is better to err by calling since you lose much less when you're wrong. For example, if the pot is greater than five times the amount of the last bet, then you only have to be right one out of five times to show a profit calling.

With the exception of an occasional skillful bluff, betting, checking and calling on the turn and river are relatively straightforward plays—not nearly as complex and demanding as betting before and after the flop.

GENERAL BASIC STRATEGY OVERVIEW

FLOP, TURN, AND RIVER

BEFORE THE FLOP

Be very selective, that is, tight. Get involved only with premium hands, especially in early positions. Don't be tempted to play mediocre hands in early position. In late or last position, the positional advantage is strong enough to justify being aggressive on lesser hands.

ON THE FLOP

Fold all hands without sound prospects unless the pot is sufficiently large to justify your draw or unless your present holding is reasonably likely to be the best hand. Basic strategy does not include "speculating" after the flop.

TURN AND RIVER

With double-size bets, turn and river card betting should be very conservative. Raise after the last card only with near-locks or occasional bluffs.

INTRODUCTION

Omaha is steadily gaining in popularity because the game is fun and has lots of action. It is seldom played "squeaky tight." The greater number of starting cards keeps more players in the hand, which generates bigger, more interesting pots, and enough action to satisfy even the cravings of home game poker players.

Omaha high-low split, which usually requires an 8 or better to qualify for low, is so addictive that most high-low aficionados now strongly prefer Omaha to all other high-low poker games. They have become *Omaholics*. Omaha high-low split has become roughly twice as popular as straight high Omaha, even though most experts consider straight high Omaha to be the game requiring more skill.

It is ironic that overall losers win more often at Omaha than at hold'em or seven-card stud. There are more than twice as many last-card turnarounds in Omaha as there are in hold'em, thus rewarding chasers more often. Another reason for the greater and more frequent success of overall losers at Omaha is that the average-caliber players at Omaha are usually less skilled and less effective than the average-caliber players at hold'em and seven-card stud.

Interestingly, it is usually the average players (not the beginners or the experts) who bad-mouth Omaha, mostly because Omaha can be so cruel on the last card. But where there is food, there are feeders. Where the losers go, the experts and the average players follow. This is the great food chain of poker.

A Big Opportunity for Winning Players

Winning players should be greatly impressed by the potential profit at Omaha because a large percentage of players typically call before the flop. More callers before the flop means more players after the flop. More loose money in the pots generally means bigger payoffs. Also, having more callers before the flop allows an expert to "get involved" in more hands per round. More volume means a greater hourly long-term profit.

Data we gathered from sessions at tables with alternating rounds of Omaha and hold'em indicate that the average hourly profit for Omaha and Omaha high-low—of two to three big bets per hour—is roughly double that of the approximately one-and-a-half big bets per hour for hold'em. That is clearly good news to those Omaha players who measure their earnings by the hour.

The four-card starting hands in Omaha create a greater frequency of big "monster" hands than in hold'em. For example, royal flushes occur roughly four times as often in Omaha. This is a benefit since many card rooms pay cash jackpots for certain big hands.

Fear and Love

In hold'em, it is better to be feared than loved. There are many pots that can be won by default, thus it is desirable to have a tight image. In Omaha, however, it is better to be loved than feared. At Omaha, most pots are won by whoever has the best hand, thus you want to have extra money in the pots that you do win.

THE GENERAL FORMULA FOR WINNING

To become a good Omaha player, you must consistently keep the percentages on your side and understand which plays are sound and which ones are marginal. Before you can make brilliant plays that depart from standard strategy, you have to understand that strategy. And before you start pounding away at your opponents with aggressive plays, you should understand the difference between aggressiveness and recklessness.

To introduce the subject of strategy properly, let's benefit from the wisdom of the ages by listing some old poker axioms, all of which contain at least a grain of truth:

- ♠ The looser you are, the harder it is to win.
- ♠ You can't be a winner if you play too many hands.
- ♠ It's not how many pots you win, but how much you lose in the pots you don't win.
- ♠ Locksmiths always win.
- ♠ Play tight in a loose game; play loose in a tight game.

Perhaps the most obvious distinction between losers and winners is the apparent looseness of most losers. You might counter that some of the best Omaha players appear to play loose much of the time. But appearances are often deceiving.

The first three wisdom-of-the-ages axioms above point to one of the most obvious truths: You cannot afford to play too many hands with inadequate cards. All winning players must know when to fold their cards.

Let's start off by telling you a big secret: It's desirable to *appear* loose at Omaha.

PLAYING LOOSE IN OMAHA

Loose players cannot consistently win at Omaha unless they're playing in games with even looser players. In other words, any player who is a consistent winner at Omaha is either not playing as loose as you think he is, or the game itself is so blessedly loose that almost any kind of decent play will win.

If you're fortunate enough to play regularly in a loose game, you probably don't need this book to win, although it will help. And regular pushover games seldom last—unless the regular big losers are so rich that they never run out of money—so enjoy it while you can.

If you want to win at poker, there's nothing like playing in a loose-as-a-goose game. You have your choice of many good strategies. You can play tight and get top dollar return on the hands that you do play. Or you can play loose and hope that your betting decisions will make you a big favorite over your opponents, many of whom are essentially throwing their money away.

"Cappelletti's theory of relativity" (apologies to Einstein) postulates that you optimize your profit by playing all profitable hands, though of course, in game situations, it is always difficult to determine which marginal hands are above the "profitability line" and which are below.

PLAYING TIGHT IN OMAHA

On the other hand, you cannot afford to be a **locksmith**, a player who only plays sure-win hands; in other words, extremely tight. Many older women and sedate men play a locksmith style. But, of the two extremes, extremely loose or extremely tight, it is far better to be a locksmith. Many locksmiths do quite well, especially if the game is weak and somewhat loose.

However, there are at least three main problems with playing a locksmith style:

1. As soon as the other players figure out that the locksmith always has a good hand when he's in the pot, they won't give much action to him when they

hold marginal hands. They'll tend to fold more often or make only minimal bets when the locksmith is in the pot.

2. Opponents will tend to give action only with real hands. This is especially true in Omaha, where the locksmith will find himself getting outdrawn on the river a larger percentage of the time than is merited by the dollars in the pot, since there are fewer callers.

3. Locksmiths don't get their share of small, uncontested pots. Opponents are folding too quickly against him.

There are certain strategies to use when you find yourself in a pot against a locksmith who is betting on the flop. For one, you should get out of his pot unless you have a very good hand.

With some good hands, when you probably are beating everyone but the locksmith, you might try the "test-the-waters" play. If you're lucky and catch him holding less than the nuts, you can frequently muscle him out with a strong raise on the flop or the turn, and go on to win with a hand weaker than his. If he does not fold, he probably does have the nuts, in which case it is right for you to fold and save the double-size bets.

Playing Tight But Looking Loose

One of the best winning strategies, not only for Omaha, but for all poker variations, is to play like a locksmith, but with enough diversionary betting that opponents don't catch on to your tight play. If you are adequately able to conceal the fact that you play mostly winning hands, you avoid the consequences of the first two locksmith problems listed above and may be able to pick up more blinds with your "diversionary" tactics.

More specifically, you should remain opportunistically tight with your calls, but be very aggressive on hands where you can take the lead and drive the betting. A good rule of thumb is that about half the hands that you start to drive should be merely good come type hands, as opposed to the good winning hands that everyone drives. The other players will soon get the message that you bet on anything and will loosen up on their calls.

Of course, if you do have a good draw hand, you're actually playing sound, not loose. The real art is to know when to continue driving, and when to fold 'em.

Depending on the degree of tightness of the game, you should determine what your own degree of tightness should be. If you plan to play somewhat tight, you should prepare some sort of poker choreography to conceal your tight strategy; that is, try running at least one bluff during the first half hour, especially if head-to-head against a player who is not a diehard caller.

In summary, it's not bad to play like a locksmith if no one realizes it.

Strategy for a Tight Game

But playing a generally tight strategy is not always right. You sometimes find yourself in a very tight game where it seems that everyone is playing like a locksmith. If that's the case, you'd be better off finding another game. Although there are ways to win in very tight games, your expected rate of winning may not be worth your while.

Always remember this cardinal rule: It's easiest to win when there is a lot of loose money floating around.

If the tight game is the only one available, there are several things you can try to improve your chances. First and foremost, start raising before the flop on any decent hand, especially when you're in or near last position. This is your best all around tool for loosening up a game. Then, follow through by driving anything reasonable on the flop. Also, consider a final bluff if you detect weakness. If you get away with bluffing once or even twice without getting caught, you'll be well ahead.

Even if you get caught bluffing every time, that loss may only be temporary: You'll be able to get much of the money back via additional callers when you finally have a good hand. After gaining everyone's hostility for disrupting the peace and tranquility of their little game, settle back for a few hands and see if anyone else loosens up before you go after them again.

You'll find that two or three rounds of this kind of investment leads to a plus situation about three out of four times. Be aware of the real principle of your actions—that the big dollars come rolling in from additional callers in pots won with real cards, not from bluffing gains. However, you need the bluffs to loosen up opponents so that you get more action when you do have the cards to back up the bets.

Psychologically, whenever you're "in control" of the game, the opponents cannot resist playing back at you.

There are times when it is right to play very loose in a tight game, but let's get the reality warning in early. If you're playing loose, either you have to have a reasonable amount of luck to come out a winner or you need a psychological advantage over your opponents so that they fold more than they should against your bets and play deeper into other hands where you have the nuts.

Bluffing Difficulties

In Omaha, a high pair is much less likely to stand up than in hold'em. So you want to be wary of overplaying such holdings as a high pair in last position, especially if the game is very tight, for the reason that you may already be beat

Also, be aware that you cannot bluff your way through in Omaha when there are too many people in the pot. You can't fool all of the people all of the time. At Omaha, bluffing works best when it's one-on-one.

But, sometimes, especially when you're on a roll and you're riding momentum, it is correct to bet aggressively at opponents even if you're not likely to have a winning hand. When you've got momentum, you're not betting your own cards, but are betting against what you think your opponents have. If you get certain lucky situations, you can bluff your way into winning a pot even if everyone at the table knows you might be bluffing!

But you have to learn to get away from bluffing situations when you expect to get one or more callers.

Remember the primary strategic objective of looseness is to get more callers and more reluctant money into future pots. But again, most of the time, you must have real cards to win.

TOO MANY PLAYERS TO BLUFF: FOUR-CARD HANDS REVEALED

Chart key: Action reads left to right, top to bottom. Each betting round begins with → and ends with ←. Other markings and symbols: a (ante); b (blind bet); • (check); = (call, including when big blind sees flop free); ↑ (raise); — (fold); ● (dealer position, a.k.a. "the button"). A seat number surrounded by asterisks (for example, * 1 *) is your seat. Any wager not preceded by a symbol is a voluntary first bet. Wagers indicate the total invested on a betting round. The money in the rightmost column indicates total pot size after the betting. For full explanation of the chart, see Appendix B.

MCU Poker Chart
$25/$50 Omaha High $25 and $50 Blinds.

1	2	3	4	5	6	7	8	9	10	Pot
		●	b25	b50						$75
Q♦ J♦ 10♥ 9♥										Starting hands <<<
					→↑100	=100	=100	=100	—	
↑150[1]	=150	—	—	=150	=150	=150	=150	↑200[2]		
=200[3]	=200			=200	=200	=200	=200[4]←			$1,425

Flop — 3♣ A♦ 4♠ — Pot $1,425

1	2	3	4	5	6	7	8	9	10	Pot
				→✓	✓	✓	✓	✓		<<<
✓[5]	✓[6]←									$1,425

Turn — 10♦ — Pot $1,825

1	2	3	4	5	6	7	8	9	10	Pot
				→✓	✓	100	100	—		<<<
=100[7]	—			=100	—[8]←					$1,825

River — 3♠ — Pot $1,175

1	2	3	4	5	6	7	8	9	10	Pot
				→100[9]		—	=100[10]			<<<
100[11]				=100						$1,175

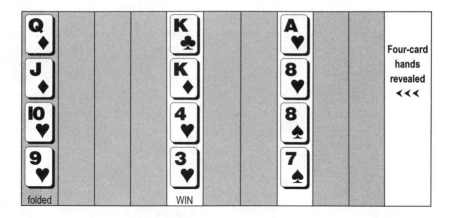

1. This is a profitable Omaha hand if played prudently. It has all kinds of straight-making power and two suits working. It's certainly worth a call, but a raise seems daring, especially since this is a speculative hand and you normally don't want to chase players out. It's usually better to just call and see what develops on the flop. But, what the heck, sometimes, you've just got to push a hand! Here, you'd like the two players to your left to fold, giving you last-to-act position on all future rounds of betting. You're conflicted, since you'd also like them to call and provide you with better pot odds.

But, you raise this time, chasing out one of those players with better position (the one on the button) and the player in the small blind. You played the hand in a way that will add a touch of unpredictability to your game if you end up showing it down. You didn't get last-to-act position, but it might have been worth a try, and you're still in good shape.

2. The player in seat #9 "caps" the betting, which means that no further raises are allowed. The tradition in most casinos is that a bet and three raises are permitted.

3. Since the cap has been reached, you can call with no fear of further raises. That $200 is all it can cost to see the flop.

4. Wow! Seven players stay to see the flop for a maximum $200 each. While this is somewhat unusual, you often get loose pots like this in Omaha when unsophisticated players compete. It's not that there are that many more great hands than in hold'em; it's just that typical players perceive their hands to be better than they are.

5. Well, you didn't expect it to be checked all the way to you after all that betting before the flop. But that's what happened. The flop was very unkind to you, leaving you with a hand you would have folded had there been any betting action.

Here's a chance to bluff. Should you?

No! It's occasionally profitable to bluff one or two opponents, but when there are this many, it's almost always a losing venture. At least one player is bound to be holding a hand strong enough so that betting will not induce him to fold. Mathematically, the likelihood of being called is in proportion to the number of players in a hand—the greater the number of players that are active, the greater the chances that at least one player, if not more, will call to see a bet.

For instance, if each player called 75 percent of the time, then a bluff into one opponent would have a 25 percent chance of success, more than enough to make a bluff attempt profitable, since you'd only be risking $50 to win $1,475. But if these six opponents all call at the same likelihood, because they don't consider the number of opponents you're betting into as a factor indicating that they need a stronger hand to call, then your bluff has less than one chance in 4,000 to 1 chance of winning right now! (It's precisely 4,095 to 1 against if that exaggerated assumption were valid.)

And, even though the pot is laying you over 29 to 1, that's not nearly enough. Of course, you can still luck out and win even if you do get called. But, you can also get lucky and win if you don't bet. And it will cost you nothing to try.

6. And that's what happens. Seat #2 checks and it costs you nothing to see the turn card.

7. You're happy with that 10♦. It gives you a possible royal flush if the K♦ comes on the river. Any king will give you a straight. And, having just paired 10s, you could easily win if another 10 shows up. Two pair might win, also, but in this instance, you shouldn't be too confident about that hand winning, even if you connect. Overall, this hand definitely merits your call.

8. Seat #6 folds, meaning the field has been reduced from seven to just four.

9. Seat #5 connects for a full house without using his kings.

10. This is a pretty pathetic call in Omaha, but players do this!

11. The river card was very disappointing, and you fold. But you had chances to win, and it didn't cost you anything to see the turn card. That turn card made it worth seeing the river. You played this hand well, but didn't win this time. Some of your opponents didn't play nearly as well, and eventually you'll win their money.

WINNING DEFAULT POTS AND BIG POTS

Although it is important to be aggressive at Omaha, is not as critical as at hold'em. Because there are a large number of **default pots**, hands where no one has much in hold'em (perhaps as many as one-third of the players in a tight game), many professionals recommend playing your hands very aggressively as frequently as two hands out of three. If aggressive betting results in your frequently winning hold'em pots uncalled, then it makes good sense to cultivate a tough tight image. Thus, in hold'em, it is better to be feared that loved.

But Omaha is a different game. There are fewer default pots. And while you can occasionally win a high pot unchallenged by lead betting all the way, at loose Omaha and Omaha high-low games, you usually have to put down the best hand to win. This is especially true in two-way Omaha high-low pots, where the players in late seats strain to call.

When you play in a game where it is likely that you'll be called, there is no point in being super aggressive and putting extra money in the pot with mediocre cards, unless you're doing it for specific psychological or tactical reasons.

For example, if you're seen betting and raising with marginal cards, your subsequent bets are more likely to be called. This works to your advantage when you have good cards because you want callers! In Omaha you make most of your money by winning big multihanded pots. The more callers, the more money in the pot, the more you win when you win. When players love to call you, your winning profits go up.

Truly, in Omaha, it is better to be loved than feared.

MAKE OPPONENTS LOVE TO CALL

Bluffing at Omaha works best when you're **driving the betting** (i.e. taking the lead), against one or two meek chasers for smaller size pots. You might try a **come-bluff** drive; that is, drive a draw hand such as an open-ended straight or four-flush, as if you have trips. If you get caught bluffing, you'll lose your investment, but you'll gain valuable "love points." Once opponents learn that you drive with draw hands, they will call more of your subsequent bets. And once they "love" to call you in Omaha, you will get extra money in your pocket.

If your bluff works, you might feel a proud temptation to show it. Most poker pros advise against this, and for good reason. It is not cheaper to advertise by showing a bluff that worked, than to wait until you get caught on a subsequent effort. You should like your prospects for further bluffing!

Keep in mind that it is difficult to bluff when the pot is medium-sized or larger because there is too much money at stake and players will have good pots odds to call bets. Unless you've set up an illusion of strength with the right combination of aggressive action and feel that a bluff will work, it is generally inadvisable to bluff good-sized pots, especially if you have not set up the situation properly.

At limit Omaha, your bluffing prospects are substantially increased when your bets are part of a consistent drive, rather than an isolated bet.

USING IMAGE TO INCREASE PROFITS

Poker players make certain assumptions about the cards opponents are likely to hold based on their previous betting. The most successful bluffing works against opponents who think they already know what you have, but are wrong. But even though the random bluff works only rarely, you might try one infrequently as part of your overall advertising campaign. And if it works once, it might work again!

Since first impressions are important, part of your overall strategy should be to bluff—or never bluff—near the beginning of a session. You want to create the opposite impression of how you want your image to seem.

From a strategic viewpoint, the importance of bluffing in Omaha should not be under-emphasized. Although bluffing is not often successful in limit Omaha, it is certainly desirable to pick up a pot or two each session. And, it is no disaster to get caught. You must advertise with a bluff or two, or else your name will be put on the locksmith scrolls.

Your image, or how the other players perceive you at the poker table, is of utmost importance to your success.

Every poker player has an image. Some are consistent with how they're perceived to play, and others are more dynamic or random or sometimes noisy. And although many high level players like to appear random, that is, have their opponents think that they might do anything, in actuality, even the most active of the top level players tries to employ standard aggressive percentage practices and put on a big show whenever they do deviate.

However, the most important consequence of your image is how it affects your opponents calling or folding in betting situations. Unwary opponents are more likely to call unknown players, since the unknowns are often perceived to be the types who bluff often. Logically, random players should not bluff too often—although they must bluff occasionally. All in all, random players are also merely trying "to be loved," which, indeed, is where the money is at Omaha.

Maximizing Profits With Your Image

We have discussed how a consistent locksmith is in the best position to be a successful bluffer, but note the price tag! At hold'em, since the pots are much smaller and there are more default up-for-grabs pots, it is good to have a tight image so you'll have greater success at stealing pots. At hold'em, it is often a matter of how many pots you win that determines your success.

But at Omaha, there are often huge pots where it takes the best hand to win. When a locksmith drives after a good flop, instead of getting two extra callers as when loved, he probably gets two *fewer* callers! His large pot wins might not even be half of what a loved player wins.

At Omaha, your overall winning results are mainly a result of how large your winning pots are.

Thus, words to the wise: Know your own image. At Omaha, you want many callers. So, plan to present an appropriate image to your opponents.

PLAYING AGGRESSIVELY

One last word about a fundamental truth of limit Omaha. Since no one hand is going to break you at limit Omaha (as opposed to pot-limit), you should play more aggressively than you might at pot-limit Omaha. Of course, it is nice and comforting to have the nuts; but unfortunately, if you sit back and wait for this type of hand, profits will be passing you by. And the nuts might get outdrawn even when you get them.

In pot-limit, you want to almost certain that you have the best hand when you have all your chips at stake. In limit Omaha, with all your speculative actions, you merely have to be a slight favorite in the long run to commit bets into the pot.

Thus, in limit Omaha, your overall strategy is to get in there and fight whenever you get into a good percentage situation. Bad hands win many pots and you should try to get your share by recognizing opportunity. You'll find that you'll accumulate a number of winning sessions during which you never had even one good, secure hand. The surest way to win is to keep the percentages on your side, play tough, and build pots. You'll eventually win your share. Remember that driving aggressively seizes the initiative and gives you an advantage over your callers.

PLAYING "GOOD ENOUGH" HANDS

Although a very tight strategy works well in loose high-low Omaha, if you take that approach in straight high Omaha, you'll miss out on more than half the number of opportunities available. You don't need high quality stuff to win if your bad stuff is good enough. Adjusting and fine-tuning the perfect strategy for any particular Omaha game is a dynamic challenge.

If possible, it is probably a good idea to keep track of the successes and failures of your more speculative plays. This is the best way to learn what works and what doesn't.

As with most forms of poker, no single aspect of your Omaha strategy determines your ultimate fate as a winner or loser more than your initial calling strategy. At Omaha, there seems to be a universal tendency for players to enter the pot with less than adequate hands. This perhaps is one reason for the popularity of Omaha. With more people staying in the pot, there is more action and bigger pots.

One night I was playing in a relatively loose and lively table of nine players where the house rules alternated one round of hold'em with one round of Omaha. In that game, it was unusual to get more than five flop-callers at hold'em, but it was also unusual to have less than seven flop-callers at Omaha! Family pots at Omaha, where everyone calls, were common.

MY FIRST OMAHA GAME

When I sat down to play Omaha for the first time, the player next to me, a lady in a wheelchair, informed me that in this game, you can call on anything. She demonstrated her beliefs by calling every single Omaha hand that night. And she still went home a winner! That happened to be a $2/$5 game in Reno and it illustrated a typical view players have of Omaha that, although unsound, is not severely punished in a limit game. On the other hand, the fact is that the person who calls every hand of hold'em or seven-card stud usually doesn't stay in the game very long and rarely goes home a winner.

Why is Omaha looser? Simply because, as you may have guessed, the difference in winning potential between the best and the worst initial four-card hand in Omaha is much less than in most other poker games. For example, a player who regularly sees the flop in hold'em with two random cards wins much less frequently than he does at Omaha with four random cards. The four starting cards in Omaha make six two-card combinations, each equivalent to a two-card hold'em hand. The result? There are many more turn and river turnarounds.

CRITERIA TO SEE THE FLOP

Even if you can survive at Omaha by calling every hand, it is obviously not an optimum strategy. You don't have to be a great mathematician to realize that if you consistently start with hands of higher potential, you'll have a higher percentage of winners. In Omaha there is a frequent last card back-in factor, but only if you have some good two-card prospects to start with.

Bottom line: If you want to increase your chances of winning, only put your money into high quality Omaha hands.

Where do you draw the line as to what constitutes a high-quality, flop-seeing hand? That is a question to which a lot of study and research by a lot of people has been done, especially at the poker table. Quite a bit of computer research has correlated initial four-card configurations with final winning hands. However, that is an erroneous approach. In real life, hands that would've won at the end often had to fold on the flop!

The best approach, therefore, is to evaluate initial four-card holdings from the standpoint of how well they expect to look on the flop. This is when it really matters. If you have good potential to improve on the flop, then it's often worthwhile to stay in the pot. If you don't hit the flop, you should not be around to see what happens on fifth street where the bets double in size.

So the key to evaluating the potential of your first four

cards is based simply on how well they'll look on the flop rather than how well they'd do if the hand was allowed to be played to completion.

PLAYING ALL FOUR CARDS

Good Omaha players play *all* four cards. Players who use only their best two-card combination are handicapping themselves, almost like a pool player who doesn't use the rails. When you have several long shot two-card combinations in addition to your main holdings, it can add more than 5 percent to your overall winning possibilities.

Weak players often play to the end because their long-shot possibilities sometimes hit. The times these long-shot hands hit and win, wreak havoc on opponents. But for all the times they miss, it adds up to big losses for them and big profits for the other players. The weak players don't care about the percentages because they are often calling anyway, and it turns out that, at least some of the time, it's right to call!

Omaha emphasizes two-card combinations more than any other form of poker. Unlike hold'em, using only one of your four cards to make a winning hand is rare in Omaha. (The only significant example is having the fourth card to a three of a kind exposed.) In Omaha, preflop hand evaluation depends on the possibilities of all the two-card combinations.

You'll be surprised at how often you back into a pot with a two-card combination other than the two-card combinations that kept you in the pot in the first place. This is the reason we emphasize that Omaha is a four-card game and your winning frequency is directly related to the number and quality of two-card combinations in the hands that you choose to play.

If you would like to test the number of flops which

connect with a particular group of pocket cards, simply take the four cards you want to test out of a regular deck of cards and then turn over the remaining 48 cards three at a time. This will give you 16 flops. Note how many of the 16 flops work well with the four-card hand you're testing. For example, if you're testing four cards containing one pair, two of the 16 flops will give you trips. If you're testing two flush cards, then approximately two of the 16 flops will yield a four-flush.

THE CAPPELLETTI OMAHA POINT-COUNT SYSTEM (FOR OMAHA-HIGH)

In order to calculate the sum total of the two-card combinations, I have quantified the combinations into a relatively simple point count system for evaluating the flop potential of the initial four cards at Omaha. This point count system assigns a certain number of points to each of the six two-card combinations, which are then added together. If the total equals 11 or more points, calling is recommended. If the total exceeds 16, raising is recommended.

However, this is subject to the game and your position. You might want to raise or call with fewer points to loosen up a tight game or in situations where the preflop bet is less

NOTE FROM CARO:

In Omaha, having three cards of the same rank is a very bad thing, because you can only use two of them, meaning one card is completely wasted. That's obvious. But...

Having three cards of the same suit usually isn't a bad enough penalty to prevent you from playing a hand you would otherwise play if you only had two of the same suit. Sure, one card of that suit is "wasted," but that same "wasted" card still has the potential power to make pairs and combine for straights.

or because you're in last betting position. If you're playing in a game where the preflop betting is vigorous and often capped, you should tighten up and play fewer hands to the flop. The point count system is detailed below.

CAPPELLETTI OMAHA POINT COUNT FOR TWO-CARD COMBINATIONS

PAIRS: Points = Denomination/2 + 2

For example: two aces = 14/2 + 2 = 9 points
two queens = 12/2 + 2 = 8 points
two fives = 5/2 + 2 = 5 points

FLUSHES: A-x = 6 points
K-x = 5 points
Q-x = 3 points
J-x = 2 points
x-x = 1.5 points (x = any card in same suit)

STRAIGHTS: 2 touching cards = 2 points
(excluding A-2 and 2-3)
(exception: J-10 = 3 points)
2 cards missing one = 2 points (excluding A-3)
(exception: 2-4 = 1 point)
2 cards missing two = 1 point (excluding A-4)
Third card bonus = 2 points (but not A or 2)
Fourth card bonus = 2 points (within five pips)

HIGH CARD (no extra bonus to paired cards)
BONUS: Aces thru tens—1 point each
Nines thru sevens—1/2 point each

POSITION   2 points for last; 1 point for next to last
BONUS:

EXAMPLES: A♣ K♣ A♦ K♦ = 9 + 9 + 6 + 6 + 2 = 32 (best hand)
Q-J-10-9 = 2 + 2+ 1 + 3 + 2 + 2 + 2 + 2 + 3 + 1/2 = 19+
(both suited = 24)
J-9-8-6 = 2 + 1 + 2 + 1 + 2 + 2 + 2 + 1 + 1 = 14
A-Q-9-8 = 2 + 1 + 2 + 2 + 2 + 1 = 10
J-8-6-4 = 1 + 2 + 2 + 2 + 1 + 1/2 = 8+

Comments

♠ Note that aces and face cards are given extra credit for their straight points, (i.e., more than their actual straight potential merits). For example, A-K = 2 points, which is more than it merits for its straight potential, but this is about right considering the overall high card potential value of the A-K. Thus the true value of high cards is reflected in points by using the high card bonus added to this inflated straight point bonus.

♠ Pairs are the best two-card holdings, since they flop a set about one out of eight times, which is slightly more often than two flush cards flop a four-flush. Although low sets can be dangerous, everyone I know would like to have more of them. Even a low pair leads to a win more frequently than an A-x suited (although the flush is more likely to be the nuts).

♠ Most players tend to overvalue the A-x suited holding, although it is one of the better holdings—since it leads to a direct lock-flush win about one out of 21 pots. Lower flush cards are seriously demoted for their second-best potential. However dangerous, low flushes sometimes back into big pots and certainly add a tangible equity to other playable holdings.

♠ The 2-point bonus for a third proximate card, and 2 additional points for a fourth one, reflect the advantages of flops with more than eight straight hit cards (nine to twenty!). For example, when you hold J-9-8-6, a 10-7 flop gives you 12 straight hit cards, all of which are nut straights.

♠ The reason why one hole straight holdings such as 8-6 are given the same two points as two touching cards like 8-7 is that both holdings have two good open-end four straight possibilities on the flop. Note that only the J-10 holding has three good four-straights.

8-6 is good with flopped 9-7 or 7-5 (eight hit cards). 8-7 is good with 9-6 or 6-5.

But 10-9 is not good—low end; however, J-10 is good with Q-9, 9-8, and K-Q, thus 3 points.

RAISING BEFORE THE FLOP

As with hold'em, the greatest tool for changing the character and tone of the game is a preflop raise. If the Omaha game is very loose, with many callers after each flop, you should be less inclined to raise, since you would rather see your flop in place than bet on the come. Remember that in Omaha, even the best possible four cards (A-K-A-K double suited) are a big underdog to the rest of the field taken as a whole.

There are certain kinds of hands in which you would like to reduce attendance in later rounds to increase your chances of winning. For example, if you raise in early position with aces and get only a few callers, the aces have a good chance of holding up. Generally, raising in an early seat—if you can get enough opponent to fold—greatly increases your chances of winning with two high pair.

There are also a number of low-card hands where you would like to raise to force the other low-card competition out. For example, a low straight will hold up better against fewer players. The value of lower-suited cards increases greatly against fewer floppers.

Raises from early position are more likely to reduce attendance due to the out-of-position strength this type of raise indicates. Most callers of the original bet will stick around for subsequent raises.

DRAWING ODDS AND OUTS

Some knowledge of basic percentages is necessary for you to understand the likelihood of improving a drawing hand.

This can be accomplished without serious mathematics. The easiest method for determining the likelihood of making your hand is to count the number of cards left in the deck that will make your hand. Since you don't know what cards are in your opponents' hands, you can consider their cards as if they were part of the remaining deck.

Flush Expectations

In poker parlance, the good cards that complete your hand are called **outs**. If you have two diamonds and the flop also contains two diamonds, then you have nine outs, the nine remaining diamonds (13 total diamonds minus the four diamonds you hold) in the deck that will give you a flush.

There are 45 unknown cards in the deck. Of the 52 starting cards, you know your four pocket cards plus the three on the flop. Thus, the odds of the turn card being a diamond are nine out of 45, or 20 percent. The mathematical combined odds of making the flush either on the turn or river are about 36 percent. That's a little more than one-third of the time.

Straight Expectations

If the flop gives you four cards in a row, that is, a two-way straight draw, then you have eight outs, and can expect to make your straight about one-third of the time. Compare this with the flush above.

Flop

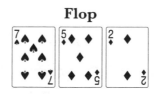

You Hold

Four 9s plus four 4s make your straight. Other possible two-way straights with eight outs:

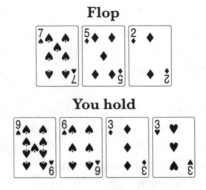

There are four 8s and four 4s that make your straight. A four-card straight missing one inside card, called a **gutshot straight**, has only four outs and will complete on the turn or river about one-sixth of the time, or 5 to 1 against.

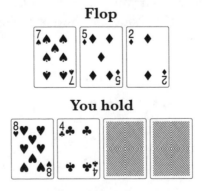

There are four 6s that make the straight. If the flop contains two suited cards, then making your straight with six of the same suit will probably make a flush for one or more opponents. If that's the case, you must make your decisions based on fewer useful outs, in this case three instead of four.

In Omaha, there are some wonderful come hands that can have as many as 20 outs for making a straight. This type of hand is the reason why my point-count system gives bonuses for the three-proximate and four-proximate cards that can surround the right flop cards.

Flop

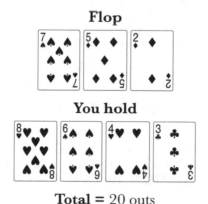

You hold

Total = 20 outs
(Four 9s, three 8s, three 6s, three 4s, three 3s, four aces)

Flop

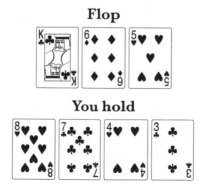

You hold

Total = 20 outs

(Four 9s, three 8s, three 7s, three 4s, four 2s)

Flop

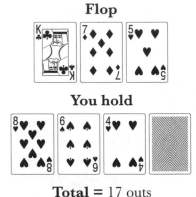

You hold

Total = 17 outs

(Four 9s, three 8s, three 6s, three 4s, four 3s)

The following table gives the approximate percentages for hitting on fourth and fifth streets given the number of outs.

OUTS AND THE CHANCES OF IMPROVING ON THE TURN AND RIVER		
Outs (2 cards to come)	Make on 4th Street	Make by 5th Street
4	.09	.17
6	.13	.25
8	.18	.33
9	.20	.36
11	.25	.43
14	.31	.53
17	.38	.62
20	.45	.70

Note: The approximate odds of hitting a straight or flush should not be equated to the odds of actually winning with that hand. Beware the possibility of losing to a better hand if the board pairs or has three cards of the same suit.

PAIRING THE BOARD

An unpaired flop has nine outs for pairing on the turn, and 12 outs for pairing on the river, minus whatever outs you hold in your hand. If no one has any of the board's outs, the last two cards would pair the board about 42 percent of the time. But that situation would not be particularly meaningful. If no one had any pairs, it would not matter if the board paired.

A more relevant calculation would be based on the assumption that some three to five outs are lurking in the players' hands. Then the board pairs on the last two cards 25 to 30 percent of the time. Generally, the more players remaining in the pot, the greater the likelihood of pair outs being held, and the less the likelihood of pairing the board.

The board pairing just seems to happen more frequently when you're holding the nut flush or straight!

In Omaha, the flop is everything. As these three cards land on the table, even the best possible hands may go down the drain and the most incredibly bad hands could turn into gold.

Strategy lesson number one comes directly from Kenny Rogers's song "The Gambler": "You've got to know when to fold 'em." When it is not your flop, or worse, when it is someone else's flop, it is time to fold. Don't chase rainbows.

TWO-CARD DRAWS

In Texas hold'em you usually cannot afford to play for **two-card draws**, when you need both the turn and river cards to complete your hand. But frequently in Omaha, the fact that you have several of these two-card draw possibilities adds enough equity to allow you to play on with marginal holdings in limit games.

AGGRESSIVE FLOP PLAY

In limit poker, since the betting on the flop is half the amount of the turn and river, you can use this round to make more plays with less cost that the latter rounds, which feature the double-size bets. This after-the-flop bet can be made with impunity, for example, with hands that would drop with fright if raised. And this after-the-flop bet can be raised with impunity as well with hands that if not improved upon, would like a free check on the turn due to the double-size bet.

The flop bet is frequently called with everything from bad hands with position to absolute locks patiently waiting for the big money.

Looking at the Flop

The flop comes—how do you like it?

If you don't like it, simply check and fold on any bet without further ado. Always remember, the main reason weak players lose at poker is because they chase with inadequate cards. It is better to quit than fight with inferior weapons.

There is also no reason to bluff right from the start unless you feel strongly that it is going to work. Save your bluffing allowance for hands that actually have reasonable winning potential. If you play too many hands—that is, find yourself staying in on hands without adequate potential—you're probably going to end up a loser.

Slowplaying a Lock

Let's take a quick look at the happy side. The flop comes and lo and behold, you have flopped quads! You look at your hand in utter disbelief and promptly check when it is your turn to bet!

Your expected value will be much higher if you check on the flop. With an *absolute lock*, you should almost always check and merely call bets on the cheap after-the-flop round. When I say **absolute lock**, I mean a king-high full house without a flopped ace on board, or a hand so good that it won't be beaten. Don't confuse the concept of absolute lock, which is independent of the last two cards, with the term **lock**, which is the best hand possible at the moment.

You would make an exception to checking with an absolute lock on the flop if you're in a game where you're very familiar with the players and want to use reverse psychology, notwithstanding that absolute locks are rare enough. Even in last position you should check and hope someone starts moving on the turn, where the bets are double-sized.

If you try to drive this lock hand, the most likely occurrence is that everyone or almost everyone will fold.

A free turn card will frequently get one or two players more involved in the pot. This is actually the main reason why you slowplay an absolute lock. With an absolute lock, since it is already a given that you're going to win this pot, it is merely a question of how many stay in and how much they contribute. Of course, a good second reason for checking a lock is that you might encourage someone else to bet.

Flopping a nut flush or straight is not an absolute lock, although like most good hands it can turn out to be a lock on the river if the board doesn't pair. You should bet and raise the nut flush or straight as much as you can, while you can. Try to get the two-pair hands out of the pot.

Remember, if the board pairs, which it will do less than 30 percent of the time—even though it seems like it happens more often—you will officially be an underdog.

Since absolute lock hands require either a pair, trips or

straight flush material on the flop, usually there is not much action since you have most of the best cards. However, if there is any kind of action on the flop, just happily call it and count your blessings. Your chance to build the pot will come later at twice the price. Bear in mind that this is purely a pull (rather than push) situation; if you show your true colors too soon, you might lose some business. You also want to give bluffers a chance to do your work for you.

All good Omaha players should be very sensitive about betting into locks and especially paranoid when raised by potential locks.

DRIVING HANDS
The Advantage of Driving

Anyone can win with good cards. Where then does the superior player gain most of his advantage? The answer is that driving properly and raising effectively are the two most important weapons in the arsenal of the good player. They not only bring more money into the pots won, but they increase the number pots won by default by forcing out the competition.

We've discussed that you should fold bad hands and extract as much as you can with the great hands. These hands are comparatively easy to play. What do you do with the in-between hands, the non-lock but good betting hands?

These hands can be called **driving hands**, and for good reason—because you should *drive* with them (i.e. bet strongly). Driving hands are your bread and butter. They occur much more frequently than the too-infrequent locks, and are played differently. Entirely so. If you get nothing else out of this book, you should learn the strategic difference between a lock and a good driving hand.

Good driving hands should not be played nonchalantly. In the finest traditions of poker, these hands should be driven with some amount of flair. A certain offensive mindset or attitude should accompany driving. Most good poker players have their own individual style and characteristic quirks when it comes to driving. But whether the money is thrown in, slammed in, delicately and politely moved in, or deposited with a song, the money goes into the pot—and that player has taken the offensive.

When a player bets aggressively, he is in effect throwing a money gauntlet at his opponents and telling them to pay up or leave his pot. Since any of these good betting hands can be beaten, it is necessary to lessen the competition. A free fourth card often changes a ho-hum, droppable hand into a potential winner, so this would the best time to reduce attendance. Perhaps the most important reason to bet a merely good hand, which can be beaten, is to drive out as much competition as possible in order to increase your own winning chances.

Good Flops for Driving

Let's take a closer look at some of these good driving situations. Note that many driving hands are related to a certain type of flop. Flops can be generally analyzed into four types, in descending order of strength:

1. **Pair:** The flop contains a pair (trips are very rare);
2. **Flush:** The flop contains two or three cards of the same suit;
3. **Straight:** The flop contains two or three adjacent cards;
4. **Random:** None of the above.

If a flop is more than one type, it is the higher type (lower number) that prevails. For example, if the flop consists of both a pair and a flush, you should be wary of your flush and straight prospects, especially if the raising starts, since there is a high likelihood of a full house. Similarly, be wary of straight prospects when there may be a flush lurking.

Good Hand/Flop Combinations for Driving

The following list of good flop-betting hands usually assumes the lack of a higher flop threat presence:

1. **Board Set:** You have a card that matches the pair flopped.
2. **Hidden Set:** One flop card matches your pair in hand.
3. **High Flush:** You hold the 1st, 2nd or 3rd highest flush draw.
4. **Straight:** You hold a made straight (beware the low end) or an eight card or more draw to a nut straight.
5. **High Two Pair:** The higher the better.
6. **High and Low Pair:** Marginal, beware the "drawing dead" possibilities (few or no win cards).

When one of the above flops hits the table and it is your turn to bet, you really don't have much choice. You simply must bet, unless you're trying to accomplish some high-level psychological ploy. You should take the opportunity to seize the initiative and become the driver. It is so imperative to do this, that it is not really a question of, "to drive or not to drive."

If your approach to poker is to sit and let other people do all the betting, you're not going to be a regular winner at poker. You need to seize the initiative. You must understand that your best chance of winning in Omaha comes from driving hands, playing offense, as opposed to chasing and playing defense.

In other words, if you fail to drive when you should, you're not taking advantage of some of your best percentage strategies. There is a tendency for new Omaha players to sit back and merely call with excellent draw hands, such as four to a nut flush or an open-ended straight with eight outs or more, reflecting perhaps their bird-in-the-hand thinking

There are a number of reasons for betting these hands, not the least of which is if you have reasonable prospects of winning, you want to get at least some initial money into the pot. The importance of building a pot, which you might win, is obvious, especially if there were no raises before the flop.

Many times you would actually rather not put any more of your own money into the pot until you see the next card, a flush come or a straight come. But you don't want to risk winning a nothing pot!

Control Factor

An additional and very strategic reason for driving is the direct effect it has on psychological considerations, such as the tightness or the looseness of the game and the control factor (which players are consciously or subconsciously competing to control the game).

Not Driving

For completeness, let's take one more look at driving from the negative point of view: what happens when you *don't* drive. Let's say that you play passively and check your hand. If your opponents play like this, it is probably a tight, dull game and it is likely that it will be checked around. You have saved a minimum bet if you lose the pot, but since you have a much better hand than most, you had a decent chance to win the pot.

By not driving you allow everyone a free chance to

improve—and probably someone did. But it won't matter much anyway due to your lack of betting, it was a nothing pot anyway.

BUILDING POTS

There is a delicate balance between saving bets and investing bets to make the pot worthy of contesting in case you hit. This first after-the-flop bet often serves the purpose of turning what might have been a nothing pot into a something pot. If it is really destined to be a nothing pot, then you might as well bet and pick up the antes before somebody else wins the raffle. If you get to drive with your nut-come hand and don't hit on the turn, which will usually be the case, then you should frequently abandon your drive and check. Less frequently, if conditions look favorable, you'll continue driving and try the bluff.

Most importantly, you want to maximize your chances of winning by driving out long-shot players who might outdraw you; for example, a player with two low pair or one pair who will normally fold on the first bet. How many times have you folded against a bet on the flop but wished you had stayed in when the fourth card turned? Well, that's the situation you want to avoid with your opponents.

Another strategic advantage in being the bettor is that there is always some chance that everyone will fold and you'll be an instant winner. If you get one or more callers, you've still gained on the hand because you seized the initiative. If you and the other callers are all on come hands and no one hits, then whoever makes the final bet will probably win a reasonably-sized pot, unchallenged. This will happen enough times to make driving bets, in the right situations, profitable plays.

If you can win more than one-third of your driving pots, you'll probably have a good night, especially if you can win one or more bluff drives. Even if you lose several bluff drive attempts, the money will usually come back from additional callers later. As you gain experience, you'll learn to distinguish when it is best to follow through with a bluff drive (certainly no more than a third of the time) or when it is best to stop driving and conserve your losses.

This is a good time to reiterate that limit Omaha is not a bluffer's game. Random efforts to spear an up-for-grabs pot have dubious success. Bluff drives are one clear exception to this. The final bet of a power drive (starting at the flop) often goes uncalled because the last person remaining has virtually nothing to call with. Of course, the best results are obtained when you correctly judge that no one has hit. Note, however, that the last cards are hard to read in Omaha; reading the average player is often easier.

THE IMPORTANCE OF DRIVING

If the game is loose and you're confident that an opponent will bet, you can check. But in this instance, you've become merely the caller, the chaser, when you could have, for the same price, been the bettor.

Are you now in position to raise? No. Unless you have a set, you don't want to raise! You don't want to put a lot of your own money into the pot at this juncture, especially if you're betting a come hand.

What you really want to do at this point is exactly what you could have done by betting first—namely, to be the driver yet another time, and to get the "half price" money into the pot. Probably the only good aspect of checking nut-come hands instead of driving is that occasionally you might trick one of the last-position players into thinking his second or third nuts hand is better than it is, and he'll do your betting for you. But normally, the overall dollars when you hit are not much more than if you had driven.

There are two points about frequency of driving that are worthy of note.

1. The more frequently you drive, the more callers (chasers) you tend to get. This is good.
2. The more frequently you drive, the more callers you get when you're trying to steal a pot. This is not good if you happen to be stealing. This should suggest something to you about when *not* to follow through.

A successful driving strategy depends on three main factors—the turn card, the remaining competition, and the quality of your driving hand.

Driving: From the Flop to the Turn

Although you should start driving on the flop with all the hand types listed earlier, you might want to discontinue driving on the turn with lesser hands. There are very good driving hands—a high set with or without extra equity—and then there are second-rate driving hands, which often lose. It is important to realize that just because you drive on the flop, does not mean that you should continue driving on the turn. You must be aware of signs that advise you to shift gears.

There are certain one-shot type hands where you won't bet on the turn unless you improve, for example, a high pair gut-straight combination. Sometimes, even after driving a hand, it is correct to fold yourself right out of the pot after the fourth card, especially when you're facing a raise or series of raises. There is no dishonor in a prudent fold.

In an average session of limit poker, you will "win" much of your money by *not* losing it; that is, you'll save money by discrete folds.

It should be clear that the player who bets first has the

best chance of winning any given pot by default. Hopefully, one or more of your bluff drives—you should have several each session—will be at the right time. In poker, as in sports, there are more opportunities to score on offense than on defense. Of course, there is also something to be said for sitting back.

However, having the initiative not only gives you an edge, but enhances your "loved" image. Even if you're the type who never bluffs, there still are many advantages in driving on the flop.

THE TRAP CHECK

One alternative to driving is the trap check, sometimes with the intention of check-raising. If one of the opponents acting before you cooperates and makes the first bet, a check-raise is probably the most effective way to get your opponents to fold.

All of the players to your left are faced with a double bet that might get raised again. They normally cannot take the pressure and will fold, sometimes with reasonable hands. The main reason for check-raising is to get enough "comers" out of the pot to increase your own chances of winning the raised pot. Borrowing a term from business, you are essentially doing a "leveraged buyout."

PLAYING A LOCK

Driving would not be a good way to play an absolute lock, except as an occasional counter ploy. Typical hands you'll want to hold for this strategy include low trips or two high pair, especially if there are middle flush or straight comes. Note that this plan does not work very well if it gets checked around.

AGGRESSIVE RAISING

Of the various moves available, raising or failing to raise is what separates the good players from the lesser players. Most raises, especially those on the flop, are tactical moves to drive out competition. And it really works. No one with a second rate hand wants to get involved in first-rate betting.

In practice, however, the raising flurry seldom continues on the turn and river. Somebody usually backs down. Of course the paradox is that good players who are making the most raising noise on the flop often don't have much. They're loosely investing half-size bets in an attempt to take advantage of the slightest edge, jockeying for position, as well as trying to reduce competition.

Most average players do not realize that when a good player bets on the flop, that good player might well be less aggressive if he had a very good hand. But even with this knowledge, you can't afford to call unless you actually have something better than they might have—unless you're a great gambler! But, if it's the latter, at these stakes, you'd better be a great gambler as well as a lucky one!

Aggressive Driving: In or Out

The message should be clear: When the raising starts, especially if there are more than two people involved, don't get involved without a hand that wins frequently enough to show a long-term profit. A lock flush draw (no pair on the flop) or a nut straight draw with eight or more outs qualifies in this category.

However, if you have a premium come hand and are a favorite to make your hand on the turn or river—for example, you have a straight draw with fourteen or more outs—it's correct to raise on the flop. Raising here not only increases the money in the pot, but, much more importantly, increases your overall chances of winning by driving out potentially dangerous two pair and lower four-flush hands.

Most of your raising strategy can be greatly simplified by what I call the "adequacy principle." When the raising starts, if you don't have an adequate hand, you should fold, even if you know the raiser usually bets on cheese. When facing potentially good hands, most of your marginal calling equity has disappeared and the increased cost of playing makes calling a bad play. If you do have an adequate hand, you may either call or raise, whatever is best for the situation; it's essentially all the same! In fact it's often correct to do the opposite of what seems best.

Sometimes putting in the second or third raise yourself puts a damper on the raising. You give your opponents something to think about. It also gives you the initiative for the turn. The converse of this is if your hand is really good (a high set, for example) and you would welcome the cap, you might reluctantly call.

In this case, you're strategically placed for fourth and fifth street double-bet action. However, if you have adequate values to call the raises, you can raise or call somewhat indiscriminately, since your mathematical expectations are about the same. Thus it becomes more a matter of feeling and art! The best time to throw in an extra raise is when you might be able to pressure somebody out, especially when a timid soul is hanging on.

The Raise as Leverage

Most players fold when confronted with a cold double raise, whereas most of the callers between the raiser and the first bettor are already on the hook and will usually call the single raise. Accordingly, with marginal hands, for example, a high two pair or low set, if you're sitting close after the bettor, you should usually take this opportunity to raise—

this should prompt many folds and also gains position and tempo on the opening bettor.

If you catch the driver and callers on come hands, your two pair might even hold up if you can get enough opponents out. With many callers it will take a straight or higher to win about 75 percent of the time. Also, you might get yourself a free last-card shot at your full house. There are some hands that are not good enough to call with, but with which you might raise. For example, a high pair by itself is not a good call from the standpoint of improvement potential; but if you raise and everyone drops out except two flushers, and they don't flush, then you'll probably win the pot.

Using the Inhibitory Raise to Take Control

Let's say that you're playing in a $5/$10 game and two of your cards are the ace of spades and another spade, and the flop contains two spades. One of the five players sitting in front of you makes a $5 bet, everyone else folds, and it is now your turn to act. There is enough money in the pot to justify a $5 call.

The turn card comes and it is not a spade. The limit is now $10 and the driver probably will bet it. At this point your $10 call is marginal.

But suppose instead that you had raised the $5 bet on the flop! Unless the original driver had an unusually good hand, he would usually call your raise, and then, being intimidated by your raise, would probably check to you on

NOTE FROM CARO:

Remember that a sophisticated Omaha player might be betting on the value of his outs alone, without even being confident that he has you beat right now. Hands that can be bet profitably because of outs are much more common in Omaha than in hold'em.

the turn. Even if the driver likes the turn card, he might check to you planning to check-raise.

If you don't hit the turn card, you can check and see the river without further investment, having invested a total of just $10 between the flop and the turn. In the original scenario it would have cost you $15 to see the final card, his $5 flop bet plus his $10 turn bet, instead of the $5 flop bet and $5 flop raise. If you did happen to hit the turn card, your "inhibitory" raise brought more money into the pot!

Whenever the driver doesn't reraise, whether you hit or not, your raise has optimized your situation, which is what winning poker is all about. Essentially, you're investing a $5 raise to grab control away from the original driver so that you have the option to be the driver on the turn. This tactical inhibitory raise is most effective when the next round of betting will be at a higher limit. It is also valuable because it gives you some control at the same limit.

THE RERAISE

If the opening driver is a good player and reraises you, he might be trying to keep the momentum for his final drive (with value or on a come bluff) or setting up a play for a turn card bet designed to oust you from the pot or see where you're at—since you'll often fold to raises after the turn. Many of these after-the-flop raising contests are analogous to two bucks showing off their horns, each hoping that the other will back down.

CHASING STRATEGIES

You have probably heard that the best poker players—or perhaps the great poker players—rarely call; they either raise or fold. Their play is based on the theory that if your hand is good enough to get involved at all, then it should be good enough to raise. While this may have validity in hold'em, it doesn't apply in Omaha.

In Omaha, there are many hands where the driver with the best hand on the turn has virtually no chance to win on the river! In fact, it is easy to construct situations where every card left in the deck gives some chaser a better hand than a driver holding a straight.

Keep this fact in mind: In Omaha, chasers win more often than in any other form of poker, even when the driver has a legitimate hand. The conclusion is that it must not be so bad to be a chaser! In fact, the mathematics of the chase is a large part of what makes Omaha so popular. And this is a primary reason why weaker players do better at Omaha than in other poker games.

Chase or Fold: Estimating the Play

The flop comes and you have a marginal hand that is not good enough to bet on. Your first choice is for everyone to check, giving you a free look at the turn. Unfortunately, as is more often the case, someone likes his hand and bets.

Do you chase or just get out cheaply?

Omaha is different than other poker games. Because you have four cards, there are a number of possibilities that should be evaluated and added together. As with all gambling, it all boils down to approximating your probability of winning versus the number of dollars expected to be at stake in the pot. Obviously, exact mathematical calculations are difficult and also usually involve assumptions about what your opponents have.

But don't avoid all this just because you feel weak in math. You need to add up your various equities (prospects of good things happening) and judge whether or not a call is reasonable. In general, as long as you have some good solid potential, even if you're unable to approximate your actual percentages, it is probably not so bad to chase a card to the turn—as long as you don't participate in chasing a bad percentage play the next round.

In these situations, position is important. There are a number of hands that you would not call in first or second position, but would willingly bet in last position, such as certain gut straights with other equity.

One of the most difficult decisions in Omaha, as in any poker game, is whether or not to make a close call as justified by current pot percentages when it is likely that there will be a raise behind you. For example, let's say there was one raise before the flop and the first-position player bets and is called by the second-position player. You're in third position with a gut straight draw, which would be the nuts, and no pair or flush flopped. There are still three players behind you, including the player who raised preflop. The current pot has fourteen times the amount of the bet you're now faced with.

If you were in last position you would happily call with your gut straight draw (10 to 1 against completing it on the turn), which, if hit, would be a big favorite to win a pot which will likely get bigger.

However, you know that the flop raiser is fond of raising and he seems to be chomping at the bit. If you call and he raises, you would be in a negative percentage situation for the duration of the pot. Still more raises this round and on the turn could be expensive. Even if you hit, you might lose or split on fifth street. Calling here is a marginal prospect indeed. Your best play is to fold. Note again that your position is critical here.

Oversimplified Rule of Thumb

There is no all-inclusive rule as to what constitutes a correct call in a certain position because of the many variables. But here is an oversimplified rule of thumb: If your position is such that the likelihood of a raise behind you is less than one third (this judgment is based upon the nature of the game itself as well as the specific individuals behind you), you may risk a call with any hand where the turn card gives you a positive expectation, based upon the amount of money in (or likely to be in) the pot.

Bad Fishing

When you have a bad hand, you'll normally need at least several cards to improve to a winner, preferably the nuts. However, there are situations where you have few or no direct winning cards, but more than half the deck will improve your hand to a good position. The presence of several additional two-card comes (they're worth, roughly, about 4 or 5 percent each) makes a big difference in the long run. There is often a thin dividing line between the good percentage investments and the bad fishing-along calls.

If it seems close, you should probably fold, especially if you may be subject to a raise after your bet goes in the middle.

MARGINAL HANDS AND POSITION
Scenario 1

To further illustrate some of the principles of hand and position evaluation, let's use a marginal hand as an example. You're playing in a nine-handed $5/$10 limit Omaha game. Seven players call the flop without raising (there is generally less preflop raising in Omaha than in hold'em). You hold A♦ 10♦ 9♦ 7♣. The flop is the K♠ 9♣ 6♦. Thus if an 8 turns (about 10 to 1 against on the next card or about 5 to 1 on either the turn or river, you would have a straight.

If two diamonds flop (about 21 to 1 against) you would have the nut flush (though the K♦ could lose to a full house).

You could get the Q-J for the highest straight, come up with a full house or the miracle straight flush! You also have various back-in possibilities that might occur if your pair of nines trip or become aces-over. This type of hand, which has no good primary draws but has a number of secondary possibilities, is usually referred to as a **combination hand**.

If you include the likely possibility that no one has a hand good enough to beat three nines or two pair, you'll probably win this pot about one out of four times. However, this estimate is contingent upon very little betting. If someone already has trip kings, you're in worse shape. In any case, all these equities add up.

If you're in late position you should clearly call and see at least the turn card. The principle illustrated here is extremely important to playing Omaha correctly. Although you normally avoid low percentage comes, such as where you need both the turn and river cards to complete your hand, if you have several of these possibilities, they might add up enough to justify seeing another card.

Let's say you're in sixth position. The first hand bets $5, three of the next four hands call, and the fifth hand raises (you suspect he has a set, kings and nines, or a tactical Q-J-10 or 8-7). Clearly you should fold. The price of fishing in has just gone up, and your chances of winning have decreased.

You want to avoid getting into big raising situations without first class stuff. It is clearly better to concede the first $5 and wait for a better hand to get involved. This might turn out to be a very expensive proposition. A reraise is not that unlikely. Even if you get your long-shot straight, you might end up losing on the river to a better hand (such as a flush or full house). Unless you have good odds of winning, you should avoid putting up a lot of money to protect only a little money. Your hand consists of only marginal values and generally bad odds.

Scenario 2

Now let's look at another scenario. The first player bets $5 and three of the next four players call. When you're in the middle positions, you have to decide if the players behind you will raise. Since your equities on this particular hand seem good, you have a chance to make a reasonable $5 investment. An 8 on the next card would make you a favorite and you might get a raise in at $10. There is also some chance that no one will bet on the next round, especially if a brick comes up, for example, a 2, 3 or 4, and that you'll get a free shot at an 8 on the river.

But just because you can justify a $5, it certainly does not justify calling two more raises this round or even $10 on the turn. In fact, at this point you should plan to fold the $10 on the turn if you don't improve. The concern: What your opponents might have.

In these marginal situations you have to stay on your toes and reevaluate your situation each round.

Also, be aware of the downside. Losing an extra $5 is obviously not the worst thing that can happen. You're concerned that the player behind you might touch off a raising contest, not only this round but next round also, especially if a diamond turns and you get sucked in!

You must avoid making bad calls or bets because you're angry or because you have a "feeling." When the odds turn against you, then it's time to get out of the hand. If you're estimating your calling odds, you have to balance the downside risks of getting involved with the benefits of the occasional huge win. Generally speaking, in these situations, if you have to put in a fair amount of money to protect a long shot, you're not playing with good odds.

The key to winning at Omaha is to correctly evaluate your prospects and to stay on the plus side of the percentages.

Scenario 3

Let's look at this hand one last time. You're in last position and everyone has checked around to you. We'll assume that no one is slowplaying a lock. But we also have to be aware that someone might have a slightly better hand than you. But if you bet, an opponent might fold in an early position.

This might be a good hand to drive, even though good players will realize you might be driving in last position and call. And if you get callers, you still have the benefit that your driving in last position might buy you the option of a free river card.

Whether or not you might want to bluff this hand all the way through to the end is a decision you can make later. For now your choice is quite clear. You should bet. Here's why. If everyone folds one time out of seven, then it would justify your bet. Let's say a few players fold. Not only have you increased your chances of winning by eliminating some players who might have improved on the turn, it is quite likely that the remaining players will check the next card around to you, giving you a free look at fifth street if you decide not to drive. Some or all of the callers may have invested $5 on the flop planning to fold on the turn if no improvement has occurred. A $10 bet on the turn might win the pot for you without further ado.

If you had not bet the $5 on the flop, you would be more likely to have a $10 bet thrown at you now and would probably fold your hand. The 10 to 1 inside straight would need at least a $100 pot to justify a $10 bet. Thus, if you calculate just the equity for your second chance, the free look at the fifth street card, to get a 10 to 1 card for the $50-plus pot, that alone will justify your initial $5 bet.

When you add up all the possibilities, even if you choose not to bluff it through, the $5 after-the-flop bet is a good percentage play. If you check with a reasonable hand in last seat, you are often passing up a ripe opportunity. Making opportunistic moves is what separates the winners from the losers.

OVERALL STRATEGY REVIEWED

In limit Omaha, you're trying to win money. It is not a question of winning any one given pot, however large (unlike pot-limit and no-limit where one huge pot can make or break a night). Nor is it the concept of playing for a lock hand and winning big pots. It is a combination of winning enough small hands and big hands where you built the pot, and minimizing your losses in hands where you were too much of a long shot to be contributing more money to someone else's pot.

As we've discussed, in Omaha, a high percentage of hands are won on the last card. Many pots are won with bad hands that outdrew the best hands on the river. Some of the best players think that the last card makes an underdog a winner on more than 50 percent of all hands! However, if you constantly play percentages, they'll come out in your favor.

The flop is the place to evaluate your hand and see where you stand. You have to decide how position, prior betting, and your opponents affect your prospects, then make the appropriate play that gives you a long-term edge.

ONE-TIER STRUCTURE GAMES

Most limit hold'em games have a two-tiered betting structure, for example, "$1/$2 limit hold'em" means that there is a $1 betting limit before the flop and after the flop, and a $2 betting limit after the turn and river. A mono-limit or one-tiered structure simply has the same betting limit on all four rounds of betting. Thus, a "$2 game" has the same $2 betting limit on the preflop, flop, turn and river.

When a driver raises before the flop in a two-tiered $1/$2 game and continues betting all four rounds—but is not raised—the total amount of his bets after all four rounds of betting would be $7 ($2+$1+$2+$2). Thus, more than half the total amount bet, $4 out of the $7, occurs after the turn. In a one-tiered structure, if the limit or maximum bet is $2, then when a driver raises before the flop and continues betting throughout, the total amount of his bets is $10 ($4+$2+$2+$2). Note that in mono-limit, more than half the total betting occurs before the turn.

Thus, in a one-tiered structure hold'em game, where more money is usually wagered before the turn rather than after the turn, there is a significant shift in strategy and tactics. If a hold'em table is loose before the flop or after the flop or both, the one-tier structure which emphasizes the first two rounds of betting, clearly benefits a player with a good starting hand. And having the maximum bet after the flop tends to give good hands more protection against chasers. Not only does the chaser have to make a larger proportionate bet after the flop to see the next card, but then, if the chaser hits, the next two "payoff" rounds are the same limit, as opposed to double bets in the two-tiered structure.

In the two-tiered structure, the half-limit bets of the first two rounds changes the initial investment threshold. Because these bets have less relative cost, the lesser amount often justifies a close call or making a speculative probing bet, for example, lead-betting a middle or low pair. And if the speculation hits, there is more potential payoff from the last two double rounds of betting. Thus, early (first two rounds) speculations are clearly more cost effective and usually generate looser action both before and after the flop. And thus the two-tiered structure tends to loosen up the game.

In the one-tiered structure, the relative investment to see

the fourth card is greater and has less payoff after a hit. And speculative probe betting (with a marginal holding) is clearly more risky at twice the relative price and hence not as cost effective as in the standard two-tiered structure. Position, very important in both structures, is even more critical after the flop in a one-tiered structure, where there could be one or more raises.

In the one-tiered structure, since the relative cost of the first two round bets to the projected final pot is greater, sensible players tend to play better starting hands before investing at twice the price. Waiting for good starting hands before the flop and not playing around after the flop with lesser hands certainly tends to tighten up the game.

Perhaps the bottom line in a mono-limit or one-tiered limit hold'em game is that good players will benefit by patiently waiting for better starting cards and weaker players will make preflop and postflop mistakes that are twice as costly.

11 OMAHA TURN AND RIVER CONCEPTS

The last two rounds in Omaha are like the last two rounds in any poker game. The seeds have already been sown, and now comes harvest time. Hopefully, you're the harvester rather than the harvestee. It's on these rounds where you want to make hay.

The turn and the river are at the higher level of the two-tier betting range; these are the big bet rounds. If just one bet with no raise occurs each round, two-thirds of what you will put into the pot will occur on these last two rounds. In other words, all of the betting on the preflop and on the flop account merely for one-third of your entire investment in an unraised pot.

These last two rounds are the key time to "know when to hold'em and know when to fold 'em."

THE TURN

The turn is a good time to make hay while the sun shines on your winning hand. Although most big pots begin with raises before and after flop, many dollars are won (or not lost) starting with the turn. Winning poker is about betting and getting more money in the pot when you have the winning hand, and folding or minimize losses when you have a loser. One of the cardinal principles of Omaha, as with other flop games, is to avoid loose-calling the turn (and the river) without adequate cards.

There are some interesting strategic fourth round considerations, particularly in situations when it is not clear whose pot it is.

First let's examine the "undriven" pot situation when the flop was checked around on the flop. At this point, unless there had been some preflop raises, the pot itself is hardly worth fighting over. In theory, since you have little to protect, there is little reason to take risks. And there is always the possibility of running into a conservative player or trapper who actually has a hand.

But we all know that if you can successfully steal a few of these little pots, it adds up to real dollars. And your sporting and competitive poker instincts might occasionally move you to go for the steal or to pick off somebody else's bluff.

So when should you invest a double bet? The answer is this: a lot depends on your overall game-plan choreography and image.

THE IMAGE
Image Development

In Omaha, it is not simply a matter of how much money you might win or lose in these little pot situations. An equal or an even more important consideration is your "image de jour" (image of the day). These little pots are a prime opportunity for "image investing," that is, you're not only investing money in winning more money, but you're also investing money in image development and enhancement.

When you make a double bet with a speculative hand, you're bluffing in the eyes of your opponents. Since it is good to be loved at Omaha, it is good PR to occasionally get caught with your hand in the cookie jar. It is difficult to quantify just how much it might be worth, but PR definitely has value. Good loose aggressive Omaha players not only show a plus in these situations when they win, but also gain "love points" when they get caught. You might easily receive two or three additional callers on your next few winning hands.

One of the main reasons to play tight on the turn of a little pot is that everyone has had a free chance to improve.

Note that the higher the card, the more likely someone improved. If that player is you, and you probably have a winner, by all means bet and hope that one or more callers think that you're trying to steal the pot. But if you did not improve substantially, why not let some other genius try to the steal this nothing pot and save your money and bluffing license for more significant endeavors.

Don't Burn Your Image

Although general poker principles tell you to occasionally take a sporting shot to steal one of these up-for-grabs little pots, for strategic reasons, you might prefer to sit back, let your "honesty" shine through, and let the other aggressive players go after it. This is especially important if you tend to drive bluff fairly frequently. It would be unfortunate if some random player decided to call you on a big driving bluff just because he remembered your "dishonesty" when you tried to bluff on one of these small pots earlier.

When you try to catch someone bluffing by calling a double bet, there is also an image consideration involved. When you expose your less-than-adequate calling hand, whether you win or whether you lose, it is usually good PR for your opponents to see that you call everything and anything. An observer might choose not to bluff you on a subsequent hand.

If you're not playing Omaha with a loose, aggressive image, there are fewer reasons to stray into someone else's pot. A player might well be sitting back with a good hand and a big net. Don't reward players who don't bet their cards adequately by betting for them. Again the key strategic principle in little-pot participation is be acutely aware of the PR and advertising impacts as well as the monetary profit involved.

The real bottom line to speculating in little pots depends

on your judgment of how often you might want to drive bluff in a given game. If you expect to drive bluff infrequently, perhaps you should do some advertising by trying more frequent bluffs in these small pots.

DRIVING OR PLAYING PASSIVELY

Let's now consider one of the most important strategic propositions; whether to continue driving or play more passively. Let's say that you liked the flop enough to bet and had several callers but no raisers. (Had there been as much as one raise, it would be an entirely different situation.)

If you hit a potentially winning card on the turn, you should continue driving about two-thirds of the time unless the game is loose enough that trapping almost always works. The remaining third of the time is written off to "trapping," "varying your style," and to protecting your future aborted drives.

When it gets checked around on the turn, it is not as potentially disastrous as checking on the flop, since most of the players who fold on the turn are not going to win the pot anyway. Note the strategic difference from the all important after-the-flop betting. Given that you just hit a good card, it is unlikely that you'll lose the pot by missing this bet.

Driving with a Brick

What happens when the turn card is neither very good nor very bad? In other words, the card didn't help you, but it likely didn't help your opponents either. (Remember, all cards that don't help you are somewhat dangerous, but some are clearly more dangerous than others.) You're now faced with a classic driving decision. If you're driving a partly made hand, for example, trips or two high pair, you should probably continue driving about 90 percent of the time—and write off the other 10 percent to varying your style.

If you're driving a four-flush or four-straight, you should probably continue driving less than 50 percent of the time. Again, to stay unpredictable, you have to vary your play. If you don't want to be considered a locksmith who always has hands when he bets, the come-bluff is one of the best times to make your occasional bluffing investment. But if you come-bluff too often, you lose much of the occasional stealing equity.

There are a number of considerations that may help you decide when to continue driving with a come-bluff. On top of the list are the number and tenacity of your opponents. Secondly, you should evaluate the strength of your own hand and the likelihood of it winning if it gets checked around. Finally, if the flop had both flush and straight potential, and the turn card was a true brick—it didn't pair, flush or straighten the board—then this is one of the best times to continue betting strongly. It is quite possible that everyone is still "coming" and that you'll win the pot by default if a brick hits on the last card and you continue to bet.

Betting here will fold most speculators who wanted to see one more card. Sometimes the domino effect kicks in; after several players have folded, the last one folds as well because of reduced calling odds. And as long as you don't bluff too frequently, you should enjoy a reasonable success rate with this play. And since you've had callers each round, the pot will have reached a reasonable size.

Drive bluffs are the most successful bluffs in Omaha. During a normal session, for every ten pots that you win, two or three should be drive bluffs (even though you might have lost several drive bluff attempts). On many occasions, those two or three drive-bluffed pots will be the margin between winning and losing. That bluffing rate is about as frequent as you can hope for to be successful. If you start bluffing too frequently, your opponents will call you more often, seriously reducing your percentage of stolen pots. Your bluffing frequency will be determined by the calling frequency of the active players. After you learn your opponents, you'll have a good idea whether the chasers are going to call you or not.

DANGEROUS TURN CARDS

Finally, in the dangerous situations when the turn card pairs or is a third card in a suit or to a straight, then you have to consider the following: The greater the number of callers, the more likely that somebody has hit.

Although the value of your cards changes drastically, your odds of a successful bluff have not substantially diminished! While you cannot bluff out a player who has hit, if no one happens to have hit, you will be more successful in bluffing out someone who believes *you* have hit.

When a dangerous card hits the turn, it is a good time to reevaluate and reconsider your options. In an early position you should probably check. You don't have that much invested at this point, about one third of what you would put in if you follow through and bet all the way. You would consider betting at this point to protect a partially made hand: for example, if you have two pair with other value, such as a straight draw. Although you don't want to give a free card, if your holding is weak, you might be better off taking it yourself.

If there were several callers, it is fairly likely that someone will bet and take over your drive, especially in a good game. If everyone checks, then your previous betting equity might allow you to drive to a win if no one hits on fifth street, although you have just indicated weakness. If you have mixed up your play well, opponents will have noticed that you sometimes check good cards on the turn, and that will increase the likelihood of this play working.

CONTINUATION DRIVES

This is a good time to introduce what is almost a black letter rule: If you continue driving on the turn—whether you have a good hand or the occasional come hand—you're just about committed to driving on the river! You'll only make an exception if an unusually bad card changes things. Once you put that turn card double bet in the pot, you should plan to bet on fifth street with all hands that would not call a fifth street bet. This is the culmination of your power drive and all unsuccessful comers will hopefully fold just as they often do when you actually have something.

This aggression is the driver's main edge. You'll win enough pots driving this way that these wins will make up for the times your fifth street bluff investments got caught. Bluffing is good for business because it gets you more callers when you have a good hand.

Managing Your Drive Moves

Once you think enough of a hand to drive it on the flop and continue driving it at twice the price on the turn, you obviously have made a significant investment. Based on your expected overall equity, you should be happy to protect this and future investments by making the high-percentage river bet. If you take the number of dollars in the pot and divide it by the amount of your last-round bet, you'll likely win the pot enough times to justify those bets. If you don't come-bluff too frequently, you might even get a possible calling hand to save money and fold against you.

But remember, it's a balancing act: if you bluff too frequently, the other players will smell blood in the waters and call frequently.

However, the above does not apply if you have an unimproved hand that might win anyway—for example, a set or two high pair. Depending on your judgment of the situation, you might try a bet, but you should probably just check and hope for the best. There is little accomplished by betting at this stage—you want to gain strategic advantages, not merely money—and if you get raised you're probably going to be that much more unhappy. If someone else bets, you'll often need to protect the pot by calling and hoping that they either made a bad bet or were bluffing.

Because of the amount of money in the pot at this point, you would only fold if you were playing against a locksmith.

Betting the last card to get more money into the pot is a simple gambling proposition with little strategic value, other than following through on a drive. Many players try to milk an extra bet from one or two callers when they judge that they have a better hand. Thin betting with a marginal hand that may or may not win is often not the best percentage play, especially when you'll get just one caller. It is certainly dubious to bet against players if you would probably fold a check-raise.

If you're less than 65 percent sure of winning, betting in this situation has a minus expectation because of the raise factor, since the size of the pot dictates that you must call if raised. Now, instead, you'll probably lose twice what you might have gained. It is also foolhardy to bet if there are few hands that your opponent would call (as opposed to folding) which are weaker than your hand. It is better to invest your money with greater return prospects, such as the earlier chips you invested in this pot. In other words, after the last card, you should be content to win the current pot with any marginal hand.

Thin-betting the last card in Omaha is mainly dependent on a last card brick and the particular opponents.

GAINING EQUITY AGAINST CONSERVATIVE PLAY

One of the golden opportunities that many less experienced players miss occurs when the driver immediately to their right stops driving. This means that a vacuum has been created. The old driver is announcing to his opponents that his original bet was based on a draw or lesser values.

The next player who bets becomes the new driver and inherits all of the equity and momentum of the original driver.

Let's say that there are four players left in the pot. The original driver, who is sitting to your right, checks, and you're in the pot with a king-high four-flush (there were two of your suit on the flop but you didn't hit on the turn). If you pick up the drive here on the turn, notice what might happen. If a brick comes on the river and you bet again, the callers between you and the old driver will be hard pressed to call. They will probably fold all medium (say two pair) to bad hands because they have two potentially legitimate bettors to contend with—you and the previous driver who is behind them.

The previous driver, who was quite likely on a draw hand (possibly the same flush you were drawing for), will usually have an even weaker holding than the marginal hands that already folded. If all works according to plan, you have bought yourself a nice fat pot. This strategy works perhaps more than one-third of the time.

You're getting great equity on your turn bet (the steal potential plus sometimes you hit on fifth street). But the picked-up drive momentum you get going into fifth street is even more valuable if you can steal the pot in this situation as often as one-third of the time!

CALLING SITUATIONS ON THE TURN

There are other draw and draw-plus hands in Omaha where all you want to do is call and hope your ship comes in. Although loose-calling at twice the price is not recommended, if you're getting good percentages on your money due to pot size (i.e., your prospects for winning are expected to bring a good return on the amount you're investing), then you'll certainly call, unless the likelihood of a raise changes your odds.

One of the fundamental differences between betting (driving) and calling is that, when you're calling, you usually don't want to drop other players out of the pot. In fact, you often need the additional money that the other callers are adding to justify your own call. If you hit on the turn, and make the temporary nuts that might get beat on the last card, then of course you bet and raise ferociously—not for the extra money, but in the hope of driving out a potential winner.

If you're still coming on the turn, the odds don't favor raising to drive out some of your opponents unless you're planning the big bluff on fifth street. But with the large pot being built, it may not be the best strategy given that the small success rate of this play. And remember, your true calling odds on the turn depend on your present odds of hitting and winning minus the threat of raises jacking up your investment.

RAISING CONSIDERATIONS
ON THE TURN

There is not nearly as much strategy to raising on the turn as there was preflop and on the flop. Mostly simple poker considerations prevail. If you have a good hand, you might raise if you think you can get more money into the pot. Occasionally, in a well-attended pot, you'll raise mainly to thin the field. And sometimes you'll make a tactical raise to force out a weak opponent and go one-on-one against a driver who you think might be bluffing.

Beware of getting caught into the trap where two or more players are making the maximum number of raises on a board showing low nut-straight possibilities. The reality is that there are more fifth street cards that lose for them than win (the two- or three-way split drastically changes the odds). If you have a piece of the low straight, it is usually right to wind it up only if you have prospects of winning the whole pot. You might make an exception to the above if there are some fish in the pot—but frequently you will turn out to be the fish.

Inhibitory raises are still valuable tactical weapons on the turn. Generally, whenever you raise a bettor who is sitting in front of you, you have a great positional advantage going into the next round. If you were raising on a draw hand that did not hit, you should frequently try the bluff if the original bettor called and checked around to you. Even if you get caught on this high percentage play, the few extra dollars are well invested, and probably will bear dividends soon in subsequent pots won.

THE BIG BLUFF PLAY

Occasionally, you might try to set up a "counter drive" or "big bluff" by raising a frequent come-bluffer on the turn. You're hoping to force out all or most of the other players with the idea that you'll continue bluffing right through on fifth street if the driver's come does not hit. Obviously, there are a lot of potential mishaps with this plan and it has a low success rate. However, if you happen to be known as a locksmith, this maneuver becomes a high percentage play, especially against players who think they "know" you. And if you're not well known and spend several hours betting like a locksmith, you're well set up to execute this counter-drive bluff.

If there are many players still in the pot and they have called around to you, you'll sometimes raise if the percentages of making your come hand compare favorably with the expected number of dollars to be returned if you hit. However, if you're drawing to the nuts—for example, you have an ace-high flush draw and there are no pairs on board—you would like as many callers as possible if you end up completing on the river. So, even if there are five players left, you should not raise on nut-draw hands if you're in a situation where you would rather not lose future customers.

In straight high Omaha, as you improve your play and get more experienced, you can frequently judge approximately what your opponents are holding by paying attention to their playing tendencies and betting patterns. If you have an idea what your opponents hold, you can make tactical bets and raises to improve your chances and sometimes win the pot outright!

FIFTH STREET CONSIDERATIONS

Although the last card in Omaha changes the winner more than in any other form of poker, the betting now becomes anticlimactic and there is amazingly little action. The hand is essentially over and everyone knows what should win and you know what you have. Then, there is the minor matter remaining as to who actually gets the pot. In most good games, after the last card, the person with the lock or near lock either bets or checks it around to the driver who often bets. Between zero and two people call. There may be a raise. And then someone gets the pot.

In Omaha there is seldom more than one raise (except when two players both have the lock), unless some inferior player miscalculates his holdings. If you have the nuts, you'll either raise or call if there are several other players yet to act. And, if your come did not come and you have nothing, it's usually best to fold.

But what if you have a pair of aces or kings, that is, a bad hand that is only good enough to beat a worse hand? If you're in last position, there were no other callers, the driver is not a locksmith, and the flop contained two suited card or straight cards that have not hit, then there is a very reasonable chance that the driver is bluffing. You should consider calling, depending of course, on your opponent!

All good players and most non-locksmith players will come-bluff more frequently than one out of five times. On reasonably sized pots, you're probably getting more than 10 to 1 odds on your money. Perhaps the main consideration in these situations is the known propensities of the driver. Most regular Omaha players will bluff well over 10 percent of the time.

Again, position is key. You should not consider calling from early position. Even with only one potential caller behind you, your odds are approximately cut in half and you should probably fold (unless the caller behind you is telegraphing his intentions to fold).

OVERCOMING THE LAST-CARD BLUES

The following text is dedicated to the memory of the thousands of hands that were best on the turn but were no longer winning hands on the river, and to the memory of the many dollars that went with them.

If you want to maintain good professional poise at the Omaha table, you must learn to treat the cruelest of last card losses like water off the back of a duck. When you play Omaha, should expect these unlucky losses to occur at least several times a session.

However, if you're playing the game correctly, you should

win just about as much money on last card draws as you lose. This includes the fact that weak players will often contribute to your winning hands when they have no business being in the pot, which, of course, boosts your profits.

In Omaha, there are a lot of hands where it is correct to call until the last card even with weaker hands. Players who play too tight are not optimizing their winning possibilities. The real skill is to be able to know the difference between investing on good odds and fishing along on bad odds. Sometimes it is correct to call the fourth card, especially in betting structures where the fourth card is cheaper than the last card, and drop if you don't hit. If the value is there, put up your money and take your chances. In the long run you should come out ahead—if you're figuring things right.

The last card blues hurt most in super big pots when you have a lot of money invested. While it is always nice to win the big pots, usually luck is in control, not you. It takes a lot of smaller pots to make up for one big loss—or a big win. However, it is practical to avoid huge swing situations where luck is a big factor by avoiding big pots, except when you have a lock or are a huge favorite.

Thus, when the pot gets to an average good size, the better players should ease up on the pot building if they're working on thin percentages. This is why you avoid making extra raises that are not likely to drop anyone. If most of the pots are roughly the same size, the good players are less likely to lose the big one—and the last card blues will hurt less.

12 OMAHA HIGH-LOW

INTRODUCTION

At high-low Omaha, the greater skill of experts compared to average players has much less financial impact then in high Omaha games. At high-low Omaha, the most significant difference in expected results occurs between losing and average players. The good news is that any average player who knows enough to play only good hands is capable of cutting up the losers and getting a share of their money. If there are several weaker players in the game, the kind who seem to stay in on almost every hand, all good players like their chances at high-low Omaha.

What usually happens is that most of the good and better players and one or two lucky losers simply split up all of the money lost by the overall losers, the weaker players, and the unlucky good players.

In high-low Omaha, the success of experts over good players is more of a long-term proposition. The expert's edge is sufficiently small that on any given occasion, the expert might have somewhere in the range of a 20 to 40 percent likelihood of losing. And if the expert is not as good as he thinks he is, or if the other players are better than he thinks they are, the self-styled expert's true chances would be worse. And of course, the expert's chances of winning are lessened by the house cut.

One main reason for the smaller skill differential between experts and average players at Omaha high-low is that there is much less correlation between what opponents have and what they're thought to have. And that inaccuracy can cost the expert serious money. Assuming the expert's objective is to win money, he might prefer hold'em and high Omaha, where his judgment is more accurate, unless, of course, there are several big losers in the high-low game.

Since no sensible gambler likes a dubious game when there are better opportunities around, if there are no truly bad players left in the high-low game, an expert is probably well advised to look elsewhere.

THE THEORY OF WINNING PLAY

High-low Omaha is completely different from straight high Omaha. High-low is a great game for solid players and a terrible game for fundamentally unsound players. Even in loose Omaha high-low games, it is difficult to win if you play too many hands, unless you're having a very lucky streak.

It is easy to lose a lot of chips when you're stuck between two good hands raising each other. And in most of these situations, if you happen to get a great last card and win, you'll only get half or perhaps one-quarter of the pot. Half pots are sustaining, but it is hard to be a winner at Omaha high-low if you don't scoop up some sizeable whole pots.

Thus, one of the most important strategies for high-low Omaha is to avoid big losses, especially the "deadly triangle" disasters where you're second-best to two lock hands raising each other on the last two double-bet rounds. Unfortunately, there are many times when you simply must call and take your licks. It takes very delicate poker judgment (and some good luck) to know when to fold or call with certain good hands. In multiple raise situations, it costs many dollars when you're wrong.

Perhaps the greatest difference between high Omaha and high-low Omaha is your basic overall strategy. In high Omaha, much of your strategy is devoted to aggressive driving, raising, and even calling, and there is a lot of benefit to taking the initiative. In high-low games, initiative is muchless important: if you don't have a made hand, you can often afford to sit back and allow others to do the pot building.

Because initiative is devalued, a key difference when playing high-low Omaha is that it's a bad percentage play to drive a high come hand if there are two or three low cards in the flop. While a raise would be more likely to drive out marginal lows, your winning odds based on going for a half pot are not adequate to justify the extra investment. Another key difference between high and high-low Omaha is the judgment aspect; that is, the good player's ability to know what each opponent is likely to have. Without an accurate appraisal of what the various remaining opponents might have, an expert high-low player is unable to concoct deep game plans.

Also, based on judgments that have a high percentage of accuracy, the high Omaha expert consistently wins more, or loses less, by taking the appropriately correct action. In high-low Omaha, the expert's judgment has much less accuracy because of the direction duality. This reflects heavily on the relative skill level of both games. Obviously, less judgment accuracy costs you dollars. Knowing that you're more likely to get into a guessing situation affects your whole strategy for getting involved with lesser hands right from the preflop.

All of these considerations suggest that a tight strategy is more effective in high-low Omaha.

NOTE FROM CARO:

In Omaha high-low, as with all high-low games, winning half the pot is never half as good as scooping it. If you have bet a total of $100 into a $400 pot, then winning half brings you $200, but only a $100 profit —your $100 must be subtracted. But scooping the pot brings you a $300 profit, three times as much!

This concept is widely overlooked in Omaha high-low, but if you always keep it in mind, you'll have a huge edge over many opponents who aren't aware of it.

One key to Omaha high-low, which holds true in all high-low poker games: Scooping a big pot is your main objective.

TWO TYPES OF HIGH-LOW GAMES

The first and most important truth about Omaha high-low is that there are actually two entirely different types of games.

1. The first type of Omaha high-low game is one where more than five players see the flop. These are lower stakes games played mostly by non-expert players who are of the "loose" variety. Since only two of the non-blind players probably have sound calling hands, that means that some of the players are playing loosely and a good player can expect to make money in the game.

If you walk into a casino in and take a seat at a typical $3/$6 to $10/$20 Omaha high-low table, you'll probably notice that an average of more than five players are seeing every flop. These are potentially profitable games for you.

2. The second type of game is one in which an average of four players or fewer see the flop. These are tight-aggressive Omaha high-low games, and have entirely different dynamics from the loose Omaha high-low described above. Tight Omaha high-low is often played at much higher stakes and often the games are shorthanded. There are frequent raises before the flop, often resulting in head-to-head confrontations, with the raiser typically squaring off against the big blind.

While most of the following information applies to the loose lower-limit version of Omaha high-low game, many of the principles and statistics are equally applicable to both.

THE TIGHT-AGGRESSIVE APPROACH

In high-low Omaha, because of the lesser degree of judgment accuracy and because of the much greater raising volatility, you have to play marginal hands cautiously. Otherwise you'll often find yourself in the unenviable position of having to guess whether to expensively protect your previous investments or fold potentially winning cards to avoid a big losing situation.

High-low Omaha calls for a more conservative approach because in many of the half pots that you win, you get back less than the amount you invested! Unless you have substantial potential, that is, whole pot potential, you should take a much more conservative approach to getting involved in a high-low Omaha pot. The bottom line is that you have to take an entirely different approach from Omaha high, although you want to disguise that fact.

As with high Omaha, playing conservatively and tight is the best approach to winning at high-low Omaha but you should make moves to conceal that fact. In other words, you should play only with good cards. You could almost carry this to the "locksmith" extreme and drop all hands except those where you're dealt high percentage cards or have an excellent come hand. In other words, you should surrender most medium hands and play mostly your no-brainers.

The problem is that it's quite possible to spend the whole session getting chewed up on blinds without getting any of the no-brainer hands. Thus, you need to expand your starting hands to include a number of good draw hands, especially if the price is right. You might be able to get away with playing a bit loose before the flop—for example, hands where you have an A-4 or A-5 for low—but you should definitely not play loose *after* the flop. You can make an exception for high-only hands, where you might try a loose call in last position. But beware: At any given time, raises are likely in high-low.

Your best approach is to let the other players speculate on their hands. If you keep track of the wins versus losses on hands where you might have fished along where the flop contains two or more low cards, you'll soon be convinced that this portion of your game is too luck-dependent to be reliable. You'll find that many of your biggest losses and smallest wins would be in hands where you played non-lock or marginal cards against two opponents.

Tight But Aggressive

However, even if your initial approach to getting involved in a pot is conservative (or almost locksmithlike), once you're involved, you should play aggressively, especially after the flop!

Once you're involved in a pot, big moves and raises often turn out to be great investments, not only for winning, but also to disguise your locksmith tendencies. Of course, big moves work best in loose games where your competition tends to play weaker hands, and these are the types of games you want to play in. That is, avoid high-low games that don't have several loose fish contributing.

Thus your overall game plan for playing high-low is to sit back and wait for very good cards and then get further involved after the flop only with sound potential. Avoid playing marginal cards. You want to avoid costly situations: for example, getting caught in a deadly triangle situation between a lock hand and another aggressive bettor, possibly also with a lock.

BEFORE THE FLOP CRITERIA: A POINT-COUNT ALTERNATIVE

In high-low Omaha, you should fold more often than you would in straight-high Omaha. A simple criteria for seeing the flop is to play only hands containing a prime low couple, that is, an A-2, A-3, or a 3-2 with two other good cards, such as two high cards, touching cards, suited cards or pairs. Four high cards 9 or higher are also playable in games where an average of five or more players are seeing the flop.

You can also play any ace-high flush couple with a 4 and a 5 (more than 17 points). Using point counts to ascertain the relative strength of the six two-card combinations in every four-card hand is an alternative approach to the various starting-hand criteria mentioned above.

Pesky Lows

If you have a high-only hand that is three or four high cards, you need more than 12 points to see the flop. There are no high-only hands good enough to raise, since most high-only hands have to be folded after a low flop. Not only will those pesky lows often take half of your pot, but sometimes they will raise you out before you get to see your winner.

The low hand point count is also based on two-card holdings. Any two low cards 8 or below are worth about 1 1/2 points because of the occasional back-in factor. Super two-card low bonuses are as follows:

SUPER TWO-CARD LOW BONUSES		
A-2	=	11
A-3	=	9
A-4	=	6
2-3	=	7
2-4	=	4
3-4	=	3
5 with a lower card = 2.5		
6 with a lower card = 2		

You pick up a four-card hand containing an A-2 or an A-3 about 6 percent of the time; you pick up a hand containing an A-2-3 (ABC) about 1 percent of the time.

In most loose high-low games, 12 or more high and low points should be required to see the flop, perhaps a bit more if raised (depending on how loose the game is), and about 18 or more high-low points to raise (but only in late seat after most callers are already in the pot). Don't raise before the flop with high-only hands.

Even if the rest of your game is undisciplined, it is to your advantage to only see the flop with good cards. Even if the game is loose enough for you to show a profit calling the flop with weaker holdings, you'll show a greater long-run profit with better starting cards.

ABAC

The best overall high-low hand in Omaha high-low is A-2-A-3 double-suited, also called ABAC. The combined high and low winning potential of ABAC makes it the best percentage winning hand in all Omaha (both high-low and high), roughly comparable to pocket aces in hold'em.

The best low flop calling hand in Omaha high-low is A-2-3-4, also called ABCD. The low bonuses alone add up to 42 points using the above point system. With this holding, even before the flop, you can expect to win low close to half the time, plus you also have whole pot potential. No high hand (even A-K,-A-K suited) has nearly that much winning potential.

PLAYING MARGINAL HANDS

At some point on the road to mastering Omaha high-low strategy, you should become aware that there are some very interesting marginal hand options. Many marginal starting hands at Omaha high-low can be played with a long-run plus expectation or with very little profit or loss. But just which marginal hands can be played at a slight profit depends on the game.

Why play "nothing" hands? Mostly to adjust your image. In most loose Omaha high-low situations, you want to be loved more than feared. You want to inject a little fun and camaraderie into the game. At Omaha high-low, it is prudent to display occasional imprudence. But, again, it all depends on the overall looseness and the other players in the game.

Many 2-3, A-4 and A-5 starting hands are borderline or worse even at most loose Omaha high-low games. Paradoxically, some borderline hands, such as A-K-7-5, actually play better at tight shorthanded games. When you play marginal starting hands, it is very important to fold most of these hands on the flop. But although you strongly prefer primary holdings to get involved after the flop, sometimes a lack of interest in betting by the other players indicates an opportunity to divvy up the antes.

Let's say you're playing an A-6-4-10 and the flop is 7-9-3. Although you have the second nut low (a deuce would give you the nut low), and an 8 or a 5 will give you a non-nut straight, this is the kind of hand you would rather have an opponent play while you draw to your usual prime A-2-plus hand ("plus" two high cards, touching cards, suited cards or pairs). In five- or six-way action, the A-2 holding should make more than double the money as the slightly above average A-6-4-10 holding.

But if the betting gets checked around to you, you should make a speculative bet to fold some opponents and improve your chances for high. After several checks, the odds change somewhat and it is now about fifty-fifty that there is an A-2 present. This lead-bet on the flop should not commit you to sticking around after the turn when the betting doubles. Whenever you find yourself playing with a marginal hand, be prepared to fold on the turn if raising occurs or is likely.

Similarly, let's say you see the flop with a A-5-4-5, one

of the best hands without an A-2 or A-3, and flop A-K-8. Your low and little flush draw are marginal holdings. But if it gets checked around to you or the person in front of you bets, you might try a bet or a raise. If you manage to narrow the action to one or two opponents, you would probably be in a marginal plus situation, which, in the long run, might show a small profit.

Marginal Hands on the Flop

Playing marginal hands after the flop is an art form. And sometimes the basic underlying mathematics are actually negative. But a slightly negative holding can sometimes be made slightly positive by aggressive raising after the flop. But even against weak and loose players, it is unsound to push too hard against a substantial mathematical disadvantage.

But what if you do?

A classic two-way marginal-minus bad player example is holding a K-2-3-Q when a 4-5-6 hits the flop. In a ten-handed game, you'll be losing low to an A-2 or A-3 about 75 percent of the time. Your ignorant end straight is a favorite to lose high, even if it happens to be high when the flop hits. But the combined odds of losing both ways are at least close to marginal if you're against only one or two loose opponents.

Even though your winning chances are dubious in a five or six-way pot, if it gets checked around to a loose player on your right who bets, it might work out well if you raise! This is not recommended as a sound money-making play, but if your raise narrows the field to two- or three-way action, you might show a slight profit in the long-run. This depends on the looseness of your one or two opponents. If either player is super solid and is likely to have one-way locked up, this would not be a good play.

But step back and take a look at the overall big picture.

If you do play to the end and get beat both ways, it makes a big splash. Everyone at the table will see your hand and realize that you're loose as a goose and perhaps not as good as they thought. If you're playing in familiar company, it's a good investment to occasionally turn over bad cards. Some players do it all the time. And sometimes the bad cards win.

In general, at Omaha high-low, it's often a good investment to occasionally make a super-aggressive raise with a two-way marginal hand, especially after the flop. If one extra caller pays you off on a subsequent hand, you get your investment back with the goodwill as ample interest.

You should expend most of your speculation budget just after the flop. If things don't look promising, give it up. Don't throw good money after bad. If your after-the-flop play is significantly better then the average player in the game, you should show a slight long-run profit playing marginal hands, especially if you only play them occasionally. Understand that the big long-run payoff in most games is the advertising value, which will significantly affect how well you're paid off on your big winning hands.

SOME HIGH-LOW ODDS

Knowing the basic odds can do wonders for your Omaha high-low bankroll. Study the following chart to get an understanding of how often the board will connect with several broad categories of starting hands. Knowing these simple odds will help a lot! See chart on the following page.

ONE- OR TWO-WAY FLOPS

If the flop contains two or more high cards (9s or greater), then, for the moment anyway, you're essentially reverting to straight high Omaha. Everything that was said earlier in high Omaha about driving and raising applies, especially if there is exactly one low card in the flop. The high hand

ODDS OF MAKING A LOW HAND	
Your hand has:	**Board makes a low with your hand**
Four (different) low cards...	
Preflop	49%
Flop has two new low cards (20 outs)	70%
Flop has one new low card (you need both)	24%
Three (different) low cards...	
Preflop	40%
Flop has two new low cards (21 outs)	72%
Flop has one new low card	26%
Two low cards...	
Preflop	24%
Flop has two new low cards (16 outs)	59%
Flop has one low card	16%

should bet to get the lows out now to maximize the chances of winning the whole pot.

If there are two or more low cards in the flop, the high hand will share the pot about three-quarters of the time. High-low is a whole new ball game and new strategies apply. Since the high hand will get only half of the pot, all of the expectations applicable to straight high Omaha are out the window—unless you have compensating low equities also.

HOW TO PLAY YOUR GOOD HANDS

In Omaha high-low as with most high-low games, you always prefer to start with prime two-way values. Of course, these are hands that you really don't have to think much about. In high-low situations, you'd simply bet it every time it is your turn. Because of the bi-directionality, both highs and lows might be betting. Thus, it is roughly twice as likely that someone will bet. And it might as well be you, since betting says little about your hands. In straight high Omaha, betting gives away more information about your hand than checking. But in high-low, checking says more (negatively) about your hand than betting.

If you want to build the pot, you should bet and hope for a raise—which is fairly likely in high-low—so that you can reraise. That will get three bets into the pot. You'll only trap with a good hand when you strongly suspect that someone else will probably bet but not raise (note that the check-raise gets two bets into the pot). And you seldom want to risk having it checked around.

On the flop, you may want to jack up the stakes on marginal or partially made hands: for example, two high pairs, especially in late position, on the theory that if you don't bet, there will be a nothing pot. Also, betting should narrow the field. But, even in last position, it is a bad play to drive high come hands without other equities. Even if you manage to push out all of the official high competition, if you have poor high holdings, one of the other low hands may beat you for high.

In high-low flop situations, you want to drive with good two-way hands, nut or near-nut high hands, good low hands that also have marginal high holdings, and sometimes with two-way marginal holdings.

PLAYING THE BLINDS

When you're on the blind, you'll often find yourself in a situation where you don't have prime values. However, if you can see the flop instead of folding for a small additional amount, it's a smart play. Certainly at 10 to 1 money odds, even many not-so-good hands are worth seeing the flop. For example, hands with two 5-or-less low cards or hands with three working high cards that would not otherwise call to see the flop, get more than adequate odds.

But don't defend your blind against a double raise without a good hand! You only invest big bucks in hands with prime values and good two-way potential. Folding is vastly better on potential big-money hands without prime values that are unlikely to flop whole pot potential.

At first glance in Omaha high-low games having an average of more than five players seeing the flop, because of the large starting pots, it might seem that you should defend your blind liberally. But there are some important qualifications you must take into account.

The most important distinction is the type of cards that you hold. Two-way potential is very important. And you can only have good low potential with very low cards. At loose Omaha high-low, you often need the nuts to win even half of the pot. Prime cards such as aces, A-2, and A-3 make the nuts much more often than medium cards.

Perhaps the most common mistake players make in loose Omaha high-low is playing medium card hands like, 9-8-7-5! Medium low cards, sixes through eights, without prime lower cards have very little two-way potential. What they do have is great second-best potential! Although these hands occasional win, they're always dangerous and highly subject to big losses, even when they flop well. And even the best flops for medium cards are very fragile. You almost should be willing to pay money *not* to play these hands!

The bottom line is that medium low cards don't increase your direct chances of winning the low half-pot, because you normally cannot afford to chase with these cards. And if you do chase and occasionally back into low, you have probably paid much more than the half-pot that you win. Similarly, although low flush cards occasionally win high, pursuing these draws without additional strength usually costs more than what you win in the long run. Indeed, low flush or big low-card holdings will cause more money to be lost by weak players than money won.

A BAD TIME TO DEFEND A BLIND

Chart key: Action reads left to right, top to bottom. Each betting round begins with → and ends with ←. Other markings and symbols: a (ante); b (blind bet); • (check); = (call, including when big blind sees flop free); ↑ (raise); — (fold); ● (dealer position, a.k.a. "the button"). A seat number surrounded by asterisks (for example, * 1 *) is your seat. Any wager not preceded by a symbol is a voluntary first bet. Wagers indicate the total invested on a betting round. The money in the rightmost column indicates total pot size after the betting. For full explanation of the chart, see Appendix B.

MCU Poker Chart. Omaha high-low 8-or-better $50/$100 with $25 and $50 blinds.

* 1 *	2	3	4	5	6	7	8	9	10	Pot
					●	b25	b50			$75
							4♣ 3♣ 6♥ 6♠			Starting hands ‹‹‹
—	100 =150	=100 =150←	—	—	↑150[1]	—	—[2]	→—	—	$525
										Flop 2♣ A♣ 6♦
	→50 =100←	↑100			=100			???[3]		‹‹‹ $825

1. This reraise wakes you up to the fact that somebody might have a serious hand this time.

2. Your Omaha high-low hand might be good enough to defend the big blind for a single raise. But it's definitely not good for two raises! Your 4-3 figures to connect for a second-best (or third-best) low much of the time and that flush is often going to lose, even if you make it. Plus, your pair of sixes just isn't very appealing in Omaha—high or high-low. Put it all together and this isn't nearly the quality of hand many novices give it credit for. And you're certainly not going to call a raise and a reraise with it. So, you fold.

3. Wish you had it back, right? Well, that's one of the main lessons you need to learn about poker. You can't go by single hand results. Sure, sometimes you would have won big hands had you played, instead of folded. That's what motivates losing players— even though they donate money to your game, they frequently get lucky and win pots where they shouldn't even have wagered. This time, you would have gotten an amazingly good flop—temporarily the "nut" low, plus three sixes, and even a straight-flush draw.

Think what would happen if you played this same hand, in the same situation, 10,000 times. Some of those times you'd scoop the pot, and some of those times you'd win a share of the pot, but often you'd win nothing.

Put it all together, and you'd average a loss by calling the reraise. So, you earned money by *not* playing this hand. If you routinely did play this hand in this situation, you'd sometimes win, but you can't just cherry pick the wins and forget about the times you'd lose. You don't know which is which in advance. You have to average it all together. The result of this hand, both theoretically and in practice in the long run, is a loss. And by folding, you didn't suffer that loss. That's all you need to know. The cards that fall after you make that correct decision are irrelevant.

STRATEGY IN TIGHT HIGH-LOW GAMES

Omaha games filled with tight-aggressive players such that there are three or less players seeing most flops, are played more like hold'em than "loose" Omaha. At tight Omaha high-low, when a tight aggressive player raises before the flop and everyone else folds, the big blind often may call liberally on sheer value.

Short-handed Omaha high-low is a very democratic game; in other words, there's more equality between good and not-so-good hands than in hold'em and Omaha high. At hold'em, if you defend your blind head-to-head by going all in against a preflop raiser with two medium low cards, you win about a third of the time. At Omaha high-low, if you play head-to-head showdown with a marginal hand against a typical preflop raiser, you win about 40-plus percent of the time!

And if you're an aggressive blind defender, you'll probably do even better. For example, if a preflop raiser follows through with a bet on the flop, on high flops, you might consider smooth-calling the flop, betting or check-raising on the turn, and then betting on the river. Assuming that your opponent routinely bets the flop, he will fold to your bets enough times to make your occasional bluffs or come bluffs profitable. It will also increase the yield on your good hands.

In order to be a consistent winner at high-low Omaha, you must be a tactical opportunist and be able to back into an occasional half pot (winning high or low) by realizing that you sometimes have a bargain call in last position. In high-low, there are numerous ways that luck presents itself, and it takes some skill and still more luck to capitalize on these occasions. But these lucky opportunities are not that frequent and also involve some amount of investment loss.

Ordinary poker bluffing is rare in high-low pots, (i.e., situations where you bet with nothing and everyone folds). On the other hand, maneuvering for half a pot, which is similar to bluffing, is prevalent. A typical maneuver is betting or raising on the flop to get a medium hand that beats your medium hand to fold. At that point, your marginal hand is good enough to win the high or low direction.

One good example of this is a "leveraged buyout" play on fifth street, when you're sitting in front of the previous driver, with some not-so-great two-way potential.

If you bet and the driver raises (who you suspect has a one-way lock), marginal hands that have you beat will often fold, fearing the deadly last-round triangle. That will leave you as the only caller chasing. And hopefully, you'll win half the pot. Not only does it take considerable skill and experience to recognize these situations, but there's also a high percentage of error rate in diagnosing them and generally a lot of luck involved. But, since these wins account for some 10 to 30 percent of your winnings, getting some piece of these creative opportunities is important if you want to be a consistent winner.

THE TURN AND RIVER

While the turn and river present many opportunities for the expert in high Omaha to exercise his skill and judgment in reading opponents and making good percentage moves, in high-low Omaha, it's much more difficult to read opponents correctly. Thus, even the best players must play more on general principles than on deep brilliant moves. However, general principles sometimes can be applied with considerable skill and psychology.

Just as all good Omaha high-low players know that they must avoid getting squeezed by the expensive raising that sometimes occurs on the last two rounds, all good Omaha players also know that this is indeed one of the best times to make money. Although a lock low hand is often reluctant to cap out the betting in fear of getting **quartered** (that is, splitting the high or low end and getting only one-quarter of the whole pot), when there is a known fish splashing around in the pot, sometimes the lock low will risk a raise or two, especially after the fourth card—if he has some extra prospects.

There are also some occasions where an expert can make fairly safe assumptions about the starting hands of other good players, which strongly affect the odds of a situation and allow the expert to make "offbeat" bets and raises on the last two rounds.

STRATEGY CONCLUSIONS

Here are some important conclusions. Heed them if you intend to make a consistent profit in Omaha high-low, a game where the simplest of mistakes, if made over and over, can kill your bankroll. Memorize the following easy tips and keep them in mind whenever you sit in a game.

1. Avoid big loss situations, especially on the turn and river.
2. Play mostly tight starting hands. In most games tight means A-2, A-3, some 2-3 hands, and four high cards all 9 or higher.
3. Once involved, be opportunistic. Consider raising after the flop on two-way marginal hands and fight fiercely if you detect weakness.
4. Avoid an Omaha high-low table if less than five players on average are seeing the flops.

SUMMARY

In summary, the impact of the skill differential of experts over merely good players is more financially significant in both hold'em and high Omaha than in high-low Omaha, because the expert wins more consistently against good players at hold'em and high Omaha than high-low Omaha. This is one reason why many average to good players like high-low. While some poker experts have wrongly evaluated the skill potential in straight high Omaha, the game is clearly more complex and, in some situations, has a higher overall skill factor than hold'em.

So, if you're an average-level to better poker player at Omaha high-low in a game with several weaker players, you have a potentially profitable game. And if there are fewer good players in a given Omaha game than at a typical hold'em table, so much the better!

Keep in mind, however, that on a bad night, not only average players, but even experts can take a pounding at Omaha high-low. At high-low, results are less predictable since few hands are sure things, and you have less control. It is much harder to gauge the likelihood of losing in a hand, and it can be disastrously expensive when you're unlucky. And because most pots are split, you win less when you win.

The staunchest of high-low aficionados admit that on a bad night, even all of their best moves can't save them from disaster. It may be some consolation that although everyone has some bad nights at high-low Omaha, most of them correlate somewhat with the lack of bad players in the game.

Even if you're a diehard high-low enthusiast, you should attempt to master the straight-high concepts of seizing the initiative and driving described in the Omaha high chapters, since whenever the flop contains three or more high cards (nines through kings), you're essentially playing straight-high Omaha.

13 ALMOST ANYONE CAN WIN AT OMAHA HIGH-LOW

This abbreviated chapter is devoted to some of the essentials that you'll need to be a winner at Omaha high-low. Although it helps to have previous poker experience, it's even more important to understand the following basic concepts and then be able to apply them in practice at the table.

You'll be pleasantly surprised to discover that in Omaha high-low, there are at least three areas where you can make or save money simply by taking advantage of opportunities and avoiding bad plays. Understanding these three areas is really not difficult. Let's look at them now.

THREE WAYS TO MAKE AND SAVE MONEY

1. Your biggest edge in Omaha high-low comes from only playing high percentage starting hands. You'll be playing fewer starting hands than most of the other players at your table.

You should understand that in a loose game—and most low stake Omaha high-low games are loose games—most of the hands played by the weaker players will lose money in the long run. The chips that they lose will float around the table and eventually be won and kept by the players playing high-percentage hands.

By playing only about one out of four starting hands, you'll be a mathematical favorite to win money at the approximate rate of one to three big bets per hour. For example, in a $5/$10 game, you should average winning about $10 to $30 per hour, depending on the other players in the game and your ability to make correct plays. But you must have sufficient discipline to invest your money only when you're the favorite. If you want to win, you must be patient.

2. A second and very important advantage you gain is based upon the principle that money saved is the same as money won. You save a lot of money in Omaha high-low by avoiding big loss situations. Weak players lose most of their money chasing, especially on the last two rounds of betting. If you chase on only half as many hands as the weak players, you'll save a lot of money.

One typical trap situation that must be avoided is the "death triangle," when two lock hands cap out the betting, splitting up the money of an unwary chaser with a second-best hand. This occurs less often at Omaha high-low than at other high-low games because a lock low hand must be cautious of being quartered, for example, when two players each have an A-2 lock low.

Perhaps the most frequent failing, even of better players, is chasing with the second nut-low on the flop. You usually save money by not competing for two-way flops when you have a second nut low draw as your only prospect.

The classic example is when you have an A-3 and the flop hits with two low cards and one high card. It is usually a bad percentage play to call unless there is a very large starting pot already built from preflop raising. Your A-3 will be the single best low draw only about 30 percent of the time. About 50 percent of the time there will be an A-2 out against you. And about 20 percent of the time, there will be another A-3 to tie with you for low, so you only get one quarter or perhaps one sixth if you hit and are not counterfeited.

The bottom line is that unless preflop raises have created a giant starting pot, you'll save money in the long run by folding money-draining chasing hands right after the flop.

But if you do call on the flop and you have inadequate prospects to continue, don't fish in for the double-size betting rounds.

3. The third important advantage is to play more aggressively than average on one-way high flops, that is, two or three high cards on the flop. This means that you should lead bet or raise with marginal or even dubious hands. If you can grab just one of these small one-way pots each hour, minus a few bets lost in the process, your hourly average would easily increase by one or two big bets per hour.

In other words, in these high Omaha situations, you're trying to steal the antes, win the sometimes sizable starting pot, or narrow the action down to few players so that your odds of ending up with the best hand easily justifies the bet or raise you invested. This aggressiveness succeeds best when you have a tight (feared) image, because both the better players and the weaker players are more likely to fold if they believe you only play sound values.

THE IMAGE GAME: LOVE AND FEAR

Omaha high-low is not simply one game, but two quite different games: a high-low split pot game and a straight high one-winner game—all depending on the flop. At Omaha high-low, the most successful players maintain a two-way image, a "loved" image for the weaker players, and a tighter or "feared" image for the better players.

Is it better to be loved or feared? There are two answers.

1. Being Loved

Answer one is that you make more money at Omaha high-low by being loved (i.e., by getting extra callers). In well-attended two-way pots, where there is little bluffing, you usually have to show the best hand to win each half of the pot. But since you're playing mainly high-percentage cards, you'll win more than your share of the pots. More callers in your pots means more money for you when you win.

Thus, in most of the big two-way, high-low pots that you play in, you prefer to have a "loved" image; that is, the other players, especially the weaker players, love to call you—because they don't fear you.

You might even attempt to publicize the few occasions when you happen to play a substandard hand since it helps to maintain a friendly non-intimidating presence that encourages weaker players to play in your pots. In these well-attended high-low two-way pots, you strive to be "loved" and attract callers.

Weaker players often don't notice specifically who is calling along with them, although they might notice who is betting or raising. So unless you have a particularly feared image, in a well attended pot your loved image has only a moderate effect on the weaker players calling. Some of the better players, however, might notice and adjust their play.

If the flop has two or three cards 8 or lower, then you're playing the high-low game and there will probably be many callers on the flop. But if the flop contains two or three high cards, then you're essentially playing high Omaha with usually one winner. The players who called to see the flop with low hands likely will fold if there is betting. If no one likes the flop, the pot is up for grabs.

2. Being Feared

When a pot is up for grabs, it might as well be you that does the grabbing at least some of the time. And you'll be more successful at grabbing if you have a tight feared image. So answer two is that when high flops hit the table, it is better to be "feared."

RANDOM CARDS

When a high flop hits the table at Omaha high-low, since most of the better players in the pot are competing with low cards like an A-2 or A-3, they'll be less likely to have enough high cards to call your bet. Most of your callers will probably be weaker players with random cards or calling stations who take one off, perhaps hoping for two good cards. Since the pot is already enlarged by the players who folded, you're usually in a highly favorable situation. And you might occasionally manage to win with a bluff.

FOUR STEPS TO WINNING AT OMAHA HIGH-LOW

Winning at Omaha high-low may seem like a bewildering goal to beginners, but there are actually just a few simple steps you need to take, steps that will serve as a quick-fix for profit. Here they are...

1. Loose Games

Play only in loose games where there is an average of more than five players seeing the flop. If an average of four or fewer players are seeing the flop, only very good poker players can expect to show a profit, especially with the house taking a rake off the top.

2. Starting Hands

In early seat play only hands containing an A-2, A-3, A-4-5 (with the ace suited), 2-3 plus another good holding, four high cards all 9 or higher, most pockets aces, and certain four all-good-card hands such as pocket kings double-suited with two prime low cards. In late position you may add slightly lesser hands such as ones containing an A-4 or A-5 if the ace is suited. Note that many high point-count hands with eights and sevens, which play very well at straight high Omaha, should be avoided at Omaha high-low because when there are corresponding cards on the board, usually a low hand will be taking half of the pot.

If you occasionally play mediocre or marginal hands, don't expect to make money on those hands in the long run. As you gain playing experience, you might occasionally play a marginal hand in late seat for image adjustment or psychological momentum purposes.

3. On The Flop

After a two-way flop (with two or three low cards), play tight and try to get more callers (loved). After some one-way high flops (two or three high cards), play aggressively unless most of your opponents are also playing aggressively and are routinely playing hands worse than yours. In this case, you should tighten up. With either type of flop, if a starting pot is unusually large because of preflop raises, the odds change significantly, and it's often correct to see the flop (take one off) if your hand can improve significantly with one good card.

If you acquire a tight image from playing tight on the two-way high-low flop hands, then it's even more advantageous to play very aggressively after a high flop. But try to maintain your tight image in these one-way pots because you would prefer less competition when you have marginal values.

Note that a bet after a flop with only one low card forces the low hands to fold or chase with bad odds. If you have two low cards when there's one low card in the flop, you'll make a backdoor low on the last two cards about one time in six.

4. Last Two Rounds

Play very conservatively on the turn and river. Don't chase, especially if raised, without at least a nut draw or when your best prospect may be second or third best if it hits. In low situations, with two low cards on the board, the two lowest cards (example A-2 in a hand with a 4 and a 6 on the board) constitute a nut low draw since four other cards (in this example, a 3, 5, 7 or 8) give you a nut low. Even though an A-3 or 2-3 are the next best low cards, only one card actually makes the nut low hand and hence the odds of your hitting the nuts on the last card are greater than 10 to 1 against. Unless you have additional prospects, bucking 10 to 1 odds for only half of the pot is not worth pursuing.

SUMMARY

Even if you lack experience and expertise, if you have enough self discipline to stick to the following three guidelines, you can win at Omaha high-low:

1. Play only high percentage starting hands.
2. Avoid heavy loss situations.
3. Compete mainly when the percentages are on your side.

The reason why you can win is because the mathematical advantage you get from playing high percentage starting hands is large enough to compensate for some amount of less-than-optimum subsequent play, especially since in Omaha high-low, less than optimum plays sometimes win.

So if you can avoid big losing situations, and perhaps occasionally gain a high board that is up for grabs, you certainly have the potential to be a winner. And with time and more experience, you may even become a big winner.

BEST OMAHA HIGH-LOW GAMES

1. Play in Omaha high-low games where an average of more than five players is seeing the flop.

2. Play in Omaha high-low games where an average of more than three players is staying in after the flop.

In order to win consistently at Omaha or hold'em or any game of skill, you must understand "basic strategy." This chapter boils down the specific strategies that were discussed earlier into a three-step process. This three-step basic strategy applies not only to Omaha high and high-low, but also to hold'em, pineapple, and most other flop games.

If you're able to perceive possible violations of basic strategy in your own playing, perhaps by playing too loosely, the problem is correctable—if you want to correct it. Basic strategy suggests a fundamental discipline, a formula for winning.

It is critical to understand your own strengths and weaknesses. If you're knowingly violating basic strategy because you're convinced that you have a superior strategy, then at the very least you should be familiar with the basic strategy to serve as a point of departure. You'll be using sophisticated finesses once you get a comfort level with this basic strategy. But, until you have reliable basic strategy to depend on, you simply can't win.

THREE STEP APPROACH TO BASIC STRATEGY

Here is a powerful three-step approach to a winning basic strategy...

Step One: Preflop Hand Evaluation

Evaluate your hand before the flop. Pick up your cards and decide whether they're worth calling with, or perhaps worth raising. Many players go wrong here by playing too many hands. If you find yourself playing half the hands or more, you're probably playing too loose.

Step Two: Flop Decisions

Upon seeing the flop, decide whether or not to get further involved. This is frequently the most difficult and complicated decision in both straight high and high-low Omaha. Gauging how your opponents' hands meshed with the flop and how they might react to checks, calls, bets, or raises is critical.

Step Three: Playing the Turn and River

On the turn and river, decide whether you still belong in the pot for the double-sized bets. Since your winning potential is fairly well clarified by the turn, this decision to compete in the big money rounds should be easier than the complexities of the flop. How you play your cards after the turn and river depends upon your basic poker skills. You have to be good at judging how your hand will fare against what your opponents are likely to have.

STEP ONE: PREFLOP HAND EVALUATION

Although the basic strategy involved in evaluating your hand before the flop is conceptually simple, this is where most players go wrong. There is a basic principle common to all poker games with blinds (as opposed to poker with individual antes): You should not put your initial money into the pot unless you have a good starting hand. The basic strategy of Omaha is to get involved only with hands that are likely to flop a playable hand more than about 30 percent of the time. The importance of hitting the flop should be self evident. Having the best hand after fifth street does you no good if you had to fold the hand on the flop.

A flop is playable in Omaha if it works with your hand so that you have at least one good draw. A good draw is one in which it is likely to hit about one third of the time or better *and* frequently win when it hits. You should shy away from lesser draws: for example, inside straights, which are about 5 to 1 against hitting with two cards coming. The possibility of raises and the likelihood of holding a bad percentage hand after the fourth card make them costly plays.

The Two-Card Combinations

Because you must use two cards from your hand, a good starting hand consists of at least several useful two-card combinations out of the six possible. Although many good Omaha players simply eyeball their four cards and use their judgment to decide whether to play or fold, there are several mathematical approaches which allow you to evaluate the total potential of your hand before the flop with reasonable accuracy—by adding up the six existing two-card combinations.

One tedious but educational method is to actually calculate the likelihood of getting a playable flop and then estimate the likelihood of hitting and winning the hand. For example, suppose you hold the ace and queen of spades and the 7 and 6 of hearts. Of your six two-card combinations (A-Q, A-7, A-6, Q-7, Q-6, 7-6) only two combinations have straight or flush potential (the A-Q and the 7-6).

Let's look at each of these two-card combinations more closely to see how they contribute to your expectations of hitting the flop and winning. This should also give you a better feel for how all Omaha hands can be evaluated using the sum of two-card combinations.

First, let's approximate the odds of the A-Q of spades winning the pot by making a flush. The board flops three spades less than 1 percent of the time but flops two spades about 1 percent of the time. This four-flush will become a flush on the turn or last card about 36 percent of the time. But even this nut flush will sometimes lose to a full house or higher. Overall, the nut flush holding will make a flush and win the pot for you only about 4 percent of the time.

The A-Q will flop a high straight much less than 1 percent of the time (only about .37 percent). This holding cannot flop a four-card multiple straight come. If only two of the three other straight cards are in the flop, conditions will often prohibit your staying in to draw for the inside straight. But, high straights do seem to win a lot of pots, so let's be generous and estimate 1 percent wins for the A-Q making the high straight.

The 7-6 holding will flop a straight less than 1 percent of the time (don't count the 8-9-10 ignorant straight—it's seldom worth playing). But, a playable two-way or better straight come will flop about 8 percent of the time. This will become a straight about a third of the time, or more for multiway straight comes. But remember, straights in general have a high mortality rate and lose close to 40 percent of the time—mostly when the flop contains two or three suited cards or a pair. Let's estimate about a 2 percent win rate for the 7-6 straight holding. And since the 7 and 6 were both hearts, let's estimate about a 1 percent win rate for a flush (mostly the backdoor flush made on the turn and river when the other potential flushers are no longer in the pot). A 7-high hand is not likely to win the flush competition.

Finally, since none of the other four two-card combinations (A-7, A-6, Q-7, Q-6) have any straight or flush potential, let's evaluate what is sometimes referred to as "single card" potential. This is essentially the likelihood of matching pairs or trips in the flop. Any single card will match a pair in the flop about .77 percent of the time. Thus, any four non-paired cards will make trips with a pair in the flop about 3 percent of the time.

Any four cards also will make two pairs with the flop about 12 percent of the time, but the two low pairs should not be played without other equities. Thus, trips plus the two high pairs (about 4 percent) and the high and low pairs (which if played, should be played very aggressively and often must be folded) give you the standard single card potential of about an 11 percent likelihood of post-flop playability. Every non-paired hand has this quality. Having an ace and another high card and no real low cards probably improves your overall winning chances by a couple of percentage points more. But even high trips require something good to win the pot, namely hitting a full house, and no opponent having a flush or straight.

There is no magic about what sort of hands are likely to hit a good flop in high Omaha. The frequency of getting a good flop is directly related to the number of good two-card combinations. Let's take a look at the likelihood of the hand A-Q-7-6 getting a good flop. Combining the 12 percent for flushes, 9 percent for straights, and the 11 percent single-card potential, the overall likelihood of hitting the flop is slightly less than 30 percent.

Based on these percentages, this is a borderline flop-seeing hand. But because of the high-card potential of the ace and the queen and the two straight flush potentials, you should probably make a loose call.

By using the above approximations, not only can you estimate your likelihood of hitting the flop, but you also can roughly calculate the odds of hitting a hand good enough to win. In the above example the likelihood of ending up with a flush, straight or higher hand is somewhere between 10 and 15 percent. But your odds of actually winning the pot are better, since more than one-third of all pots are won with lesser hands (depending a great deal on the characteristics of the particular game).

Good Starting Hands are Essential

Using the above approach, any Omaha hand can be evaluated for flop potential and for final winning potential. In order to quickly evaluate the total potential of a four-card Omaha hand, it would be more practical to have some simple systemic method for adding up the potential of each of the two-card combinations. The Cappelletti Omaha Point Count System detailed earlier provides such a method. It assigns an appropriate value to each possible two-card combination based on both flop expectation and overall winning potential. You simply add together the points of all six of the two-card combinations and fold, call, or raise based on the resulting total.

Using the point-count system, which recommends calling on hands that add up to 11 points or more, the above A-Q-7-6 hand computes to 12 points—6 points for the A-x flush, 2 points for the 7-6, 2 points for the ace and queen high cards, and 2 indirect "intangible" bonus points for the straight flush.

But whether you evaluate your initial four cards using this formula or simply have years of experience, the bottom line is you must play only good hands to be a winner. Anyone who has experienced the last-card blues in Omaha knows

NOTE FROM CARO

There are concepts that apply to all forms of poker and concepts specific to just some of them. For instance, specific to high-low games, when it's clear that two or more players are going for the same side, the first one to bet will often force rational opponents to fold, even if their hands are slightly better.

This is because astute opponents know they can't afford to compete in a costly betting war for just half of the pot. They're essentially forced to surrender to the first bettor going the same way. This concept implies that you should bet into a knowledgeable foe who seems to have a one-way hand, even if it's slightly better than your own.

that you need to go into the last card with one or more good draws in addition to other values you may be betting.

Good draws come from good starting hands. And that's your basic preflop strategy.

One-Way and Two-Way Hands

In Omaha high-low, because of the likelihood of a split pot whenever two or more low cards flop, a two-way strategy replaces the traditional one-way strategy. Although a one-way high hand of four high cards (nine or higher) are playable before the flop, nevertheless, most of these one-way high hands have to be folded after a flop with two or more low cards, because of the inadequate payoff of only going high.

Thus, in Omaha high-low, two-way hands which contain an ace, deuce, or three give you the best chances of winning.

STEP TWO: FLOP DECISIONS

Basic strategy dictates that in an early position—where you have fewer opportunities to employ skill and there is a potential for raises by players behind you—you should only bet or call according to the strength of your hand compared to the flop.

You modify your strategy further when there is a lot of money in the pot to protect. In other words, if the pot was capped before the flop, you'll drop one of the below hands because an even higher threat is present. For example, you'll avoid playing flush or straight comes when there is a pair on the flop. Note that each of the situations involves *two* or more flop cards working in conjunction with your hand. There is also no mention made of the possibility of pushing a high pair. In Omaha high-low, however, a high pair with a nut low draw may be pushed to pressure the better highs.

In straight high Omaha and in Omaha high-low when two or three high cards are on the board, the following good flops, in descending order of strength, are playable:

Locks: Straight flush or quads.

Board Set: Trips, you have a card that matches a pair in the flop.

Hidden Set: Trips, one flop card matches your pair in hand.

Flush: You hold first, second, or third highest two-suited cards that match two or three of the same suit in the flop.

Straight: You hold two or more proximate cards that work with two or three cards in the flop to make a straight or one or more good straight comes.

High Two Pair: Play aggressively if there is a reasonable chance that they might hold up and win the pot.

High and Low Two Pair: Play very aggressively if conditions seem favorable, otherwise fold.

Early Position

Because everyone has four cards, you should always assume the worst in an early position and tend to play conservatively. Murphy's Law applied to Omaha is that somebody hits any given flop. For example, if there is a pair on board, assume somebody holds one of the other two cards. Again, keep this in mind: Omaha is not like hold'em where many flops are missed and up for grabs.

Late Position

In late positions you should be more opportunistic. However, there is a significant difference between opportunistic and stupid. This is where much of the skill in Omaha comes into play.

In late positions there are at least two situations you should look for.

1. If a single bet comes around to you, and no one behind you is likely to raise, you might venture a call any time the pot odds justify your particular long shot. The classic example is drawing to an inside straight. In Omaha, your odds going into the turn are almost always better than you think, because with four good cards in your hand, seeing the turn frequently presents additional opportunities that you may not have foreseen.

2. The second situation to look for, one that stirs the blood of all natural-born poker players, is when it gets checked around to you. Just the fact that no one has taken the opportunity to bet means something. What you might do depends a lot on the character of the game you're playing in. Without going into all the various bluff possibilities, let's look solely at value betting.

If you have as much as the high pair or any decent come, you can justify betting on values simply by noting that everyone will fold some percentage of the time. Or someone with a come hand may call and not draw. If you don't bet, everyone gets a free card, and both your odds of winning and expected value in the pot go way down. If you're the timid type, perhaps you should think of it as being much more scary *not* to bet than to bet.

Playing Secondary Potential

In Omaha, you should fold on the flop about two-thirds of the time. If you're getting involved on the flop as much as half the time, you're probably chasing too much and losing money. On the other hand, on the one-third of the time that you get involved—this assumes that you're seeing the flop with only good hands—some borderline decisions will be involved. Many tight players fold hands that are good percentage investments, that instead, should have been played. Of course, the real skill is to understand the various factors involved and to make the good plays.

The simple rule of thumb is this. Think of each secondary two-card prospect where you need a good card on both the turn *and* river to complete a flush or straight as having a 4 percent equity. Though each situation is different, rather than trying to remember every nuance, you'll use this as a very rough estimate. If these secondary potentials added to your other direct prospects yield enough potential wins compared to the dollars in the pot, you may try a loose call, preferably in a later seat, if you judge that a raise is unlikely to follow your call. If a bad turn card turns, you simply fold your half-bet investment. But if the turn card helps, then you have earned the honor of being officially sucked in for the infamous Omaha last-card roulette.

Flop Strategy Summary

The essence of after-the-flop basic strategy is to get further involved only with good percentage hands. Once you make the key decision to stay in the pot, tactics come into play. Depending on position and other conditions, it might be advisable to raise, even with some not-so-great hands. Raises in early positions tend to reduce competition while raises in later seats tend to get it checked around to you next time (which might save fourth round maximum-bet money if you miss). Sometimes all your opponents will fold to your raise.

Remember, Omaha is the game where the last card changes the winner more than any other form of poker. You have to become accustomed to the fact that a relatively large percentage of winning hands will come from chasing. Quite frequently, the driver is actually a vast underdog to the various chasers. You want to get your share of those "chasing wins" as well. So when the right circumstances present themselves, start playing those combination hands to get your share. It all boils down to a matter of good evaluation and keeping the percentages on your side.

STEP THREE: PLAYING THE TURN AND RIVER

One of the biggest differences between Omaha and hold'em is the increased risk of losing on the infamous last card due to the four-card hands having many more possibilities of combining with the board to make a winner. In Omaha, when you have the nuts after the turn, you usually live in fear of the last card forming a better hand than yours. The natural order of things on the river is that chasers hope for miracle cards to complete their hands and the leader prays for a brick.

After the turn very few hands are totally secure. Even four-of-a-kind hands can lose to higher quads or a straight flush if respectively, a higher card than the quads gets paired on the river or a third proximate suited card appears. For example, suppose that after the turn you happen to have four fives and that two of the four board cards are the three and five of diamonds. Of the 44 outstanding cards, there are 39 bricks and 5 dangerous cards, namely the 7, 6, 4, 2 and ace of diamonds that would create the possibility of a straight flush.

Also, all single cards on the board that are of higher denomination than the quads are potential non-bricks. For example, if you have four 5s and a second 8 comes on the river, there is a possibility that someone might have four 8s. While any exact two-card holding is very unlikely at hold'em, in four-card Omaha anything can happen.

After the Turn Card

With 44 cards remaining on the river, the odds of two

specific cards being in one four-card hand are around one-half percent (.634 percent). If you were playing against eight opponents, all of whom were still in the pot after the turn, it would be eight times more likely that any two specific cards would be held by one of the eight players, or about 5 percent. The better the two specific cards happen to be, for example, two kings, or the king and queen of spades, the more likely that the holder, on seeing a favorable flop would still be around after the turn. Thus, in these instances, the odds are about 19 to 1. But clearly, if the two specific cards happened to be something like the 2 and 3 of diamonds, the odds of two such specific cards being out against you would be less since players would be unlikely to see the flop with these cards in Omaha high games.

One typical Omaha situation occurs when you're driving a nut straight after the turn, but the board has two suited cards (and no pairs). If the feared last card is a third card of that suit, or if the board pairs, it is often best to fold your no-longer-nut-straight to the expected last round bets. It would certainly be foolish for you to bet.

For example suppose your hand is an 8-6-5-4, and the four board cards are K-9-7-5, with two spades. At this point, after the turn, you have a 9-high straight which is the best possible hand given the board. Although it is always correct to drive here in order to thin the competition, few players realize how tenuous these hands really are.

In the above example there are only 11 or 12 bricks (depending on which two of the four board cards are the spades). All last cards from kings down to fives are dangerous! The only last cards that are bricks are aces, deuces, threes or fours, but definitely not in spades! Note how the presence of the innocuous king on the board works with the 9 to make all queens, jacks and tens into dangerous cards.

The main lesson to be learned here is that, although it is

correct to make the first bet after the turn with these hands in order to drive out some of the competition, it is often wrong to raise! If you can raise or reraise before there have been intervening callers, it is definitely good to do so because the increased pressure might drive out lesser flush or two-pair hands. But if you're in last position and there have been several intervening callers, a raise, even with a reraise by the first bettor, is unlikely to drop anyone who has already called a bet in the round. Once stuck for a bet, a player will usually see it through to the end.

In this situation, you should raise only if you think that you might drop some competition. But you don't raise just to get more money into the pot. Your equity in this situation is often less than that of the chasers! If the lead bettor who you would be raising has the same holding as you, your money odds really plunge.

Counting Bricks

Thus, the three main variables in this type of the turn situation:

1. How many bricks exist.
2. How many of the dangerous holdings are likely to be lurking.
3. How likely it is that you'll split the pot if you manage to hang on and win.

Although you can count bricks, the last two variables require good table judgment. Based on these evaluations, you can estimate your pot odds and calculate whether or not a raise is good business. When in doubt, the simple rule stated above is usually correct: Don't raise when only a dozen or less cards are bricks and you don't have other draws, unless you judge that the raise is very likely to drop some competition.

AVOID BATTLING FOR
HALF THE THREE-WAY POT

MCU Poker Chart. Omaha high-low 8-or-better $50/$100 with $25 and $50 blinds.

1	2	3	4	5	6	7	8	9	10	Pot
4♦ A♣ K♦ 10♣								●	b25	$75
										Starting hands ‹‹‹
=100[1] ←	→—	—	—	—	—	—	—	↑100	==100	$300
✓								√[2] ←	→✓ ‹‹‹	Flop 7♠ 6♠ 9♣ $575
✓ —[4] ←								100[3]	→✓ =100 ‹‹‹	Turn 8♠ $775

Chart key: Action reads left to right, top to bottom. Each betting round begins with → and ends with ←. Other markings and symbols: a (ante); b (blind bet); • (check); = (call, including when big blind sees flop free); ↑ (raise); — (fold); ● (dealer position, a.k.a. "the button"). A seat number surrounded by asterisks (for example, * 1 *) is your seat. Any wager not preceded by a symbol is a voluntary first bet. Wagers indicate the total invested on a betting round. The money in the rightmost column indicates total pot size after the betting. For full explanation of the chart, see Appendix B.

1. This is okay to call, because:
> **a.** It only costs you half price, since you have the $50 big blind.
>
> **b.** The raise and call came from the latest possible positions (the button and the small blind), making them less threatening.
>
> **c.** Your call closes the betting, meaning there is no possibility of further raising after you act (as there would be if the player in the button had just called and then the player in the small blind had raised).

2. It's a good thing that the button checked, because you probably wouldn't have been able to justify a call.

3. Shucks, you got bet into. You were hoping for another free card here—the final river card.

4. The free turn card provided you with the fourth-best-possible low hand. A-2, A-3, and 3-2 are all better lows. You were hoping to get another free card, but after you check, there's a bet and a call.

Should you overcall? No! You must fold here, because if you call, you'll only be hoping to win or split half the pot. And it's likely to cost you even more money on the river. It's very likely that one of these players has a high hand that you can't possibly beat, no matter what happens on the river and that one or both players have a better low hand than yours. You must fold. And, so, you do.

AVOIDING COMMON OMAHA ERRORS

There are many mistakes that you'll see again and again in Omaha. Some are so common that it's hard to sit at a table of average players for more than a few minutes without spotting some of them. Almost as frequently as not using two cards from their hands, inexperienced Omaha players make the following mistakes:

Example 1: Over-Evaluating Two Low Flush Cards

Flop

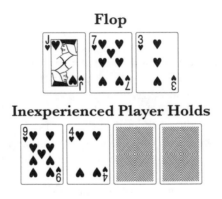

Inexperienced Player Holds

On any given nine-handed deal, three or four players will have a queen or higher flush holdings such as A-x, K-x or Q-x. Try dealing out nine hands and see for yourself. This fact should help you understand why king- and queen-high flush draws usually win the flush competition, jack-high is a definite underdog, and other flush cards, believe it or not, will win the flush competition less than 20 percent of the time! So, on two- and three-card flush flops, fold those weak flush draws before they cost you money. If the betting is unusually mild, or unless you want to overplay your cards and bet them like the nuts to scare out a tight player who may you beat with a jack or queen flush draw (but he won't scare with the ace or king), this play is generally not a good idea.

You best chance of winning with a weak flush draw is via the backdoor flush route: this is when the flop has only one card in your suit and the other players with two higher cards in your suit fold. In that situation, you are in the hand because you have other strengths you're playing. If, lo and behold, fate chooses to give you a backdoor flush on fourth and fifth streets, a 20 to 1 shot, you have a better chance of having that flush hold up. Although some big pots are won via the long shot backdoor flush, many dollars are lost paying off higher flushes.

Example 2: Over-Evaluating Low End Straight

Flop

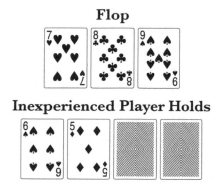

Inexperienced Player Holds

Since even the J-10 nut straight will lose this pot a fair amount of the time, the 10-7 is indeed a marginal holding, and the 6-5 ignorant straight should usually fold. Occasionally the low-end straight will win a pot, but it is most likely to win backing-in on the turn and river. It is similar to the low flush above, that is, after other straight competition has folded. If the board is, in order, K-7-9-8, a 6-5 will beat high sets and win the pot, since the higher straight competition probably folded on the A-K-7 flop.

Example 3: Over-Evaluating Two Card Straight Draw Holdings

Flop

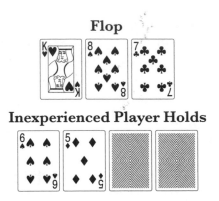

Inexperienced Player Holds

This is actually a better hand than the made straight above, since at least you have the gutshot 4 to give you a good hand. Note that the 9 probably will be a loser, giving you the ignorant end of the straight as in Example 2.

Example 4: Over-Evaluating a Straight Draw

Your best hand here is likely to be better for somebody else.

Flop

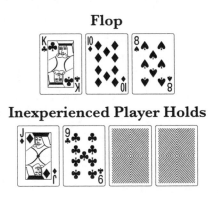

Inexperienced Player Holds

Although this J-9 open-ended straight come is normally a good hand (eight outs hit about one-third of the time), the presence of the king makes the queen draw a winner for the A-J holder and the J-9 ignorant straight gets you the usual prize for second place. Thus, because of the presence of the king, this holding is reduced to essentially a gutshot needing a 7 to complete, very similar to Example 3.

Example 5: Over-Evaluating a Low Compromised Set

Flop

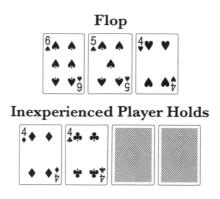

Inexperienced Player Holds

Although a set is usually one of the best all-around hands, in this particular situation, the low set should fold if the raising starts. This is the type of flop that often leads to expensive pots. If there is a lot of betting, unless you get the miracle fourth 4, you'll lose this pot about 90 percent of the time (over two-thirds of the time you won't fill and lose to a straight or flush; of the remaining one-third of the time you'll often lose to a higher full house when the board pairs). If the betting is tame with only one bettor, you might limp along optimistically.

This might be a good hand for an overplay (bluffing), especially with two spades on the flop. You'll attempt to get a low straight out and the flush comers to call—but forget this plan if another spade hits the table! This both-ends-against-the-middle tactic requires some amount of luck, but would maximize your chances if you decided to come into the pot.

CONCLUSION

Now it is time to try out your newly acquired skills. Most importantly, remember that you should be voluntarily playing less than half the hands. If you find yourself playing considerably more than 50 percent of the hands, you're giving up too much equity. It is better to have three to six two-card combinations going for you than merely one or two. It is not a coincidence that hands with all four cards working seem to win more frequently. Second, when hands are worth playing on the flop, drive and raise more frequently. And think positively. Psychology does have its place in poker.

When an expert plays a three-hour session of high-low Omaha in relatively weak games, he wins about 80 percent of the time. Your overall winning frequency will reflect your skill level. There is a lot of luck in Omaha and you will lose some of the time. But for every bad streak there will be good streaks. You have to be patient.

In Gambling 101 you learn that if you strive to keep the odds on your side, you'll win in the long run.

If you're losing too frequently you're either very unlucky or you're doing something wrong—probably the latter. Most likely you're calling too often or not betting enough. If you're losing because you're playing too tight—the classic symptoms are "you're only getting a few hands worth playing" and "you're constantly getting outdrawn on the last card"—then you're probably dropping out on a lot of hands that should be played for at least one more card. If you're constantly the *screwee* and seldom the *screwor* on the last card, you're probably playing too tight.

If you continue to lose, perhaps you should try a game with lower stakes until you have your overall strategic game better adjusted. In a retrenching situation, it is normal to think in terms of losing less rather than winning more. But remember, on any given hand, if you fail to push your advantage and are playing scared, you're probably not playing winning poker.

Accordingly, it is fine to tighten up and play higher-quality starting hands, but if you do have adequate cards to be involved on the flop, remember that aggressive poker is usually winning poker.

Sometime within the past thirty years, hold'em quietly replaced seven-card stud as the most popular and significant poker game on this planet. Hold'em's offspring, Omaha, came along in the 1980s; but it is Omaha high-low which has been snowballing in popularity. It would not be surprising if Omaha (high-low and straight high) surpassed hold'em in popularity sometime within the next 40 years.

Both hold'em and Omaha are deep games that enable skillful play on many levels. They also retain the usual poker potential for guile and psychology, as well as that many-dimensioned commodity called "fun." The concepts of fun and mass appeal should not be underestimated. Perhaps the main reason that hold'em and Omaha have proliferated is because they're both captivating games.

> Whereas it is better to be "feared" at hold'em, it is better to be "loved" at Omaha.

CARO ON HOLD'EM VS. OMAHA

Is it easier to get a big hand in Omaha than in hold'em? The most obvious answer is that, sure, it's easier to connect for a big hand in Omaha, because there are many more combinations that can be married to the board with Omaha's four private cards than there are with hold'em's two private cards.

Fine. That's true—there are more combinations. But, wait! Does that mean it's easier to get a really powerful hand in Omaha? That depends on how you define "powerful hand."

You see, "powerful" must be measured in context. If a

full house is easier to get, then it's not as powerful. Think about it. So, yes, it's much easier to hold a straight in Omaha when the board shows…

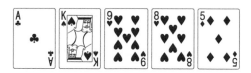

When you see that board in hold'em or Omaha, you know that no flush is possible because there aren't three cards of the same suit on the board, and no full house or four-of-a-kind is possible, because there isn't a pair on the board. So, next you look to see if a straight is possible, and, by golly, it is! But, you'd need a 7-6 to connect.

Well, in hold'em you have only one combination of cards to qualify as 7-6. How many do you have in Omaha? The answer is six. In hold'em, you can only match the first card with the second card. But in Omaha, you can also match the first card with the third card or the fourth card, and the second card with the third card or the fourth card, and the third card with the fourth card. Count 'em folks—that's six. It's much more likely that you hold 7-6 in Omaha.

So, back to the original question: Is it easier to get a powerful hand in Omaha? Not really, because hands that are easier to get aren't as powerful. So, it's easier to get hands that would be powerful in hold'em, but when you get them in Omaha, they aren't as strong.

How many possible hands can you have in hold'em, combining your starting cards with the board? The answer is 21. That's because you can use the two cards from your hand to match any of 10 combinations of three cards on the board, plus use either card from your hand to match any of five four-card combinations on the board (10 combinations, counting both cards), plus you can play all five cards on the board, using neither card from your hand (1 combination).

How many possible hands can you have in Omaha, combining your starting cards with the board? First, keep in mind that in Omaha you must use exactly two cards from your hand and exactly three cards from the board. Those are the rules. So, there's no such thing as playing the board or using just one card in your hand to make, say, a straight.

So, you can pair any of six two-card combinations of cards from your hand with any of 10 three-card combinations from the board. That's 60 combinations. That makes our comparison 21 for hold'em, versus 60 for Omaha. However, it's not quite as simple as saying you're about three times more likely (60 to 21) to get a "powerful" hand in Omaha. There are many other strange things to consider.

For instance, in hold'em, if you have…

and the board is…

Then you have a full house (K-K-K-4-4) and cannot possibly be beat by a flush.

But, in Omaha, if you have…

and the board is the same…

Then you only have three kings with a queen kicker (K-K-K-Q-4) and must worry about losing to a flush! This happens because you need to use exactly two cards from your hand. You can't use just one king and the pair of fours on the board.

Listen closely to the other differences Mike C. cites in the next section, and you'll understand that differences between hold'em and Omaha are critically important for you to understand.

CAPPELLETTI ON HOLD'EM VS. OMAHA

Straight high Omaha has approximately the same skill level as hold'em, although the two games are very different. Both games allow a significant gradient of skill levels from super-expert to beginner. And pot-limit straight high Omaha is generally recognized as one of the most skillful poker games.

My view of Omaha high-low is that it is a "fun variation" of poker but not in the same league with straight high Omaha and hold'em in regards to skill level. But just how important is skill? How does skill fit into the overall picture? Are there different types of skill?

Poker skill is a combination of many ingredients, but certainly intelligence and sensitivity are two of them. It takes intelligence to evaluate card situations objectively, such as possible holdings and percentages of winning. It takes sensitivity to judge opponents and recognize opportunity.

Hold'em hands have only two cards. Most hold'em hands miss the flop about two-thirds of the time. If your opponents have missed the flop, the pot is up for grabs— and it might as well be you who grabs it—as long as you don't try to grab too often. Often someone else also tries grabbing it, for example, the preflop raiser, and a lot of fancy maneuvering occurs. Hold'em is the more skillful game from the standpoint of sensitivity, reading your opponents (judging their likely holdings) and playing your position (position is more significant in hold'em).

Each four-card Omaha hand has six two-card combinations. At Omaha, someone holds the nuts about 10 times more frequently than at hold'em, which is why more players stay in to see the flop in Omaha!

Considerable skill is required to optimize your play in Omaha. You need to evaluate the various potentials of a given hand both objectively (estimating your odds) and subjectively (relative to your opponents and momentum of the game). If you could judge your opponent's probable holdings at Omaha as well as at hold'em, then Omaha would probably entail more overall skill. But you can't! And guessing your opponents holdings at Omaha high-low is often pure conjecture!

Although an Omaha expert might correctly guess what two-card holding an opponent is playing, that opponent not only has *that* two-card holding but also might have several additional prospects with his other two cards. It is difficult even for an expert to evaluate the whole picture. And, at Omaha high-low, there is much more uncertainty.

At hold'em, an expert quickly sizes up his opponents and learns what range of two-card holdings they play. From their betting and mannerisms, an expert gains a much better read on his opponents than a good player at Omaha. At hold'em, there is more skill involved in reading your opponents and using that information, especially when you have a positional advantage. One oversimplification is that hold'em requires more subjective skills whereas Omaha requires more objective skills.

The mathematical subtleties at Omaha are probably not as significant as stealing default pots at hold'em. Thus, there is probably more "poker skill" at hold'em than at Omaha. The question of which game inherently requires more skill is not as consequential as asking in which game does skill have the greatest impact! Note that having a slightly greater skill advantage in a hold'em game, where most players are folding bad hands, will probably not make you as much money as an Omaha game where seven players are seeing the flop!

And therein lies the rub. Although poker is a game of skill and there are many poker skills to be learned, the most consequential skill in poker is the overall ability to recognize opportunity! Choosing the right game and the right situation has more impact on your success than any other aspect of poker.

In many hold'em games, especially at higher stakes, many of the decent-to-better players play reasonably well. Even if these players deviate somewhat from what is considered optimum hold'em strategy, sometimes their variations or "instinctive" plays are based on table situations (of which you may be unaware) and hence these plays may actually be equal or superior to what you believe is the correct play. And there is always the possibility, however small, that your perception of reality is slightly off.

PROFIT OPPORTUNITIES: HOLD'EM VS. OMAHA

At hold'em, if too many of your opponents are playing textbook hold'em, it may have a noticeable negative impact on your results. If about half or more of your opponents play well enough to win a little or break even, your hourly rate of winning, minus the "time" dollars or rake, is probably less than what you would stand to win in a lower-stake, more favorable game.

In other words, if too many of your opponents are playing the same tight-aggressive textbook hold'em formula—even if they play somewhat inferior to you—they may well be taking money out of the game rather than putting money in. If there are several weak players feeding the game—most of your equity at hold'em is from weak-player confrontations—then there is less overall money in that game. The more winning players who take money out of a game, the less you win.

For many players, it is much easier to win at Omaha than hold'em simply because few players play Omaha correctly! Even most decent-to-good Omaha players cost themselves money by playing incorrectly both before and after the flop. Add that better-player money to what the weak players in the game contribute and there is ample money to be won. This also means that even the weak players win more often and hence are more likely to keep coming back.

It is not unusual to find an Omaha game where half the players see every flop and where three or more callers—often the same ones from hand to hand—routinely play weak hands after the flop. In such games you're usually well paid off when you win. It is preferable to play in a game where more players are contributing and you love your odds, rather than struggle in a game where a lot of players are playing fairly accurately.

Hourly Win Rate

A typical hold'em winner averages between one to one-and-a-half big bets per hour. The tighter you play, the more likely you are to be winning that one big bet per hour if you're playing well (assuming luck is more or less even). At loose Omaha, it is not unusual to average two to three big bets per hour. The average dollars-per-hour win will increase as more players see the flop.

If your average hourly win rate at Omaha high-low is between two and three big bets-per-hour—for example, at $5/$10 Omaha, you might be averaging about $25 per hour—that amount is approximately the same as what you would be winning at $10/$20 hold'em if indeed you were averaging between one to one-and-a-half big bets per hour.

If you win approximately the same hourly amount playing $5/$10 Omaha as when playing $10/$20 hold'em, are the two games equally advantageous?

Yes and no.

If your average hourly win were approximately equal in both games, because your units-above-average is twice as high at Omaha, you would be less likely to have a losing session at Omaha. This was tested on a computer model with wins at the given rates, and showed losses 37 percent of the time at hold'em and 27 percent of the time at Omaha. Thus, if the long run bottom line is approximately equal, you would be less likely to have a losing session at Omaha.

Since the swings from plus to minus are significantly higher in the $10/$20 hold'em game because of the higher stakes, your biggest wins would be bigger in the hold'em game; but your occasional big losses at hold'em figure to be more than twice your largest loss at Omaha— and possibly twice as financially uncomfortable. Given the above conditions, you would need considerably less bankroll at Omaha.

Bottom Line Profit Potential

So what is the overall bottom line? As observed earlier, it depends largely on your overall objective in playing poker. If making money is your prime objective, you should determine whether you can make more money playing hold'em or Omaha.

If you have substantial hold'em skills and are consistently making good money at hold'em, common sense tells you not to throw away a good thing since the grass is not always greener on the other side. But if you have few or no profits at hold'em, you may find a home at the Omaha tables. If you're adequate or good at both, then it becomes a matter of finding the best available table and making hay where the sun shines. And since it is usually easier to find a nice plump loose Omaha game, the choice is often made for you.

16 BANKROLL REQUIREMENTS

Here's a word of caution about playing for stakes higher than you can afford. If you will be a long-run winner in any given game at a given stake, then the more money you are playing for, the more money you will win in the long run. But, unfortunately, in the short run, you sometimes encounter a serious losing streak and go broke before you've had a chance to stash away enough winnings to maintain an adequate reserve. If you are attempting to play poker professionally and you go broke, you are out of action until you acquire more capital, which might even require you to get a "real" job.

You are strongly advised to stay within safe limits while you are acquiring a sufficient bankroll to stabilize your situation in life. We have all heard stories about the precipitous excitement of having all your worldly money on the table in front of you. Try bungee jumping or extreme skiing; they are probably safer.

In the short run, there is a lot of luck in poker. Not only will gambling above your head make you at least somewhat uncomfortable, even for those with nerves of steel, but you might be deterred from making good plays because of the money pressure.

Once you find a game at an appropriate stake within your means, either settle down to business and earn a livelihood, or use some of this income to build up your bankroll so that you can afford to play at higher stakes.

Your general game plan should include a practical decision about which games to play, assuming you have a choice, and how much you can afford to risk. Everyone loses some of the time, so you should not play for stakes that can jeopardize your bankroll. You cannot play your best if you're intimidated by a game that, if it goes sour, can wipe you out.

Minimum Bankroll Needed

If you're trying to survive as a professional poker player, the minimum size of the bankroll you'll need to survive your inevitable losing streaks depends mostly on the size of the stakes at which you play. Obviously the higher the stakes, the more money you'll need in reserve.

Since it is possible to encounter long losing streaks that exhaust any limited bankroll, many professional players suggest that a *winning player* should have a bankroll of between 250 to 300 times the big bet to survive about five or six large losses. We define a winning player as one capable of averaging a win of more than one big bet per hour in the game he plays. Let's further define a typical large loss for a session as about 50 times the big bet size. For example, a typical large loss in a $20/$40 game would be $2,000.

Thus, a $10,000 bankroll should enable a $20/$40 pro to survive the typical dry spells. Again, that assumes that the pro is indeed a winning player and actually wins an average of at least one big bet per hour in the long run. Of course, if he is not a winning player, then he should expect to lose any size bankroll in the long run. It is just a matter of time.

If you're fortunate enough to be a winning player, the following question must be asked: Can you spend some of your basic bankroll capital on other things? The answer, emphatically, is no. Your bankroll money is the tool of your trade. If you sell off your tools, you jeopardize your ability to make money at your profession.

Here are some strong words of advice from Mike Caro...

MIKE CARO'S BANKROLL ADVICE

NOTE FROM CARO:

Important survival warning!

Don't spend your bankroll.

One reason skilled players put themselves out of action is that they spend their bankrolls. This is a very common mistake. What happens is players seldom anticipate a long run of misfortune. But count on this: The cards will turn bad for many days in a row. And you've got to plan for it.

It's a good idea to keep more bankroll in reserve than you think you'll need. Violation of this advice results in this common example:

A player starts with a $12,000 bankroll. Gets lucky. Builds it to $27,000. Buys refrigerator, watch, 157 DVDs, a new stereo system, a wall-size TV, and a motorcycle. Bankroll is still $12,000. Player now, having promoted himself to larger limits, loses $12,000. Player is now broke. Player feels like a loser.

Yep. Happens all the time, my friends. Now this same player, who actually won $15,000 in a short time, and who is possibly averaging $300 an hour at poker, crawls around humbly trying to borrow money to play in a small-limit game.

Mike Caro expounds further on this…

Don't Cannibalize.

If you can avoid it, don't spend any portion of your bankroll until you've accumulated so much money that you can siphon off profit with almost no risk. Your bankroll is your equipment for doing business. It's hard to convince players that they shouldn't cannibalize their bankroll to buy groceries for their family (as an extreme example). But, in fact, winning players shouldn't. It's the same as having a print shop, and the first time you're short on cash selling off the printing press. That might fix you up in cash for a week or two, but you then have no means of survival, no way to earn an income tomorrow.

I'll say it one last time. Please, don't spend your bankroll.

Money Management

Money management can be something of a foreign concept to many gamblers. It is sometimes given an almost mystical importance as if just managing your money, in itself, is enough to overcome any odds that may be against you.

In contrast, here are some words of wisdom from guru Mike Caro.

NOTE FROM CARO:

Nothing intrigues gamblers as much as the mystical, magical concept of money management. What is it? How can it help? The topic of money management isn't about to disappear, so we might as well deal with it.

In the real world you can be more reckless with a small bankroll than with a large one. But most players treat their bankrolls just the opposite.

The whole concept of money management offends me. Not that the idea is bad. Not that the term is bad. It's just that money management has come to mean something to most people that is more akin to witchcraft than to science. Pseudo-scientists come up with pseudo-formulas for protecting a bankroll. They don't work, because they aren't borne of reason, and they can't be fitted into logical arguments. These systems just don't work, that's all there is to it.

There's J. L. Kelly's famous criterion, a mathematical formula for finding your best chance of success by considering the amount of money you have and the amount of risk. This formula is correct beyond question. That's because it's a rational, logical, mathematically precise strategy. The main feature of Kelly's Criterion that makes it accurate is simply that there are no unexplained conclusions.

By contrast, silly systems, those by the pseudo-scientists, often take into account the past outcomes of random events. For instance, if a roulette wheel has seen a ball land red eleven times in a row, the system might assume that black is due. Or, it might say that red is hot and you should still keep betting it. It depends on the whim of the pseudo-scientist devising the system.

Of course, the truth is that any truly random event has no ties to independent random events that already occurred. The past, in most casino games, does not influence the future.

But, I even have a problem with Kelly. Not the picky problem some people suggest. You can't easily find games where you can bet as much as you want and still divide your bets into convenient amounts to fit the formula. Forget that. The problem I see is with real life. A small bankroll may simply not be worth protecting by mathematical formula, because you can usually go somewhere beyond gambling and put together another small bankroll. Then you can try again.

I'm not saying that you can't use a mathematically correct formula to take real-world factors into account. But nobody does.

CARO'S UNUSUAL WINNING HOLD'EM STRATEGY

What you're about to see is controversial. It's so controversial, in fact, that several years ago Mike Caro stopped distributing it, because it was taking too much of his time to explain. You see, it varies substantially from most of his other teachings about hold'em.

It partially violates Caro's guidelines about being extremely selective in choosing the hands you enter pots with, although, on balance, the strategy will have you playing much tighter than your opponents in loose games that supply the majority of your profit. It seems to go against common advice by having you sometimes just call with hands you'd usually like to raise with. And sometimes it has you raise with hands you might not consider playing and with hands you'd just call with if you did play them.

Using a Deceptive Strategy for Profit

All this is described in *Caro's Professional Hold'em Report*, in which he talks about "balancing" a strategy. By balancing, he means elevating some hands so that they will be played more aggressively than they should and demoting others so that they'll be played less aggressively. This is done for deception. It was my arguments that swayed Caro and convinced him to include the table here, despite the likely criticism from some sources who have their own strategies to argue.

The desired effect of the chart is to construct a strategy that is powerful, but suitably deceptive against weak-to-average real-world opponents. It can even hold its own against stronger opponents, as long as they don't understand the strategy being used. The built-in deception is the key to success. Although it's easy to argue that some hands might be dominated, these same hands actually tend to dominate opponents who surprising play even weaker hands. You could argue that if you follow the chart, certain hands will be played too timidly, and the deliberately inconsistent ways some of the hands are played relative to stronger and weaker ones will lose more money in practice than it gains through deception. Those are good arguments against this strategy, but not good enough—and they not accurate.

Selective, Unpredictable and Dominating

After analyzing millions of hands (with computer assistance) that were actually played online for real money, using an anonymous database that did not identify players by strength, name, or individual strategies, Caro has found that most of the hands in the chart below that were previously criticized because they would be dominated, would often actually dominate. That's assuming you were playing against typical opponents.

For this reason, and others, Caro has reaffirmed his long-standing pronouncement that this strategy will win substantially against weak or average opponents. It will also win against many more accomplished opponents.

The key behind that assertion is that the charts lead you to play substantially more conservatively than most typical players, making the strategy selective, yet unpredictable, and thus, is a powerful alternative winning formula.

However, as Caro points out, caution is required when playing the strategy. First, you cannot take one hand out of context and argue that the recommended action is wrong. Caro knows it's "wrong." It's deliberately "wrong" for deceptive reasons, as clearly explained in the original report, allowing you to play similar hands more profitably. And that's what makes it "right."

Middle of the Ranges

Also, keep in mind that some of the categories are too broad and could benefit from subdivision. For instance, the "Players to Act" column shows "5 to 9" and "2 to 8," corresponding to a description of the action. Obviously, these cover a lot of ground, and the suggested tactic is aimed mostly at something in the middle of those ranges. For instance, you can think of the suggested tactic for "2 to 8" players to act to be ideally aimed at "5" players to act.

It works okay for more or for fewer, but isn't ideal. You often should choose a significantly more conservative approach at the high end of the players to act (confronting more opponents) and a significantly more liberal one at the low end (confronting fewer opponents). In extreme cases, you might fold, instead of call or raise, when the number is at the high end and call; or you might raise, instead of fold, when the number is at the low end. The strategy is designed to work even if you don't make these adjustments, as long as you're against mostly weak to average opponents.

On the charts in the following pages, you'll find the categories of hands subdivided, beginning with the "Major pairs" heading and ending with "3-2."

Good Luck—and Go Win

So, we close this book with the following table. We don't expect you to memorize it all at once. In fact, most players won't attempt to memorize it at all. But even so, you'll probably find it instructional. It's an example of a powerful hold'em strategy that can be used to destroy weaker opponents when taken as a whole. That last part is important. In order for this strategy to work, you must use it all. You can't pick and choose which advice you like, because it's deliberately balanced for deception. Some hands are played in ways you normally wouldn't choose to play them if just those specific hands and situations were examined in isolation.

We hope you've found this book rewarding. Go win!

KEYS TO READING THE CHART

Here are some key explanations that will help you interpret the chart:

1. If an asterisk (*****) follows the ranks shown in the "Hand" column, that means the cards are of the same suit.

2. When you see the word "**other**" in the heading for a category of hand, it means the main (higher) rank is dealt with a card that is outside the straight range for that combination. For instance "9 high (other)" shows listings "9-42*" and "9-42" in the "Hand" column—which means that the hand can be 9-4, 9-3, or 9-2. (The asterisk means the two cards are of the same suit, as noted above.)

3. "**Players to act**" means the number of opponents still holding hands, including one or more of the blinds.

4. "**1/small**" in the "Players to act" column means there is only one opponent left to act behind you and everyone else has folded, so you are the small blind. The "**small**" to the right of the slash is just an added reminder of the fact that "**1**" implies you're the small blind and only the big blind is still a threat.

5. "**2/deal**" in the "Players to act" column means only the two blinds remain as a threat; everyone else has folded. The "**deal**" to the right of the slash is just an added reminder of the fact that "**2**" implies that you're in the dealer position (on the button).

6. "**Blinds only**" in the "Action" column means nobody has either called or raised the big blind yet, so the only "action" is the blind bets.

7. "**Big only**" in the "Action" column means nobody has either called or raised the big blind yet, and you're in the small blind position with only the big blind left as a threat.

8. "**R, R-C** or **C-R**" in the "Action" column means that before the action reaches you, the big blind has been raised, raised and then called or called and then raised. Obviously, the exact order of action and the number of participants makes a difference, but the strategy should work well, even if you don't adjust to that fact.

9. "**2 raises**" in the "Action" column means the blind has been raised and there has also been a reraise by the time the action reaches you.

10. "**R by sml bld**" in the "Action" column means you are in the big blind and everyone folded until the small blind raised. ("Raised by small blind.")

11. Under the "Strategy" column, you'll find four sets of recommendations: "**LM**," (limit) "**LX**," (limit, experimental) "**PL**," (pot limit) and "**NL**" (no limit). Whichever strategy line you're interested in, it's always in the relative position in the column: first LM, then LX, then PL, and finally NL. Actually both LM and LX are advanced experimental strategy lines with built-in deception and advice that deliberately differs from Caro's normal teaching. But the LX line is even more experimental than the LM line (which is the one you should probably use first).

12. The advice given for each strategy line should be interpreted as follows:

o **P** = pass (or, more precisely, fold, since there's a blind bet pending);

o **C** = call;

o **R** = raise in limit games (or reraise, if it's already raised); or make a typical-size raise in pot-limit and no-limit games;

o **r** = make a small raise in pot-limit and no-limit games;

o **+** = bet the maximum possible in pot-limit and no-limit games.

13. Often you'll see two or three tactics recommended for a single situation. The recommendation to the left always takes precedence. You should use it more often. In fact, the strategy suggests you use a recommendation to the left twice as often as one to the right. So, if the recommendation says "**CP**," then you should usually call, but sometimes fold (pass). Specifically, you should call four times for every two times you fold. If there are three possible choices (this only happens in the PL and NL strategy lines), such as "**RrC**," this means you should raise a typical amount (**R**) more often than you should raise a small amount (**r**), but raise a small amount more often than you should call (**C**).

The ratio would be 4:2:1, four typical raises for every two small raises and every one call.

14. There is no specific advice given for when you're in the big blind and have been just called (not raised). In this and other semi-common situations, such as when there are three or more raises, you should use your best judgment. Too much depends on the characteristics of opponents to provide set-in-stone advice for all situations—particularly those with a higher than usual probability of deception.

Major pairs...

HAND	PLAYERS TO ACT	ACTION	STRATEGY LM LX PL NL
A-A	5 to 9	Blinds only	RC CR RC rC
A-A	3 or 4	Blinds only	R RC RC rCR
A-A	2/deal	Blinds only	R R RC RrC
A-A	1/small	Big only	R RC R rRC
A-A	2 to 8	R,R-C or C-R	CR CR rCR R+C
A-A	2 to 7	2 raises	RC RC +RC +RC
A-A	1/small	R,R-C or C-R	RC CR CR Cr+
A-A	1/small	2 raises	RC CR R+C R+C
A-A	0/big	R,R-C or C-R	CR C RC+ RrC
A-A	0/big	2 raises	CR C R+C R+C
A-A	0/big	R by sml bld	R RC RC R+C
K-K	5 to 9	Blinds only	RC CR RC RCr
K-K	3 or 4	Blinds only	R RC RC RrC
K-K	2/deal	Blinds only	R R R rC
K-K	1/small	Big only	R RC RC RC
K-K	2 to 8	R,R-C or C-R	R RC RC C+R
K-K	2 to 7	2 raises	R RC +RC +CR
K-K	1/small	R,R-C or C-R	R C CR C+
K-K	1/small	2 raises	CR C C+ C+
K-K	0/big	R,R-C or C-R	RC C CR C+
K-K	0/big	2 raises	RC C C+ C+
K-K	0/big	R by sml bld	R R RC RC+

Q-Q	5 to 9	Blinds only	R CR CR CR
Q-Q	3 or 4	Blinds only	R RC RC RC
Q-Q	2/deal	Blinds only	RC RC RC RC
Q-Q	1/small	Big only	R RC RC rC
Q-Q	2 to 8	R,R-C or C-R	R RC R+C RC+
Q-Q	2 to 7	2 raises	RC CR C+R +C
Q-Q	1/small	R,R-C or C-R	RC C CR CR
Q-Q	1/small	2 raises	RC C CR CR
Q-Q	0/big	R,R-C or C-R	CR C CR CR+
Q-Q	0/big	2 raises	CR CR C+R C+
Q-Q	0/big	R by sml bld	R R rR+ RC+

Middle pairs...

HAND	PLAYERS TO ACT	ACTION	STRATEGY LM LX PL NL
J-J	5 to 9	Blinds only	RC C RC RC
J-J	3 or 4	Blinds only	R CR RC RC
J-J	2/deal	Blinds only	R R RC rRC
J-J	1/small	Big only	R R R r
J-J	2 to 8	R,R-C or C-R	RC CR CR C
J-J	2 to 7	2 raises	C C C CR+
J-J	1/small	R,R-C or C-R	CR C CP CP
J-J	1/small	2 raises	CP PC P P+
J-J	0/big	R,R-C or C-R	C C C C+
J-J	0/big	2 raises	CP PC P P+
J-J	0/big	R by sml bld	R RC RC R+C
10-10	5 to 9	Blinds only	CR C CP Cr
10-10	3 or 4	Blinds only	RC CR RC rC
10-10	2/deal	Blinds only	R R RC RrC
10-10	1/small	Big only	R RC RC rC
10-10	2 to 8	R,R-C or C-R	CP CP CP+ CP+
10-10	2 to 7	2 raises	PC PC PC+ PC+

10-10	1/small	R,R-C or C-R	C C PC PC
10-10	1/small	2 raises	PC P P P
10-10	0/big	R,R-C or C-R	C C C C
10-10	0/big	2 raises	PC P P P
10-10	0/big	R by sml bld	R RC RC Rr+
9-9	5 to 9	Blinds only	CP PC CP Cr
9-9	3 or 4	Blinds only	RC CR RC RCr
9-9	2/deal	Blinds only	R RC RC RrC
9-9	1/small	Big only	R RC RC RC
9-9	2 to 8	R,R-C or C-R	PC PC CP PC+
9-9	2 to 7	2 raises	P P PC+ PC+
9-9	1/small	R,R-C or C-R	C P PC PC
9-9	1/small	2 raises	P P P P
9-9	0/big	R,R-C or C-R	C C C C
9-9	0/big	2 raises	P P P P
9-9	0/big	R by sml bld	R RC RC RC
8-8	5 to 9	Blinds only	CP PC PC Cr
8-8	3 or 4	Blinds only	RC CR CR Cr
8-8	2/deal	Blinds only	R RC RC rC
8-8	1/small	Big only	R RC RC RC
8-8	2 to 8	R,R-C or C-R	PC PC PC PC
8-8	2 to 7	2 raises	P P P P+
8-8	1/small	R,R-C or C-R	C P P PC
8-8	1/small	2 raises	P P P P
8-8	0/big	R,R-C or C-R	C C PC C
8-8	0/big	2 raises	P P P P
8-8	0/big	R by sml bld	R RC RC rC+

Minor pairs...

HAND	PLAYERS TO ACT	ACTION	STRATEGY LM LX PL NL
7-7	5 to 9	Blinds only	C P PR PCr
7-7	3 or 4	Blinds only	CR CR RC rC
7-7	2/deal	Blinds only	R R R Rr
7-7	1/small	Big only	R RC RC rC
7-7	2 to 8	R,R-C or C-R	PC P PR PR
7-7	2 to 7	2 raises	P P P P
7-7	1/small	R,R-C or C-R	C P P PC
7-7	1/small	2 raises	P P P P
7-7	0/big	R,R-C or C-R	C C PC CP
7-7	0/big	2 raises	P P P P
7-7	0/big	R by sml bld	R RC RC CrR
6-6	5 to 9	Blinds only	PC P P Pr
6-6	3 or 4	Blinds only	CR CR CP CP
6-6	2/deal	Blinds only	R R R r
6-6	1/small	Big only	RC RC RC rRC
6-6	2 to 8	R,R-C or C-R	P P P PrC
6-6	2 to 7	2 raises	P P P P
6-6	1/small	R,R-C or C-R	C P P P
6-6	1/small	2 raises	P P P P
6-6	0/big	R,R-C or C-R	C CP PC PC
6-6	0/big	2 raises	P P P P
6-6	0/big	R by sml bld	RC RC RC RC
5-5	5 to 9	Blinds only	P P P P
5-5	3 or 4	Blinds only	CR C PC PC
5-5	2/deal	Blinds only	RC R R r
5-5	1/small	Big only	RC RC RC rC
5-5	2 to 8	R,R-C or C-R	P P P PR
5-5	2 to 7	2 raises	P P P P
5-5	1/small	R,R-C or C-R	CP P P P

5-5	1/small	2 raises	P P P P
5-5	0/big	R,R-C or C-R	C CP PC PC
5-5	0/big	2 raises	P P P P
5-5	0/big	R by sml bld	CR RC CR Cr
4-4	5 to 9	Blinds only	P P P P
4-4	3 or 4	Blinds only	CR C P PC
4-4	2/deal	Blinds only	RC RC RC rCR
4-4	1/small	Big only	CR CR CR Cr
4-4	2 to 8	R,R-C or C-R	P P P P
4-4	2 to 7	2 raises	P P P P
4-4	1/small	R,R-C or C-R	CP P P P
4-4	1/small	2 raises	P P P P
4-4	0/big	R,R-C or C-R	C PC P P
4-4	0/big	2 raises	P P P P
4-4	0/big	R by sml bld	CR CR CRP CrP
3-3	5 to 9	Blinds only	P P P P
3-3	3 or 4	Blinds only	C P P PC
3-3	2/deal	Blinds only	CR PC CR rC
3-3	1/small	Big only	C C CR C
3-3	2 to 8	R,R-C or C-R	P P P P
3-3	2 to 7	2 raises	P P P P
3-3	1/small	R,R-C or C-R	CP P P P
3-3	1/small	2 raises	P P P P
3-3	0/big	R,R-C or C-R	CP P P P
3-3	0/big	2 raises	P P P P
3-3	0/big	R by sml bld	C CP CPR CrP
2-2	5 to 9	Blinds only	P P P P
2-2	3 or 4	Blinds only	P P P P
2-2	2/deal	Blinds only	C P RC CR
2-2	1/small	Big only	C C C C
2-2	2 to 8	R,R-C or C-R	P P P P

2-2	2 to 7	2 raises	P P P P
2-2	1/small	R,R-C or C-R	CP P P P
2-2	1/small	2 raises	P P P P
2-2	0/big	R,R-C or C-R	CP P P P
2-2	0/big	2 raises	P P P P
2-2	0/big	R by sml bld	C PC PC CrP

Ace high (straight range)...

HAND	PLAYERS TO ACT	ACTION	STRATEGY LM LX PL NL
A-K*	5 to 9	Blinds only	RC RC RC rC
A-K*	3 or 4	Blinds only	RC RC RC CR
A-K*	2/deal	Blinds only	R RC RC RC
A-K*	1/small	Big only	R RC RC rCR
A-K*	2 to 8	R,R-C or C-R	CR CR RC rRC
A-K*	2 to 7	2 raises	CR CR CR+ CR+
A-K*	1/small	R,R-C or C-R	CR C C C
A-K*	1/small	2 raises	C C PC PC+
A-K*	0/big	R,R-C or C-R	C C CR CR
A-K*	0/big	2 raises	C C PC PC
A-K*	0/big	R by sml bld	R R RC rR+
A-K	5 to 9	Blinds only	RC RC RC rC
A-K	3 or 4	Blinds only	R RC RC RC
A-K	2/deal	Blinds only	R RC RC RC
A-K	1/small	Big only	R R R rR
A-K	2 to 8	R,R-C or C-R	RC RC RC RC+
A-K	2 to 7	2 raises	CP CP CP CPR
A-K	1/small	R,R-C or C-R	CR C C C
A-K	1/small	2 raises	C PC PC PC
A-K	0/big	R,R-C or C-R	CR CR C C
A-K	0/big	2 raises	C CP PC PC
A-K	0/big	R by sml bld	R RC R RC+

A-Q*	5 to 9	Blinds only	RC RC RC rC
A-Q*	3 or 4	Blinds only	RC RC RC CR
A-Q*	2/deal	Blinds only	R RC RC RC
A-Q*	1/small	Big only	R RC RC rC
A-Q*	2 to 8	R,R-C or C-R	CR CR CR CR
A-Q*	2 to 7	2 raises	CP PC PC PC
A-Q*	1/small	R,R-C or C-R	C C C C
A-Q*	1/small	2 raises	CP PC PC PC
A-Q*	0/big	R,R-C or C-R	C C C C
A-Q*	0/big	2 raises	CP PC PC PC
A-Q*	0/big	R by sml bld	RC RC RC RCr
A-Q	5 to 9	Blinds only	RC RC RC rC
A-Q	3 or 4	Blinds only	RC RC RC RC
A-Q	2/deal	Blinds only	R RC RC rRC
A-Q	1/small	Big only	R R R R
A-Q	2 to 8	R,R-C or C-R	CR C CR Cr
A-Q	2 to 7	2 raises	PC PC P P
A-Q	1/small	R,R-C or C-R	C C CP C
A-Q	1/small	2 raises	PC PC P P
A-Q	0/big	R,R-C or C-R	C C C C
A-Q	0/big	2 raises	PC P P P
A-Q	0/big	R by sml bld	R R R rRC
A-J*	5 to 9	Blinds only	CR C CR Cr
A-J*	3 or 4	Blinds only	RC RC CR CR
A-J*	2/deal	Blinds only	R RC RC rC
A-J*	1/small	Big only	R RC RC rC
A-J*	2 to 8	R,R-C or C-R	C C C C
A-J*	2 to 7	2 raises	P P P P
A-J*	1/small	R,R-C or C-R	C C PC CP
A-J*	1/small	2 raises	P P P P
A-J*	0/big	R,R-C or C-R	C C C C

A-J*	0/big	2 raises	PC P P P
A-J*	0/big	R by sml bld	R R RC rCR
A-J	5 to 9	Blinds only	C CP CP CP
A-J	3 or 4	Blinds only	RC CR RC Cr
A-J	2/deal	Blinds only	R RC RC RC
A-J	1/small	Big only	R RC R rC
A-J	2 to 8	R,R-C or C-R	CP PC PC PC
A-J	2 to 7	2 raises	P P P P
A-J	1/small	R,R-C or C-R	C PC P P
A-J	1/small	2 raises	P P P P
A-J	0/big	R,R-C or C-R	C CP CP CP
A-J	0/big	2 raises	P P P P
A-J	0/big	R by sml bld	CR CR RC RC
A-10*	5 to 9	Blinds only	C CP C C
A-10*	3 or 4	Blinds only	C CR CR CR
A-10*	2/deal	Blinds only	RC CR RC rC
A-10*	1/small	Big only	R RC RC rC
A-10*	2 to 8	R,R-C or C-R	C C CP CP
A-10*	2 to 7	2 raises	P P P P
A-10*	1/small	R,R-C or C-R	C CP PC PC
A-10*	1/small	2 raises	P P P P
A-10*	0/big	R,R-C or C-R	C C C C
A-10*	0/big	2 raises	P P P P
A-10*	0/big	R by sml bld	RC RC CR CR
A-10	5 to 9	Blinds only	P P P PC
A-10	3 or 4	Blinds only	CR C RC RC
A-10	2/deal	Blinds only	RC CR RC RC
A-10	1/small	Big only	R RC RC rC
A-10	2 to 8	R,R-C or C-R	PC P P P
A-10	2 to 7	2 raises	P P P P
A-10	1/small	R,R-C or C-R	CP P P P

A-10	1/small	2 raises	P P P P
A-10	0/big	R,R-C or C-R	C CP PC PC
A-10	0/big	2 raises	P P P P
A-10	0/big	R by sml bld	CR C R R

Ace high (other)...

HAND	PLAYERS TO ACT	ACTION	STRATEGY LM LX PL NL
A-96*	5 to 9	Blinds only	P P P PC
A-96*	3 or 4	Blinds only	CR C C Cr
A-96*	2/deal	Blinds only	RC CR CR Cr
A-96*	1/small	Big only	R RC RC rC
A-96*	2 to 8	R,R-C or C-R	P P PC PC
A-96*	2 to 7	2 raises	P P P P
A-96*	1/small	R,R-C or C-R	PC P P P
A-96*	1/small	2 raises	P P P P
A-96*	0/big	R,R-C or C-R	CR PC PC PC
A-96*	0/big	2 raises	P P P P
A-96*	0/big	R by sml bld	RC CR C C
A-96	5 to 9	Blinds only	P P P P
A-96	3 or 4	Blinds only	CR CP PR Pr
A-96	2/deal	Blinds only	RC CR R r
A-96	1/small	Big only	R RC RC rC
A-96	2 to 8	R,R-C or C-R	P P P P
A-96	2 to 7	2 raises	P P P P
A-96	1/small	R,R-C or C-R	PC P P P
A-96	1/small	2 raises	P P P P
A-96	0/big	R,R-C or C-R	C PC P P
A-96	0/big	2 raises	P P P P
A-96	0/big	R by sml bld	CR C CR CR

Ace high (low straight)...

HAND	PLAYERS TO ACT	ACTION	STRATEGY LM LX PL NL
A-52*	5 to 9	Blinds only	PC PC PC CP
A-52*	3 or 4	Blinds only	R C C Cr
A-52*	2/deal	Blinds only	RC C CR Cr
A-52*	1/small	Big only	R RC RC r
A-52*	2 to 8	R,R-C or C-R	PC P PC CP
A-52*	2 to 7	2 raises	P P P P
A-52*	1/small	R,R-C or C-R	C PC PC PC
A-52*	1/small	2 raises	P P P P
A-52*	0/big	R,R-C or C-R	C C CP CP
A-52*	0/big	2 raises	P P P P
A-52*	0/big	R by sml bld	CR C C C
A-52	5 to 9	Blinds only	P P P P
A-52	3 or 4	Blinds only	CR PC PRC PrC
A-52	2/deal	Blinds only	R CR RC rC
A-52	1/small	Big only	RC RC R r
A-52	2 to 8	R,R-C or C-R	P P P P
A-52	2 to 7	2 raises	P P P P
A-52	1/small	R,R-C or C-R	PC P P P
A-52	1/small	2 raises	P P P P
A-52	0/big	R,R-C or C-R	CP PC P P
A-52	0/big	2 raises	P P P P
A-52	0/big	R by sml bld	C C C Cr

King high (straight range)...

HAND	PLAYERS TO ACT	ACTION	STRATEGY LM LX PL NL
K-Q*	5 to 9	Blinds only	RC CR RC rC
K-Q*	3 or 4	Blinds only	RC RC RC Cr
K-Q*	2/deal	Blinds only	R RC RC rCR
K-Q*	1/small	Big only	R R RC rCR

K-Q*	2 to 8	R,R-C or C-R	CR CR C Cr
K-Q*	2 to 7	2 raises	P P PC PC
K-Q*	1/small	R,R-C or C-R	C C C C
K-Q*	1/small	2 raises	C PC PC PC
K-Q*	0/big	R,R-C or C-R	C C CR CR
K-Q*	0/big	2 raises	C CP PC PC
K-Q*	0/big	R by sml bld	R RC CR CrR
K-Q	5 to 9	Blinds only	R RC RC rC
K-Q	3 or 4	Blinds only	R RC RC rC
K-Q	2/deal	Blinds only	R RC RC RC
K-Q	1/small	Big only	R R R rR
K-Q	2 to 8	R,R-C or C-R	C CP CPR CPR
K-Q	2 to 7	2 raises	P P P P
K-Q	1/small	R,R-C or C-R	C CP PC CP
K-Q	1/small	2 raises	P P P P
K-Q	0/big	R,R-C or C-R	C C PC PC
K-Q	0/big	2 raises	P P P P
K-Q	0/big	R by sml bld	RC RC RC RC+
K-J*	5 to 9	Blinds only	CR CR CR Cr
K-J*	3 or 4	Blinds only	R RC RC CrR
K-J*	2/deal	Blinds only	R RC RC rC
K-J*	1/small	Big only	R RC RC rC
K-J*	2 to 8	R,R-C or C-R	C C CR CR
K-J*	2 to 7	2 raises	P P P PC
K-J*	1/small	R,R-C or C-R	C C C C
K-J*	1/small	2 raises	P P P P
K-J*	0/big	R,R-C or C-R	C C C C
K-J*	0/big	2 raises	CP PC PC PC
K-J*	0/big	R by sml bld	R R CR CRr
K-J	5 to 9	Blinds only	C PC PCR PCr
K-J	3 or 4	Blinds only	R RC RC rC

K-J	2/deal	Blinds only	R RC RC RCr
K-J	1/small	Big only	R R R RCr
K-J	2 to 8	R,R-C or C-R	C CP PCR PCR
K-J	2 to 7	2 raises	P P P P
K-J	1/small	R,R-C or C-R	C C P PC
K-J	1/small	2 raises	P P P P
K-J	0/big	R,R-C or C-R	C C CP CP
K-J	0/big	2 raises	P P P P
K-J	0/big	R by sml bld	R RC RC RC
K-10*	5 to 9	Blinds only	C C CR Cr
K-10*	3 or 4	Blinds only	R RC RC CR
K-10*	2/deal	Blinds only	R RC RC CR
K-10*	1/small	Big only	R RC RC C
K-10*	2 to 8	R,R-C or C-R	C C C C
K-10*	2 to 7	2 raises	P P P P
K-10*	1/small	R,R-C or C-R	C C PC PC
K-10*	1/small	2 raises	P P P P
K-10*	0/big	R,R-C or C-R	C C CP CP
K-10*	0/big	2 raises	P P P P
K-10*	0/big	R by sml bld	R RC CR CRr
K-10	5 to 9	Blinds only	PC P PC PCr
K-10	3 or 4	Blinds only	R CR CRP Cr
K-10	2/deal	Blinds only	R RC RC RC
K-10	1/small	Big only	R RC RC RC
K-10	2 to 8	R,R-C or C-R	PC P P P
K-10	2 to 7	2 raises	P P P P
K-10	1/small	R,R-C or C-R	CP PC P P
K-10	1/small	2 raises	P P P P
K-10	0/big	R,R-C or C-R	C CP P PC
K-10	0/big	2 raises	P P P P
K-10	0/big	R by sml bld	RC CR RC rC

K-9*	5 to 9	Blinds only	PC P PC PC
K-9*	3 or 4	Blinds only	R CR C C
K-9*	2/deal	Blinds only	R CR RC Cr
K-9*	1/small	Big only	R RC RC rC
K-9*	2 to 8	R,R-C or C-R	C C CP PC
K-9*	2 to 7	2 raises	P P P P
K-9*	1/small	R,R-C or C-R	C PC P PC
K-9*	1/small	2 raises	P P P P
K-9*	0/big	R,R-C or C-R	C C CP CP
K-9*	0/big	2 raises	P P P P
K-9*	0/big	R by sml bld	RC CR CR CRr
K-9	5 to 9	Blinds only	P P P P
K-9	3 or 4	Blinds only	RP CP RP RP
K-9	2/deal	Blinds only	R CR R C
K-9	1/small	Big only	R RC RC rRC
K-9	2 to 8	R,R-C or C-R	P P P P
K-9	2 to 7	2 raises	P P P P
K-9	1/small	R,R-C or C-R	CP PC P P
K-9	1/small	2 raises	P P P P
K-9	0/big	R,R-C or C-R	C CP P P
K-9	0/big	2 raises	P P P P
K-9	0/big	R by sml bld	R C RC RC

King high (other)...

HAND	PLAYERS TO ACT	ACTION	STRATEGY LM LX PL NL
K-82*	5 to 9	Blinds only	P P P P
K-82*	3 or 4	Blinds only	RP PC PCR PCR
K-82*	2/deal	Blinds only	R CR CR Cr
K-82*	1/small	Big only	R CR CR Cr
K-82*	2 to 8	R,R-C or C-R	P P P P
K-82*	2 to 7	2 raises	P P P P

K-82*	1/small	R,R-C or C-R	CP P P P
K-82*	1/small	2 raises	P P P P
K-82*	0/big	R,R-C or C-R	C PC P P
K-82*	0/big	2 raises	P P P P
K-82*	0/big	R by sml bld	CR C CR CR
K-82	5 to 9	Blinds only	P P P P
K-82	3 or 4	Blinds only	PR P P Pr
K-82	2/deal	Blinds only	R CR RC RrC
K-82	1/small	Big only	R CR RC rC
K-82	2 to 8	R,R-C or C-R	P P P P
K-82	2 to 7	2 raises	P P P P
K-82	1/small	R,R-C or C-R	P P P P
K-82	1/small	2 raises	P P P P
K-82	0/big	R,R-C or C-R	CP P P P
K-82	0/big	2 raises	P P P P
K-82	0/big	R by sml bld	RC C RC RC

Queen high (straight range)...

HAND	PLAYERS TO ACT	ACTION	STRATEGY LM LX PL NL
Q-J*	5 to 9	Blinds only	C C CR CrR
Q-J*	3 or 4	Blinds only	R RC RC CrR
Q-J*	2/deal	Blinds only	R RC RC CR
Q-J*	1/small	Big only	R C CR Cr
Q-J*	2 to 8	R,R-C or C-R	C C C Cr
Q-J*	2 to 7	2 raises	P P PC PC
Q-J*	1/small	R,R-C or C-R	C C CP C
Q-J*	1/small	2 raises	PC P P P
Q-J*	0/big	R,R-C or C-R	C C CR Cr
Q-J*	0/big	2 raises	C P P PC
Q-J*	0/big	R by sml bld	R RC CR CrR
Q-J	5 to 9	Blinds only	C PC CP CP

278

Q-J	3 or 4	Blinds only	R CR CR Cr
Q-J	2/deal	Blinds only	R RC RC RC
Q-J	1/small	Big only	R C RC rC
Q-J	2 to 8	R,R-C or C-R	PC P PC PC
Q-J	2 to 7	2 raises	P P P P
Q-J	1/small	R,R-C or C-R	C PC PC PC
Q-J	1/small	2 raises	P P P P
Q-J	0/big	R,R-C or C-R	C PC CP C
Q-J	0/big	2 raises	P P P P
Q-J	0/big	R by sml bld	R CR RC RC
Q-10*	5 to 9	Blinds only	C PC CPR CPr
Q-10*	3 or 4	Blinds only	R CR CR Cr
Q-10*	2/deal	Blinds only	R RC RC rC
Q-10*	1/small	Big only	R C CR Cr
Q-10*	2 to 8	R,R-C or C-R	C C C C
Q-10*	2 to 7	2 raises	P P P P
Q-10*	1/small	R,R-C or C-R	C PC PC CP
Q-10*	1/small	2 raises	P P P P
Q-10*	0/big	R,R-C or C-R	C C C C
Q-10*	0/big	2 raises	P P P P
Q-10*	0/big	R by sml bld	CR CR CR Cr
Q-10	5 to 9	Blinds only	PC P P Pr
Q-10	3 or 4	Blinds only	RC CP PC PrC
Q-10	2/deal	Blinds only	R CR RC rC
Q-10	1/small	Big only	R RC RC RC
Q-10	2 to 8	R,R-C or C-R	P P P PR
Q-10	2 to 7	2 raises	P P P P
Q-10	1/small	R,R-C or C-R	CP P P P
Q-10	1/small	2 raises	P P P P
Q-10	0/big	R,R-C or C-R	C CP P PC
Q-10	0/big	2 raises	P P P P

Q-10	0/big	R by sml bld	RC C CR Cr
Q-9*	5 to 9	Blinds only	CP PC CP CPR
Q-9*	3 or 4	Blinds only	RC RC RC Cr
Q-9*	2/deal	Blinds only	RC RC CR CR
Q-9*	1/small	Big only	RC RC CR Cr
Q-9*	2 to 8	R,R-C or C-R	C C C C
Q-9*	2 to 7	2 raises	P P P P
Q-9*	1/small	R,R-C or C-R	C PC P PC
Q-9*	1/small	2 raises	P P P P
Q-9*	0/big	R,R-C or C-R	C C PC CP
Q-9*	0/big	2 raises	P P P P
Q-9*	0/big	R by sml bld	CR CR C CR
Q-9	5 to 9	Blinds only	P P P P
Q-9	3 or 4	Blinds only	RC PC PR PRC
Q-9	2/deal	Blinds only	R C RCP CPR
Q-9	1/small	Big only	R CR RC rC
Q-9	2 to 8	R,R-C or C-R	P P P P
Q-9	2 to 7	2 raises	P P P P
Q-9	1/small	R,R-C or C-R	PC P P P
Q-9	1/small	2 raises	P P P P
Q-9	0/big	R,R-C or C-R	C PC P P
Q-9	0/big	2 raises	P P P P
Q-9	0/big	R by sml bld	RC C RC RC
Q-8*	5 to 9	Blinds only	CP P P P
Q-8*	3 or 4	Blinds only	CR C CR Cr
Q-8*	2/deal	Blinds only	R CR RC Cr
Q-8*	1/small	Big only	R CR CR Cr
Q-8*	2 to 8	R,R-C or C-R	CP CP CP CP
Q-8*	2 to 7	2 raises	P P P P
Q-8*	1/small	R,R-C or C-R	C PC P P
Q-8*	1/small	2 raises	P P P P

Q-8*	0/big	R,R-C or C-R	C CP PC PC
Q-8*	0/big	2 raises	P P P P
Q-8*	0/big	R by sml bld	CR C C C
Q-8	5 to 9	Blinds only	P P P P
Q-8	3 or 4	Blinds only	RP P PR Pr
Q-8	2/deal	Blinds only	R CP RP CP
Q-8	1/small	Big only	R C RC Cr
Q-8	2 to 8	R,R-C or C-R	P P P P
Q-8	2 to 7	2 raises	P P P P
Q-8	1/small	R,R-C or C-R	PC P P P
Q-8	1/small	2 raises	P P P P
Q-8	0/big	R,R-C or C-R	C P P P
Q-8	0/big	2 raises	P P P P
Q-8	0/big	R by sml bld	R C C C

Queen high (other)...

HAND	PLAYERS TO ACT	ACTION	STRATEGY LM LX PL NL
Q-72*	5 to 9	Blinds only	P P P P
Q-72*	3 or 4	Blinds only	P P P P
Q-72*	2/deal	Blinds only	C CP C CP
Q-72*	1/small	Big only	RC CR CPR CrP
Q-72*	2 to 8	R,R-C or C-R	P P P P
Q-72*	2 to 7	2 raises	P P P P
Q-72*	1/small	R,R-C or C-R	PC P P P
Q-72*	1/small	2 raises	P P P P
Q-72*	0/big	R,R-C or C-R	CP P P P
Q-72*	0/big	2 raises	P P P P
Q-72*	0/big	R by sml bld	C C C CR
Q-72	5 to 9	Blinds only	P P P P
Q-72	3 or 4	Blinds only	P P P P
Q-72	2/deal	Blinds only	CR CP RPC rP

Q-72	1/small	Big only	RC C C CPR
Q-72	2 to 8	R,R-C or C-R	P P P P
Q-72	2 to 7	2 raises	P P P P
Q-72	1/small	R,R-C or C-R	P P P P
Q-72	1/small	2 raises	P P P P
Q-72	0/big	R,R-C or C-R	P P P P
Q-72	0/big	2 raises	P P P P
Q-72	0/big	R by sml bld	C C C C

Jack high (straight range)...

HAND	PLAYERS TO ACT	ACTION	STRATEGY LM LX PL NL
J-10*	5 to 9	Blinds only	CR C C CR
J-10*	3 or 4	Blinds only	RC CR RC rCR
J-10*	2/deal	Blinds only	R RC CR CR
J-10*	1/small	Big only	R CR RC rC
J-10*	2 to 8	R,R-C or C-R	C C C CR
J-10*	2 to 7	2 raises	PC P P PC
J-10*	1/small	R,R-C or C-R	C C C C
J-10*	1/small	2 raises	CP P P P
J-10*	0/big	R,R-C or C-R	C C C C
J-10*	0/big	2 raises	C PC P PC
J-10*	0/big	R by sml bld	RC CR CR Cr
J-10	5 to 9	Blinds only	P P P PCR
J-10	3 or 4	Blinds only	RC C RC rC
J-10	2/deal	Blinds only	R RC RC rC
J-10	1/small	Big only	R RC RC rC
J-10	2 to 8	R,R-C or C-R	PC P PCR PC
J-10	2 to 7	2 raises	P P P P
J-10	1/small	R,R-C or C-R	C CP PC PC
J-10	1/small	2 raises	P P P P
J-10	0/big	R,R-C or C-R	C C PC PC

J-10	0/big	2 raises	P P P P
J-10	0/big	R by sml bld	R CR CR CR
J-9*	5 to 9	Blinds only	CP PC PRC rCP
J-9*	3 or 4	Blinds only	C C RC CrR
J-9*	2/deal	Blinds only	RC RC RC CrR
J-9*	1/small	Big only	C C CR Cr
J-9*	2 to 8	R,R-C or C-R	C C C C
J-9*	2 to 7	2 raises	P P P P
J-9*	1/small	R,R-C or C-R	C C PC CP
J-9*	1/small	2 raises	P P P P
J-9*	0/big	R,R-C or C-R	C C C C
J-9*	0/big	2 raises	PC P P P
J-9*	0/big	R by sml bld	CR CR CR CR
J-9	5 to 9	Blinds only	P P P P
J-9	3 or 4	Blinds only	PC PC PR PrC
J-9	2/deal	Blinds only	RC CR RC rC
J-9	1/small	Big only	R CR RC rC
J-9	2 to 8	R,R-C or C-R	P P P PCR
J-9	2 to 7	2 raises	P P P P
J-9	1/small	R,R-C or C-R	PC P P P
J-9	1/small	2 raises	P P P P
J-9	0/big	R,R-C or C-R	C P P P
J-9	0/big	2 raises	P P P P
J-9	0/big	R by sml bld	CR C CR C
J-8*	5 to 9	Blinds only	C PC PC PCR
J-8*	3 or 4	Blinds only	CR CR CR Cr
J-8*	2/deal	Blinds only	RC RC RC RC
J-8*	1/small	Big only	RC CR RC rC
J-8*	2 to 8	R,R-C or C-R	C CP CP CP
J-8*	2 to 7	2 raises	P P P P
J-8*	1/small	R,R-C or C-R	CP P P P

J-8*	1/small	2 raises	P P P P
J-8*	0/big	R,R-C or C-R	C PC PC CP
J-8*	0/big	2 raises	P P P P
J-8*	0/big	R by sml bld	CR CR R Cr
J-8	5 to 9	Blinds only	P P P P
J-8	3 or 4	Blinds only	PC PC PRC PCR
J-8	2/deal	Blinds only	CP CP PR PrC
J-8	1/small	Big only	RC CR RC rC
J-8	2 to 8	R,R-C or C-R	P P P P
J-8	2 to 7	2 raises	P P P P
J-8	1/small	R,R-C or C-R	P P P P
J-8	1/small	2 raises	P P P P
J-8	0/big	R,R-C or C-R	PC P P P
J-8	0/big	2 raises	P P P P
J-8	0/big	R by sml bld	CR C RC C
J-7*	5 to 9	Blinds only	P P P PC
J-7*	3 or 4	Blinds only	CR C CR Cr
J-7*	2/deal	Blinds only	RC CR CR Cr
J-7*	1/small	Big only	RC CR CR Cr
J-7*	2 to 8	R,R-C or C-R	CP PC PC PC
J-7*	2 to 7	2 raises	P P P P
J-7*	1/small	R,R-C or C-R	CP P P P
J-7*	1/small	2 raises	P P P P
J-7*	0/big	R,R-C or C-R	C PC P PC
J-7*	0/big	2 raises	P P P P
J-7*	0/big	R by sml bld	C C C CR
J-7	5 to 9	Blinds only	P P P P
J-7	3 or 4	Blinds only	P P P P
J-7	2/deal	Blinds only	RP CP RC rC
J-7	1/small	Big only	R R CR Cr
J-7	2 to 8	R,R-C or C-R	P P P P

J-7	2 to 7	2 raises	P P P P
J-7	1/small	R,R-C or C-R	P P P P
J-7	1/small	2 raises	P P P P
J-7	0/big	R,R-C or C-R	P P P P
J-7	0/big	2 raises	P P P P
J-7	0/big	R by sml bld	C RC C C

Jack high (other)...

HAND	PLAYERS TO ACT	ACTION	STRATEGY LM LX PL NL
J-62*	5 to 9	Blinds only	P P P P
J-62*	3 or 4	Blinds only	P P P P
J-62*	2/deal	Blinds only	PC P CPR CPr
J-62*	1/small	Big only	CR CP CP CPr
J-62*	2 to 8	R,R-C or C-R	P P P P
J-62*	2 to 7	2 raises	P P P P
J-62*	1/small	R,R-C or C-R	PC P P P
J-62*	1/small	2 raises	P P P P
J-62*	0/big	R,R-C or C-R	CP P P P
J-62*	0/big	2 raises	P P P P
J-62*	0/big	R by sml bld	CR C C C
J-62	5 to 9	Blinds only	P P P P
J-62	3 or 4	Blinds only	P P P P
J-62	2/deal	Blinds only	P P PC Pr
J-62	1/small	Big only	PR PC CP CPr
J-62	2 to 8	R,R-C or C-R	P P P P
J-62	2 to 7	2 raises	P P P P
J-62	1/small	R,R-C or C-R	P P P P
J-62	1/small	2 raises	P P P P
J-62	0/big	R,R-C or C-R	P P P P
J-62	0/big	2 raises	P P P P
J-62	0/big	R by sml bld	CR C CP CP

10 high (straight range)...

HAND	PLAYERS TO ACT	ACTION	STRATEGY LM LX PL NL
10-9*	5 to 9	Blinds only	C C C Cr
10-9*	3 or 4	Blinds only	RC C CR CrR
10-9*	2/deal	Blinds only	RC CR RC Cr
10-9*	1/small	Big only	R CR CR Cr
10-9*	2 to 8	R,R-C or C-R	C C C+ Cr+
10-9*	2 to 7	2 raises	P P P P
10-9*	1/small	R,R-C or C-R	C C PC CP
10-9*	1/small	2 raises	P P P P
10-9*	0/big	R,R-C or C-R	C C C C
10-9*	0/big	2 raises	P P P P
10-9*	0/big	R by sml bld	RC CR CR CR
10-9	5 to 9	Blinds only	P P P P
10-9	3 or 4	Blinds only	P P PC PCr
10-9	2/deal	Blinds only	RC CR RCP rC
10-9	1/small	Big only	R CR CR Cr
10-9	2 to 8	R,R-C or C-R	P P PC PCR
10-9	2 to 7	2 raises	P P P P
10-9	1/small	R,R-C or C-R	C P P P
10-9	1/small	2 raises	P P P P
10-9	0/big	R,R-C or C-R	C PC PC PC
10-9	0/big	2 raises	P P P P
10-9	0/big	R by sml bld	RC C RC RC
10-8*	5 to 9	Blinds only	PC PC PC PRC
10-8*	3 or 4	Blinds only	CP CP CP Cr
10-8*	2/deal	Blinds only	RC CR C Cr
10-8*	1/small	Big only	R CR CR rC
10-8*	2 to 8	R,R-C or C-R	CP PC PC PC
10-8*	2 to 7	2 raises	P P P P
10-8*	1/small	R,R-C or C-R	C PC PC PC

10-8*	1/small	2 raises	P P P P
10-8*	0/big	R,R-C or C-R	C C C C
10-8*	0/big	2 raises	P P P P
10-8*	0/big	R by sml bld	RC CR CR CR
10-8	5 to 9	Blinds only	P P P P
10-8	3 or 4	Blinds only	PR PR PCR PCr
10-8	2/deal	Blinds only	RC CR RP rPC
10-8	1/small	Big only	R CR CR R
10-8	2 to 8	R,R-C or C-R	P P P P
10-8	2 to 7	2 raises	P P P P
10-8	1/small	R,R-C or C-R	P P P P
10-8	1/small	2 raises	P P P P
10-8	0/big	R,R-C or C-R	PC P P PC
10-8	0/big	2 raises	P P P P
10-8	0/big	R by sml bld	RC C RC RC
10-7*	5 to 9	Blinds only	PC P PC PCR
10-7*	3 or 4	Blinds only	CR C RC CRP
10-7*	2/deal	Blinds only	R CR RC rC
10-7*	1/small	Big only	R C CR CrR
10-7*	2 to 8	R,R-C or C-R	P PC PC PC
10-7*	2 to 7	2 raises	P P P P
10-7*	1/small	R,R-C or C-R	CP P P P
10-7*	1/small	2 raises	P P P P
10-7*	0/big	R,R-C or C-R	C PC PC PC
10-7*	0/big	2 raises	P P P P
10-7*	0/big	R by sml bld	CR CR C RC
10-7	5 to 9	Blinds only	P P P P
10-7	3 or 4	Blinds only	P P P PC
10-7	2/deal	Blinds only	PR P PR Pr
10-7	1/small	Big only	PR PR RCP PC
10-7	2 to 8	R,R-C or C-R	P P P P

10-7	2 to 7	2 raises	P P P P
10-7	1/small	R,R-C or C-R	P P P P
10-7	1/small	2 raises	P P P P
10-7	0/big	R,R-C or C-R	P P P P
10-7	0/big	2 raises	P P P P
10-7	0/big	R by sml bld	PC PC C C
10-6*	5 to 9	Blinds only	P P P P
10-6*	3 or 4	Blinds only	CP CP CP CrP
10-6*	2/deal	Blinds only	RC PC CRP rCR
10-6*	1/small	Big only	RC C CR Cr
10-6*	2 to 8	R,R-C or C-R	PC PC PC PC
10-6*	2 to 7	2 raises	P P P P
10-6*	1/small	R,R-C or C-R	PC P P P
10-6*	1/small	2 raises	P P P P
10-6*	0/big	R,R-C or C-R	C P P P
10-6*	0/big	2 raises	P P P P
10-6*	0/big	R by sml bld	C C C C
10-6	5 to 9	Blinds only	P P P P
10-6	3 or 4	Blinds only	P P P P
10-6	2/deal	Blinds only	RP PC PR PrR
10-6	1/small	Big only	RP PR PR P
10-6	2 to 8	R,R-C or C-R	P P P P
10-6	2 to 7	2 raises	P P P P
10-6	1/small	R,R-C or C-R	P P P P
10-6	1/small	2 raises	P P P P
10-6	0/big	R,R-C or C-R	P P P P
10-6	0/big	2 raises	P P P P
10-6	0/big	R by sml bld	C CP CP C

10 high (other)...

HAND	PLAYERS TO ACT	ACTION	STRATEGY LM LX PL NL
10-52*	5 to 9	Blinds only	P P P P
10-52*	3 or 4	Blinds only	P P P P
10-52*	2/deal	Blinds only	PR PR PCR CPR
10-52*	1/small	Big only	PR PC PC PCr
10-52*	2 to 8	R,R-C or C-R	P P P P
10-52*	2 to 7	2 raises	P P P P
10-52*	1/small	R,R-C or C-R	P P P P
10-52*	1/small	2 raises	P P P P
10-52*	0/big	R,R-C or C-R	PC P P P
10-52*	0/big	2 raises	P P P P
10-52*	0/big	R by sml bld	C C CP CP
10-52	5 to 9	Blinds only	P P P P
10-52	3 or 4	Blinds only	P P P P
10-52	2/deal	Blinds only	PR P P P
10-52	1/small	Big only	RP P P P
10-52	2 to 8	R,R-C or C-R	P P P P
10-52	2 to 7	2 raises	P P P P
10-52	1/small	R,R-C or C-R	P P P P
10-52	1/small	2 raises	P P P P
10-52	0/big	R,R-C or C-R	P P P P
10-52	0/big	2 raises	P P P P
10-52	0/big	R by sml bld	PC P PC PC

9 high (straight range)...

HAND	PLAYERS TO ACT	ACTION	STRATEGY LM LX PL NL
9-8*	5 to 9	Blinds only	CR CP C C
9-8*	3 or 4	Blinds only	RC CR CR Cr
9-8*	2/deal	Blinds only	RC CR CR Cr
9-8*	1/small	Big only	RC CR CR Cr

9-8*	2 to 8	R,R-C or C-R	C C CP CrP
9-8*	2 to 7	2 raises	P P P P
9-8*	1/small	R,R-C or C-R	C CP CP CP
9-8*	1/small	2 raises	P P P P
9-8*	0/big	R,R-C or C-R	C C C CR
9-8*	0/big	2 raises	P P P P
9-8*	0/big	R by sml bld	RC CR CR CR
9-8	5 to 9	Blinds only	P P P P
9-8	3 or 4	Blinds only	PR P PC Pr
9-8	2/deal	Blinds only	RP CR RP Cr
9-8	1/small	Big only	R CR CR Cr
9-8	2 to 8	R,R-C or C-R	P P P PC
9-8	2 to 7	2 raises	P P P P
9-8	1/small	R,R-C or C-R	P P P P
9-8	1/small	2 raises	P P P P
9-8	0/big	R,R-C or C-R	CP P P P
9-8	0/big	2 raises	P P P P
9-8	0/big	R by sml bld	CR C CR C
9-7*	5 to 9	Blinds only	PC PC PC PCr
9-7*	3 or 4	Blinds only	RP CP CPR Cr
9-7*	2/deal	Blinds only	RC RC CR Cr
9-7*	1/small	Big only	RC CR CR rC
9-7*	2 to 8	R,R-C or C-R	CP PC PC PC
9-7*	2 to 7	2 raises	P P P P
9-7*	1/small	R,R-C or C-R	C P PC PC
9-7*	1/small	2 raises	P P P P
9-7*	0/big	R,R-C or C-R	C C C C
9-7*	0/big	2 raises	P P P P
9-7*	0/big	R by sml bld	CR C CR CR
9-7	5 to 9	Blinds only	P P P P
9-7	3 or 4	Blinds only	P P PRC PC

9-7	2/deal	Blinds only	RP CP PR PC
9-7	1/small	Big only	R PC C PCR
9-7	2 to 8	R,R-C or C-R	P P P P
9-7	2 to 7	2 raises	P P P P
9-7	1/small	R,R-C or C-R	PC P P P
9-7	1/small	2 raises	P P P P
9-7	0/big	R,R-C or C-R	CP P P P
9-7	0/big	2 raises	P P P P
9-7	0/big	R by sml bld	C C CP CP
9-6*	5 to 9	Blinds only	PC P P PC
9-6*	3 or 4	Blinds only	PR PC PC PRC
9-6*	2/deal	Blinds only	RP CP CR Cr
9-6*	1/small	Big only	RC C CR Cr
9-6*	2 to 8	R,R-C or C-R	PC P P PC
9-6*	2 to 7	2 raises	P P P P
9-6*	1/small	R,R-C or C-R	CP P P P
9-6*	1/small	2 raises	P P P P
9-6*	0/big	R,R-C or C-R	C PC P PC
9-6*	0/big	2 raises	P P P P
9-6*	0/big	R by sml bld	RC CR CR CR
9-6	5 to 9	Blinds only	P P P P
9-6	3 or 4	Blinds only	P P P P
9-6	2/deal	Blinds only	PR PC PR Pr
9-6	1/small	Big only	RP PR PR PR
9-6	2 to 8	R,R-C or C-R	P P P P
9-6	2 to 7	2 raises	P P P P
9-6	1/small	R,R-C or C-R	P P P P
9-6	1/small	2 raises	P P P P
9-6	0/big	R,R-C or C-R	PC P P P
9-6	0/big	2 raises	P P P P
9-6	0/big	R by sml bld	CR CP CP CP

9-5*	5 to 9	Blinds only	P P P P
9-5*	3 or 4	Blinds only	RP CP CP CrP
9-5*	2/deal	Blinds only	RP CP CPR Cr
9-5*	1/small	Big only	R C C Cr
9-5*	2 to 8	R,R-C or C-R	PC P P PC
9-5*	2 to 7	2 raises	P P P P
9-5*	1/small	R,R-C or C-R	CP P P P
9-5*	1/small	2 raises	P P P P
9-5*	0/big	R,R-C or C-R	CP P P P
9-5*	0/big	2 raises	P P P P
9-5*	0/big	R by sml bld	RC C C C
9-5	5 to 9	Blinds only	P P P P
9-5	3 or 4	Blinds only	P P P P
9-5	2/deal	Blinds only	PR PC P Pr
9-5	1/small	Big only	RP PR PR PRC
9-5	2 to 8	R,R-C or C-R	P P P P
9-5	2 to 7	2 raises	P P P P
9-5	1/small	R,R-C or C-R	P P P P
9-5	1/small	2 raises	P P P P
9-5	0/big	R,R-C or C-R	PC P P P
9-5	0/big	2 raises	P P P P
9-5	0/big	R by sml bld	C CP CP CP

9 high (other)...

HAND	PLAYERS TO ACT	ACTION	STRATEGY LM LX PL NL
9-42*	5 to 9	Blinds only	P P P P
9-42*	3 or 4	Blinds only	P P P P
9-42*	2/deal	Blinds only	PR PC PC CP
9-42*	1/small	Big only	RP P P P
9-42*	2 to 8	R,R-C or C-R	P P P P
9-42*	2 to 7	2 raises	P P P P

9-42*	1/small	R,R-C or C-R	P P P P
9-42*	1/small	2 raises	P P P P
9-42*	0/big	R,R-C or C-R	CP P P P
9-42*	0/big	2 raises	P P P P
9-42*	0/big	R by sml bld	C C PC PC
9-42	5 to 9	Blinds only	P P P P
9-42	3 or 4	Blinds only	P P P P
9-42	2/deal	Blinds only	P P P P
9-42	1/small	Big only	P P P P
9-42	2 to 8	R,R-C or C-R	P P P P
9-42	2 to 7	2 raises	P P P P
9-42	1/small	R,R-C or C-R	P P P P
9-42	1/small	2 raises	P P P P
9-42	0/big	R,R-C or C-R	P P P P
9-42	0/big	2 raises	P P P P
9-42	0/big	R by sml bld	PC PC P P

8 high (straight range)...

HAND	PLAYERS TO ACT	ACTION	STRATEGY LM LX PL NL
8-7*	5 to 9	Blinds only	CR CR C CR
8-7*	3 or 4	Blinds only	RC CR CR Cr
8-7*	2/deal	Blinds only	R RC CR Cr
8-7*	1/small	Big only	R CR C Cr
8-7*	2 to 8	R,R-C or C-R	C C CP CrR
8-7*	2 to 7	2 raises	P P PR+ P
8-7*	1/small	R,R-C or C-R	C PC CP CP
8-7*	1/small	2 raises	P P P P
8-7*	0/big	R,R-C or C-R	C C C C
8-7*	0/big	2 raises	P P P P
8-7*	0/big	R by sml bld	R CR C C
8-7	5 to 9	Blinds only	P P P P

8-7	3 or 4	Blinds only	PR P PR PrC
8-7	2/deal	Blinds only	R CR CPR Cr
8-7	1/small	Big only	R PR CRP CrP
8-7	2 to 8	R,R-C or C-R	P P P P
8-7	2 to 7	2 raises	P P P P
8-7	1/small	R,R-C or C-R	PC P P P
8-7	1/small	2 raises	P P P P
8-7	0/big	R,R-C or C-R	CP P PC PC
8-7	0/big	2 raises	P P P P
8-7	0/big	R by sml bld	RC C CP CP
8-6*	5 to 9	Blinds only	PC PC PC PCr
8-6*	3 or 4	Blinds only	RC CP CP Cr
8-6*	2/deal	Blinds only	R RC CR Cr
8-6*	1/small	Big only	R C CR Cr
8-6*	2 to 8	R,R-C or C-R	CP CP CP CP
8-6*	2 to 7	2 raises	P P P P
8-6*	1/small	R,R-C or C-R	C P P P
8-6*	1/small	2 raises	P P P P
8-6*	0/big	R,R-C or C-R	C C CP C
8-6*	0/big	2 raises	P P P P
8-6*	0/big	R by sml bld	RC C C C
8-6	5 to 9	Blinds only	P P P P
8-6	3 or 4	Blinds only	P P P PRC
8-6	2/deal	Blinds only	PR PC P PC
8-6	1/small	Big only	RC PC CP CP
8-6	2 to 8	R,R-C or C-R	P P P P
8-6	2 to 7	2 raises	P P P P
8-6	1/small	R,R-C or C-R	PC P P P
8-6	1/small	2 raises	P P P P
8-6	0/big	R,R-C or C-R	CP P P P
8-6	0/big	2 raises	P P P P

8-6	0/big	R by sml bld	CR C PC CP
8-5*	5 to 9	Blinds only	PC P P P
8-5*	3 or 4	Blinds only	PR P PC PC
8-5*	2/deal	Blinds only	RC C C C
8-5*	1/small	Big only	RC C CR Cr
8-5*	2 to 8	R,R-C or C-R	PC P P PC
8-5*	2 to 7	2 raises	P P P P
8-5*	1/small	R,R-C or C-R	CP P P P
8-5*	1/small	2 raises	P P P P
8-5*	0/big	R,R-C or C-R	C PC P P
8-5*	0/big	2 raises	P P P P
8-5*	0/big	R by sml bld	CR C CR C
8-5	5 to 9	Blinds only	P P P P
8-5	3 or 4	Blinds only	P P P P
8-5	2/deal	Blinds only	PR P PR Pr
8-5	1/small	Big only	R P P P
8-5	2 to 8	R,R-C or C-R	P P P P
8-5	2 to 7	2 raises	P P P P
8-5	1/small	R,R-C or C-R	P P P P
8-5	1/small	2 raises	P P P P
8-5	0/big	R,R-C or C-R	PC P P P
8-5	0/big	2 raises	P P P P
8-5	0/big	R by sml bld	C C PC PC
8-4*	5 to 9	Blinds only	P P P P
8-4*	3 or 4	Blinds only	PR P PC PrC
8-4*	2/deal	Blinds only	PR PC CP C
8-4*	1/small	Big only	RC C C C
8-4*	2 to 8	R,R-C or C-R	P P P P
8-4*	2 to 7	2 raises	P P P P
8-4*	1/small	R,R-C or C-R	P P P P
8-4*	1/small	2 raises	P P P P

8-4*	0/big	R,R-C or C-R	CP P P P
8-4*	0/big	2 raises	P P P P
8-4*	0/big	R by sml bld	CR C CP C
8-4	5 to 9	Blinds only	P P P P
8-4	3 or 4	Blinds only	P P P P
8-4	2/deal	Blinds only	PR PC P PRC
8-4	1/small	Big only	PR P P P
8-4	2 to 8	R,R-C or C-R	P P P P
8-4	2 to 7	2 raises	P P P P
8-4	1/small	R,R-C or C-R	P P P P
8-4	1/small	2 raises	P P P P
8-4	0/big	R,R-C or C-R	PC P P P
8-4	0/big	2 raises	P P P P
8-4	0/big	R by sml bld	CP CP P PC

8 high (other)...

HAND	PLAYERS TO ACT	ACTION	STRATEGY LM LX PL NL
8-32*	5 to 9	Blinds only	P P P P
8-32*	3 or 4	Blinds only	P P P P
8-32*	2/deal	Blinds only	P P P Pr
8-32*	1/small	Big only	PC P P P
8-32*	2 to 8	R,R-C or C-R	P P P P
8-32*	2 to 7	2 raises	P P P P
8-32*	1/small	R,R-C or C-R	P P P P
8-32*	1/small	2 raises	P P P P
8-32*	0/big	R,R-C or C-R	PC P P P
8-32*	0/big	2 raises	P P P P
8-32*	0/big	R by sml bld	CP CP PC CP
8-32	5 to 9	Blinds only	P P P P
8-32	3 or 4	Blinds only	P P P P
8-32	2/deal	Blinds only	P P P P

8-32	1/small	Big only	P P P P
8-32	2 to 8	R,R-C or C-R	P P P P
8-32	2 to 7	2 raises	P P P P
8-32	1/small	R,R-C or C-R	P P P P
8-32	1/small	2 raises	P P P P
8-32	0/big	R,R-C or C-R	P P P P
8-32	0/big	2 raises	P P P P
8-32	0/big	R by sml bld	P P P P

7 high (straight range)...

HAND	PLAYERS TO ACT	ACTION	STRATEGY LM LX PL NL
7-6*	5 to 9	Blinds only	CP PC CP C
7-6*	3 or 4	Blinds only	RC CR C Cr
7-6*	2/deal	Blinds only	R C CR RC
7-6*	1/small	Big only	RC C CR rRC
7-6*	2 to 8	R,R-C or C-R	CP PC C C
7-6*	2 to 7	2 raises	P P P P
7-6*	1/small	R,R-C or C-R	C P PC PC
7-6*	1/small	2 raises	P P P P
7-6*	0/big	R,R-C or C-R	C C CP CP
7-6*	0/big	2 raises	P P P P
7-6*	0/big	R by sml bld	RC C CR CR
7-6	5 to 9	Blinds only	P P P P
7-6	3 or 4	Blinds only	P P P PCr
7-6	2/deal	Blinds only	PR PC PC C
7-6	1/small	Big only	RP PC C rCP
7-6	2 to 8	R,R-C or C-R	P P P P
7-6	2 to 7	2 raises	P P P P
7-6	1/small	R,R-C or C-R	PC P P P
7-6	1/small	2 raises	P P P P
7-6	0/big	R,R-C or C-R	CP P P PC

7-6	0/big	2 raises	P P P P
7-6	0/big	R by sml bld	CR C C C
7-5*	5 to 9	Blinds only	PC P P PC
7-5*	3 or 4	Blinds only	CR PC CP CrP
7-5*	2/deal	Blinds only	RC RC C Cr
7-5*	1/small	Big only	RC CR C C
7-5*	2 to 8	R,R-C or C-R	PC P PC PC
7-5*	2 to 7	2 raises	P P P P
7-5*	1/small	R,R-C or C-R	CP P P P
7-5*	1/small	2 raises	P P P P
7-5*	0/big	R,R-C or C-R	C PC PC PC
7-5*	0/big	2 raises	P P P P
7-5*	0/big	R by sml bld	CR C CR C
7-5	5 to 9	Blinds only	P P P P
7-5	3 or 4	Blinds only	P P P P
7-5	2/deal	Blinds only	PR P P PrC
7-5	1/small	Big only	RP P PR PC
7-5	2 to 8	R,R-C or C-R	P P P P
7-5	2 to 7	2 raises	P P P P
7-5	1/small	R,R-C or C-R	PC P P P
7-5	1/small	2 raises	P P P P
7-5	0/big	R,R-C or C-R	CP P P P
7-5	0/big	2 raises	P P P P
7-5	0/big	R by sml bld	C CP PC PC
7-4*	5 to 9	Blinds only	P P P P
7-4*	3 or 4	Blinds only	P P PCR PCr
7-4*	2/deal	Blinds only	RC CP R C
7-4*	1/small	Big only	CR C CR Cr
7-4*	2 to 8	R,R-C or C-R	P P P P
7-4*	2 to 7	2 raises	P P P P
7-4*	1/small	R,R-C or C-R	PC P P P

7-4*	1/small	2 raises	P P P P
7-4*	0/big	R,R-C or C-R	PC P P P
7-4*	0/big	2 raises	P P P P
7-4*	0/big	R by sml bld	CR C PC CP
7-4	5 to 9	Blinds only	P P P P
7-4	3 or 4	Blinds only	P P P P
7-4	2/deal	Blinds only	P P P P
7-4	1/small	Big only	PR P P P
7-4	2 to 8	R,R-C or C-R	P P P P
7-4	2 to 7	2 raises	P P P P
7-4	1/small	R,R-C or C-R	P P P P
7-4	1/small	2 raises	P P P P
7-4	0/big	R,R-C or C-R	P P P P
7-4	0/big	2 raises	P P P P
7-4	0/big	R by sml bld	CP CP P PC
7-3*	5 to 9	Blinds only	P P P P
7-3*	3 or 4	Blinds only	P P P Pr
7-3*	2/deal	Blinds only	PR PC PC PCr
7-3*	1/small	Big only	R C C C
7-3*	2 to 8	R,R-C or C-R	P P P P
7-3*	2 to 7	2 raises	P P P P
7-3*	1/small	R,R-C or C-R	P P P P
7-3*	1/small	2 raises	P P P P
7-3*	0/big	R,R-C or C-R	PC P P P
7-3*	0/big	2 raises	P P P P
7-3*	0/big	R by sml bld	C C PC CP
7-3	5 to 9	Blinds only	P P P P
7-3	3 or 4	Blinds only	P P P P
7-3	2/deal	Blinds only	P P P P
7-3	1/small	Big only	PR P P P
7-3	2 to 8	R,R-C or C-R	P P P P

7-3	2 to 7	2 raises	P P P P
7-3	1/small	R,R-C or C-R	P P P P
7-3	1/small	2 raises	P P P P
7-3	0/big	R,R-C or C-R	P P P P
7-3	0/big	2 raises	P P P P
7-3	0/big	R by sml bld	PC PC P P

7-2…

HAND	PLAYERS TO ACT	ACTION	STRATEGY LM LX PL NL
7-2*	5 to 9	Blinds only	P P P P
7-2*	3 or 4	Blinds only	P P P P
7-2*	2/deal	Blinds only	P P P P
7-2*	1/small	Big only	PR P P P
7-2*	2 to 8	R,R-C or C-R	P P P P
7-2*	2 to 7	2 raises	P P P P
7-2*	1/small	R,R-C or C-R	P P P P
7-2*	1/small	2 raises	P P P P
7-2*	0/big	R,R-C or C-R	PC P P P
7-2*	0/big	2 raises	P P P P
7-2*	0/big	R by sml bld	CP PC P CP
7-2	5 to 9	Blinds only	P P P P
7-2	3 or 4	Blinds only	P P P P
7-2	2/deal	Blinds only	P P P P
7-2	1/small	Big only	P P P P
7-2	2 to 8	R,R-C or C-R	P P P P
7-2	2 to 7	2 raises	P P P P
7-2	1/small	R,R-C or C-R	P P P P
7-2	1/small	2 raises	P P P P
7-2	0/big	R,R-C or C-R	P P P P
7-2	0/big	2 raises	P P P P
7-2	0/big	R by sml bld	P P P P

6 high...

HAND	PLAYERS TO ACT	ACTION	STRATEGY LM LX PL NL
6-5*	5 to 9	Blinds only	PC PC PC CP
6-5*	3 or 4	Blinds only	RC CR CR Cr
6-5*	2/deal	Blinds only	RC RC CR CR
6-5*	1/small	Big only	RC C CR rC
6-5*	2 to 8	R,R-C or C-R	PC P CP C
6-5*	2 to 7	2 raises	P P P P
6-5*	1/small	R,R-C or C-R	PC P P PC
6-5*	1/small	2 raises	P P P P
6-5*	0/big	R,R-C or C-R	C CP PC PC
6-5*	0/big	2 raises	P P P P
6-5*	0/big	R by sml bld	CR C C C
6-5	5 to 9	Blinds only	P P P P
6-5	3 or 4	Blinds only	P P P P
6-5	2/deal	Blinds only	PR P PC CP
6-5	1/small	Big only	RC PC PC CPr
6-5	2 to 8	R,R-C or C-R	P P P P
6-5	2 to 7	2 raises	P P P P
6-5	1/small	R,R-C or C-R	P P P P
6-5	1/small	2 raises	P P P P
6-5	0/big	R,R-C or C-R	PC P P P
6-5	0/big	2 raises	P P P P
6-5	0/big	R by sml bld	CR C PC CP
6-4*	5 to 9	Blinds only	P P P PC
6-4*	3 or 4	Blinds only	PR PC PC rPC
6-4*	2/deal	Blinds only	RC CR C C
6-4*	1/small	Big only	RC CP CP CR
6-4*	2 to 8	R,R-C or C-R	P P PC PC
6-4*	2 to 7	2 raises	P P P P
6-4*	1/small	R,R-C or C-R	PC P P P

Mike Caro and Mike Cappelletti

6-4*	1/small	2 raises	P P P P
6-4*	0/big	R,R-C or C-R	CP PC PC PC
6-4*	0/big	2 raises	P P P P
6-4*	0/big	R by sml bld	CR C C C
6-4	5 to 9	Blinds only	P P P P
6-4	3 or 4	Blinds only	P P P P
6-4	2/deal	Blinds only	P P P PC
6-4	1/small	Big only	P P P P
6-4	2 to 8	R,R-C or C-R	P P P P
6-4	2 to 7	2 raises	P P P P
6-4	1/small	R,R-C or C-R	P P P P
6-4	1/small	2 raises	P P P P
6-4	0/big	R,R-C or C-R	P P P P
6-4	0/big	2 raises	P P P P
6-4	0/big	R by sml bld	CP PC P PC
6-3*	5 to 9	Blinds only	P P P P
6-3*	3 or 4	Blinds only	P P PR PC
6-3*	2/deal	Blinds only	CR CP CP C
6-3*	1/small	Big only	CR CP CR C
6-3*	2 to 8	R,R-C or C-R	P P P P
6-3*	2 to 7	2 raises	P P P P
6-3*	1/small	R,R-C or C-R	P P P P
6-3*	1/small	2 raises	P P P P
6-3*	0/big	R,R-C or C-R	PC P P P
6-3*	0/big	2 raises	P P P P
6-3*	0/big	R by sml bld	C C CP C
6-3	5 to 9	Blinds only	P P P P
6-3	3 or 4	Blinds only	P P P P
6-3	2/deal	Blinds only	P P P P
6-3	1/small	Big only	P P P P
6-3	2 to 8	R,R-C or C-R	P P P P

6-3	2 to 7	2 raises	P P P P
6-3	1/small	R,R-C or C-R	P P P P
6-3	1/small	2 raises	P P P P
6-3	0/big	R,R-C or C-R	P P P P
6-3	0/big	2 raises	P P P P
6-3	0/big	R by sml bld	CP PC P PC
6-2*	5 to 9	Blinds only	P P P P
6-2*	3 or 4	Blinds only	P P P Pr
6-2*	2/deal	Blinds only	PR PC PC PC
6-2*	1/small	Big only	CR C PC P
6-2*	2 to 8	R,R-C or C-R	P P P P
6-2*	2 to 7	2 raises	P P P P
6-2*	1/small	R,R-C or C-R	P P P P
6-2*	1/small	2 raises	P P P P
6-2*	0/big	R,R-C or C-R	PC P P P
6-2*	0/big	2 raises	P P P P
6-2*	0/big	R by sml bld	C C P PC
6-2	5 to 9	Blinds only	P P P P
6-2	3 or 4	Blinds only	P P P P
6-2	2/deal	Blinds only	P P P P
6-2	1/small	Big only	P P P P
6-2	2 to 8	R,R-C or C-R	P P P P
6-2	2 to 7	2 raises	P P P P
6-2	1/small	R,R-C or C-R	P P P P
6-2	1/small	2 raises	P P P P
6-2	0/big	R,R-C or C-R	P P P P
6-2	0/big	2 raises	P P P P
6-2	0/big	R by sml bld	PC P P P

5 high...

HAND	PLAYERS TO ACT	ACTION	STRATEGY LM LX PL NL
5-4*	5 to 9	Blinds only	PC PC PC CP
5-4*	3 or 4	Blinds only	R C C Cr
5-4*	2/deal	Blinds only	RC CR C C
5-4*	1/small	Big only	R C C r
5-4*	2 to 8	R,R-C or C-R	PC P PC CP
5-4*	2 to 7	2 raises	P P P P
5-4*	1/small	R,R-C or C-R	C PC P PR+
5-4*	1/small	2 raises	P P P P
5-4*	0/big	R,R-C or C-R	CP PC PC PC
5-4*	0/big	2 raises	P P P P
5-4*	0/big	R by sml bld	C C C CR
5-4	5 to 9	Blinds only	P P P P
5-4	3 or 4	Blinds only	P P P P
5-4	2/deal	Blinds only	P P PC PC
5-4	1/small	Big only	P P P PC
5-4	2 to 8	R,R-C or C-R	P P P P
5-4	2 to 7	2 raises	P P P P
5-4	1/small	R,R-C or C-R	P P P P
5-4	1/small	2 raises	P P P P
5-4	0/big	R,R-C or C-R	PC P P P
5-4	0/big	2 raises	P P P P
5-4	0/big	R by sml bld	C C P CP
5-3*	5 to 9	Blinds only	P P P P
5-3*	3 or 4	Blinds only	P P PC PC
5-3*	2/deal	Blinds only	RP CP CR C
5-3*	1/small	Big only	RC CP CP C
5-3*	2 to 8	R,R-C or C-R	P P P P
5-3*	2 to 7	2 raises	P P P P
5-3*	1/small	R,R-C or C-R	PC P P P

Mastering Hold'em and Omaha • Cardoza Publishing

5-3*	1/small	2 raises	P P P P
5-3*	0/big	R,R-C or C-R	C PC P P
5-3*	0/big	2 raises	P P P P
5-3*	0/big	R by sml bld	C C CP C
5-3	5 to 9	Blinds only	P P P P
5-3	3 or 4	Blinds only	P P P P
5-3	2/deal	Blinds only	P P P P
5-3	1/small	Big only	P P P P
5-3	2 to 8	R,R-C or C-R	P P P P
5-3	2 to 7	2 raises	P P P P
5-3	1/small	R,R-C or C-R	P P P P
5-3	1/small	2 raises	P P P P
5-3	0/big	R,R-C or C-R	P P P P
5-3	0/big	2 raises	P P P P
5-3	0/big	R by sml bld	CP P P PC
5-2*	5 to 9	Blinds only	P P P P
5-2*	3 or 4	Blinds only	P P P PC
5-2*	2/deal	Blinds only	CP P CP CP
5-2*	1/small	Big only	CP P P P
5-2*	2 to 8	R,R-C or C-R	P P P P
5-2*	2 to 7	2 raises	P P P P
5-2*	1/small	R,R-C or C-R	P P P P
5-2*	1/small	2 raises	P P P P
5-2*	0/big	R,R-C or C-R	PC P P P
5-2*	0/big	2 raises	P P P P
5-2*	0/big	R by sml bld	C CP P PC
5-2	5 to 9	Blinds only	P P P P
5-2	3 or 4	Blinds only	P P P P
5-2	2/deal	Blinds only	P P P P
5-2	1/small	Big only	P P P P
5-2	2 to 8	R,R-C or C-R	P P P P

305

5-2	2 to 7	2 raises	P P P P
5-2	1/small	R,R-C or C-R	P P P P
5-2	1/small	2 raises	P P P P
5-2	0/big	R,R-C or C-R	P P P P
5-2	0/big	2 raises	P P P P
5-2	0/big	R by sml bld	P P P P

4 high...

HAND	PLAYERS TO ACT	ACTION	STRATEGY LM LX PL NL
4-3*	5 to 9	Blinds only	P P P P
4-3*	3 or 4	Blinds only	PR PC PC CP
4-3*	2/deal	Blinds only	RP CP CP C
4-3*	1/small	Big only	C C C C
4-3*	2 to 8	R,R-C or C-R	P P P PC
4-3*	2 to 7	2 raises	P P P P
4-3*	1/small	R,R-C or C-R	P P P P
4-3*	1/small	2 raises	P P P P
4-3*	0/big	R,R-C or C-R	CP P P PC
4-3*	0/big	2 raises	P P P P
4-3*	0/big	R by sml bld	CR C CP C
4-3	5 to 9	Blinds only	P P P P
4-3	3 or 4	Blinds only	P P P P
4-3	2/deal	Blinds only	P P P P
4-3	1/small	Big only	P P P P
4-3	2 to 8	R,R-C or C-R	P P P P
4-3	2 to 7	2 raises	P P P P
4-3	1/small	R,R-C or C-R	P P P P
4-3	1/small	2 raises	P P P P
4-3	0/big	R,R-C or C-R	P P P P
4-3	0/big	2 raises	P P P P
4-3	0/big	R by sml bld	PC P P PC

4-2*	5 to 9	Blinds only	P P P P
4-2*	3 or 4	Blinds only	P P P P
4-2*	2/deal	Blinds only	PR PC PC PCr
4-2*	1/small	Big only	P P PC CP
4-2*	2 to 8	R,R-C or C-R	P P P P
4-2*	2 to 7	2 raises	P P P P
4-2*	1/small	R,R-C or C-R	P P P P
4-2*	1/small	2 raises	P P P P
4-2*	0/big	R,R-C or C-R	PC P P P
4-2*	0/big	2 raises	P P P P
4-2*	0/big	R by sml bld	PC P P PC
4-2	5 to 9	Blinds only	P P P P
4-2	3 or 4	Blinds only	P P P P
4-2	2/deal	Blinds only	P P P P
4-2	1/small	Big only	P P P P
4-2	2 to 8	R,R-C or C-R	P P P P
4-2	2 to 7	2 raises	P P P P
4-2	1/small	R,R-C or C-R	P P P P
4-2	1/small	2 raises	P P P P
4-2	0/big	R,R-C or C-R	P P P P
4-2	0/big	2 raises	P P P P
4-2	0/big	R by sml bld	P P P P

3-2

HAND	PLAYERS TO ACT	ACTION	STRATEGY LM LX PL NL
3-2*	5 to 9	Blinds only	P P P P
3-2*	3 or 4	Blinds only	P P P P
3-2*	2/deal	Blinds only	PR PC CP CPR
3-2*	1/small	Big only	P P PCR PC
3-2*	2 to 8	R,R-C or C-R	P P P P
3-2*	2 to 7	2 raises	P P P P

3-2*	1/small	R,R-C or C-R	P P P P
3-2*	1/small	2 raises	P P P P
3-2*	0/big	R,R-C or C-R	PC P P P
3-2*	0/big	2 raises	P P P P
3-2*	0/big	R by sml bld	PC P P PC
3-2	5 to 9	Blinds only	P P P P
3-2	3 or 4	Blinds only	P P P P
3-2	2/deal	Blinds only	P P P P
3-2	1/small	Big only	P P P P
3-2	2 to 8	R,R-C or C-R	P P P P
3-2	2 to 7	2 raises	P P P P
3-2	1/small	R,R-C or C-R	P P P P
3-2	1/small	2 raises	P P P P
3-2	0/big	R,R-C or C-R	P P P P
3-2	0/big	2 raises	P P P P
3-2	0/big	R by sml bld	P P P P

Thanks for letting us share our thoughts with you. End of book.

APPENDIX A: KILL GAMES

The *kill* feature at both hold'em and Omaha has become popular in many cardrooms. A **kill** game is a table at which all players have agreed that if they win a pot with more than a specified threshold amount, they agree to play the next hand at twice the stakes with the winner posting an extra blind of $20. For example, in a $10/$20 game, the specified kill amount might be $200, which, if reached, would up the stakes in the following game to $20/$40.

If, instead, the game is $10/$20 with a *half kill*, then if someone scoops a pot with more than the specified threshold amount, the next hand is played at $15/$30, with the winner posting a $15 blind. There would then be three blinds; the $5 small blind, the $10 big blind, and the position-independent $15 kill blind.

Why are there kill pots? Presumably, to increase the action. When there is more money in a kill starting pot, there is more incentive to win the pot. Although many players tend to tighten up when the stakes temporarily double, the better ones will get more aggressive with preflop raises. Many weaker players view the kill as a plot by the better players to increase the stakes. I have often heard statements like, "If I wanted to play $20/$40, I would sit at a $20/$40 table."

Nevertheless, kill games are popular, because there is

NOTE FROM CARO:

Always remember that you are being penalized whenever you're forced to put in a kill on the next hand. What this really means is that the pot you are currently trying to win is less valuable to you and, theoretically, not as large as it may seem. Keep this in mind when you choose whether to call, raise or fold.

more excitement at a table where huge pots occur. Players like the extra action, as long as the threshold for activating the kill is not set too low. If the kill threshold is too low, it changes the size of the game because frequent kill pots essentially raise the stakes. Players must take risky moves into consideration because the winner of the previous pot is forced to ante a substantial portion of his profit. For example, in a $5/$10 kill game, the winner of a threshold $70 pot, of which only $30 to $40 might be profit—and that would be lessened by the, say, a $3 house rake—has to post $10 in the next pot. That makes some marginally profitable starting hands unprofitable. This has the result of causing knowledgeable players to tighten up their starting hand selection.

APPENDIX B: HOW TO USE MCU POKER CHARTS

This appendix presents illustrations of some of the principles that have been described in this book. First it explains how to use MCU Poker Charts.

USING MCU POKER CHARTS

Mike Caro devised MCU Poker Charts because there was clearly a need for a common method of presenting poker hands in printed form and on the Web. The poker charts are found in this book and many other publications, along with a guide to interpretation similar to this one. MCU Poker Charts are designed to be read from left to right and top to bottom, just like you're reading this book.

Actions take place in sequence. So, wherever you see a wager, a fold, or cards appearing, that's when it happened. Everything in the chart that appears earlier—reading left to right, top to bottom—happened earlier. Everything that appears later—reading left to right, top to bottom—happened later.

For your convenience, each MCU Poker Chart has a legend at the bottom, briefly explaining how to interpret it, in case you forget. We'll use two flavors of MCU Poker Charts in this book—one each for hold'em and Omaha (both high and high-low).

On the next pages are examples of each of these charts, beginning with hold'em.

MCU Poker Chart. *Game*: Hold 'em *Structure*: $25 and $50 blinds, $50 bets on starting hand and flop, $100 thereafter.

1	2	3	4	5	6	7	8	9	10	Pot
		•	b25	b50						$75
J♠ 10♦										Starting hands <<<
					→—	—	—	—	—	
=50[1]	↑100[2]	=100	—	=100						
=100←										$425
										Flop: J♣ J♥ 2♠ <<<
✓[3]	50	=50		→✓						
=50←				—						$575
										Turn: K♥ <<<
→✓[4]	✓	100								
=100	—←									$775
										River: 7♣ <<<
→✓		100								
↑200		=200[5]←								$1,175
J♠ 10♦		K♦ Q♦								Two-card hands revealed <<<
WIN										

> **Chart key:** Action reads left to right, top to bottom. Each betting round begins with → and ends with ←. Other markings and symbols: a (ante); b (blind bet); • (check); = (call, including when big blind sees flop free); ↑ (raise); — (fold); ● (dealer position, a.k.a. "the button"). A seat number surrounded by asterisks (for example, * 1 *) is your seat. Any wager not preceded by a symbol is a voluntary first bet. Wagers indicate the total invested on a betting round. The money in the rightmost column indicates total pot size after the betting. For full explanation of the chart, see Appendix B.

Okay, here's a fuller explanation. At the top, you see what kind of game we're playing and the betting structure. On the next row, you see the seat numbers. If a number is surrounded by asterisks, such as "*** 1 ***" above, that's the seat on which we're focusing our strategy. Often, we will expose the facedown cards for this hand and not for the others until later in the strategy discussion. Private, hidden cards have a line beneath (underline) to differentiate them from exposed cards.

Below the seat numbers is the starting hands row. You can see that this is a full table, because everyone received cards. We're in seat #1, so we see only those cards.

The ● indicates that the #3 seat has the dealer button, so wagers begin to the right with a small $25 blind, marked "**b25**" and a $50 big blind, marked "**b50**." Still reading left to right in the starting-hand action row (see rightmost column for description of betting round), you see → in seat #6, meaning the voluntary action on this rounds starts here. After the starting arrow, you see a dash (—), meaning the player folded. You can always look upward from the bottom in any column. Where you see the dash, that's where the player exited the pot. You see nothing in the betting round columns beneath that fold indicator.

Seats #7, #8, #9, and #10 also fold (note the dashes). Now we skip down to the next line (just like reading a book, remember, left to right, top to bottom). Your seat, #1, says "=50[1]" and is interpreted this way: The equal sign means call, the "50" indicates the amount (equal to the big blind), and the superscript [1] means that you should look for that number in the comments following the table (omitted here) to see what is said about the strategy at that point in the action.

Seat #2 is marked "↑100[2]"—and this means the player raised to a total of $100 for the betting round (a $50 raise) and that a strategy note (footnote number 2) follows the chart. The rest of the action in this betting round is easy to follow. The ← symbol follows the very last action on the betting round. The cumulative size of the pot at the end of the betting round is shown last in the rightmost column. Here it's $425. The pot size, after the betting, is provided for every betting round.

The Flop

Now we move down to the second betting round, the action on the flop. First you see the flop over in the right hand column. Then comes the wagering. The only thing you need to know here is that a check mark (✓) means that the player checked.

The betting round following the fourth communal board card ("Turn") and the final one ("River") are shown in separate rows. On the bottom row, you see the showdown to determine the winner—and the winning hand is indicated with the word, "**WIN**." (Those adopting the MCU Poker Charts can also use the bottom row to expose, for instructive purposes, other hands that did not reach the showdown. These should be marked as non-showdown hands, such as by including the word "**FOLDED**" at the bottom. These non-showdown private cards can also be revealed in the text following the table or they can be shown exposed in the table, instead of concealed, as they are dealt. The method used should be the one that is most useful for the purpose.)

Again, the strategy notes that correspond to the superscripts are not relevant for this example, and are not included here. In the actual strategy charts used in this book, any superscript numbers have corresponding explanations following the chart.

Optionally, the areas on the chart pertaining to a player's actions can be shaded for betting rounds after a hand is folded. This makes it easier to see who's still active, and that's the method used in this book.

Okay, here's a fuller explanation. At the top, you see what kind of game we're playing and the betting structure. On the next row, you see the seat numbers. If a number is surrounded by asterisks, such as "*** 1 ***" above, that's the seat on which we're focusing our strategy. Often, we will expose the facedown cards for this hand and not for the others until later in the strategy discussion. Private, hidden cards have a line beneath (underline) to differentiate them from exposed cards.

Below the seat numbers is the starting hands row. You can see that this is a full table, because everyone received cards. We're in seat #1, so we see only those cards.

The • indicates that the #3 seat has the dealer button, so wagers begin to the right with a small $25 blind, marked "**b25**" and a $50 big blind, marked "**b50**." Still reading left to right in the starting-hand action row (see rightmost column for description of betting round), you see → in seat #6, meaning the voluntary action on this rounds starts here. After the starting arrow, you see a dash (—), meaning the player folded. You can always look upward from the bottom in any column. Where you see the dash, that's where the player exited the pot. You see nothing in the betting round columns beneath that fold indicator.

Seats #7, #8, #9, and #10 also fold (note the dashes). Now we skip down to the next line (just like reading a book, remember, left to right, top to bottom). Your seat, #1, says "=50[1]" and is interpreted this way: The equal sign means call, the "50" indicates the amount (equal to the big blind), and the superscript [1] means that you should look for that number in the comments following the table (omitted here) to see what is said about the strategy at that point in the action.

Seat #2 is marked "↑100[2]"—and this means the player raised to a total of $100 for the betting round (a $50 raise) and that a strategy note (number 2) follows the chart. The rest of the action in this betting round, I'm sure you can follow. The ← symbol follows the very last action on the betting round. The cumulative size of the pot at the end of the betting round is shown last in the rightmost column. Here it's $425. The pot size, after the betting, is provided for every betting round.

Now let's look at an Omaha MCU Poker Chart.

Chart key: Action reads left to right, top to bottom. Each betting round begins with → and ends with ←. Other markings and symbols: a (ante); b (blind bet); • (check); = (call, including when big blind sees flop free); ↑ (raise); — (fold); ● (dealer position, a.k.a. "the button"). A seat number surrounded by asterisks (for example, * 1 *) is your seat. Any wager not preceded by a symbol is a voluntary first bet. Wagers indicate the total invested on a betting round. The money in the rightmost column indicates total pot size after the betting.

MCU Poker Chart. *Game*: Omaha high-low, 8-or-better *Structure:* $25 and $50 blinds, $50 bets on starting hand and flop, $100 thereafter.

1	2	3	4	5	6	7	8	9	10	Pot
		●	b25	b50						$75
4♦ **2♦** **A♣** **A♥**										Starting hands ◄◄◄
		—			→↑100	—	—	=100	—	
↑150[1]	=150		—	=150	=150			=150←		$625
										Flop **A♦ 7♦ 6♣** ◄◄◄
				→✓	✓			→50[2]		
↑100	=100[3]			=100	—			=100←		$575
										Turn **Q♦** ◄◄◄
				→100				=100		
=100[4] =200←	↑200			=200				=200		$775
										River **8♣** ◄◄◄
				→✓				✓		
100[5]	=100			=100				=100		$1,175

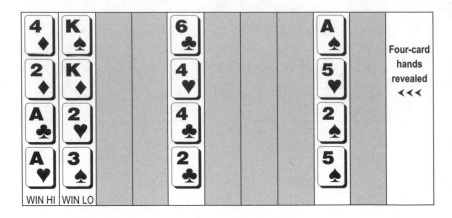

Now that we've walked through the hold 'em chart together, you probably already understand how to read this Omaha high-low version. Remember, each player's cards are individual and appear as they are dealt.

Other Details

MCU Poker Charts don't require the graphical cards shown here. That's the way they are presented in this book, but you can substitute other graphics or text symbols to define a card. So you can, alternatively, present your starting hand like this: J♠ 10♦. (You can even just make it "Jc 10d," if no symbols are available. It's the flow of the MCU charts that's important to standardize, so we have a common way to illustrate and explain poker hands, from book to book, article to article—in print, on the web, and beyond.)

And even those symbols explained at the bottom of the chart don't need to be used, if unavailable. Substitutions may be needed on websites, for instance. In such cases, these are the sanctioned changes:

- ♠ Use * instead of ● for the dealer-position button.
- ♠ Use > instead of → to indicate the first voluntary action.

♠ Use < instead of ← to indicate the last action on the betting round.

♠ Use r instead of ↑ to indicate a raise or reraise ("r150," instead of "↑150").

♠ Use k instead of ✓ to indicate a check.

♠ Use -- (two hyphens) instead of — (typographical dash) to indicate a fold.

♠ Use <<< instead of ◄◄◄ as ornamental indicators pointing from the "Pot" column at right to the action at left.

♠ Use c d h s instead of ♣ ♦ ♥ ♠, if the card symbols are unavailable and you're not using full card graphics.

♠ Use (1), (2), (3), and so forth, instead of [1], [2], [3] (superscripts) to indicate places in the action that match comments following the MCU Poker Chart.

The table format, with bordered rows and columns, should be maintained. This is standard fare for the Web as well as almost all word processors.

It's Free to Everyone

Finally, I have given the concept and the design for these MCU Poker Charts to the public. I am not claiming any rights to them. Anyone can use them. I hope they become universally accepted. I also hope nobody changes the concept or the specific way information is presented. There may be ways to improve these charts, but if we all go our own way, we won't have a universal method for communicating poker strategy. And we need one.

There is also a Type II MCU Poker Chart (the one we're using is Type I) that I won't describe in detail here. It depicts a clockwise spiral pathway leading toward the pot at center. Superimposed on the spiral is a geometric "pie" with each slice representing a poker seat. All the action takes place in order, within the appropriate player slices, including wagers and cards received, as you mentally travel along the spiral toward the pot. It is worthy of future use, but deemed too cumbersome to employ in this book.

I'm open to suggestions for future improvement in the MCU Poker Chart standard. Any improvements accepted will be formally announced periodically, and none should be so radical that people reading older charts cannot easily understand the new ones. This is my dream. I hope other publishers adopt MCU Poker Charts as their standard[1], that they comment freely on the design, and that they become a part of the team in our united effort to popularize poker worldwide.

---

[1]Publishers, instructors, and others wanting to adopt the MCU Poker Charts as a standard can find Microsoft Word templates at www.poker1.com.

CARDOZA POKER BOOKS
POWERFUL INFORMATION YOU MUST HAVE

HOLD'EM WISDOM FOR ALL PLAYERS *by Daniel Negreanu*. Superstar poker player Daniel Negreanu provides 50 easy-to-read and right-to-the-point hold'em strategy nuggets that will immediately make you a better player at cash games and tournaments. His wit and wisdom makes for great reading; even better, it makes for killer winning advice. Conversational, straightforward, and educational, this book covers topics as diverse as the top 10 rookie mistakes to bullying bullies and exploiting your table image.176 pages, paperback, $14.95.

CHAMPIONSHIP NO-LIMIT & POT-LIMIT HOLD'EM *by T. J. Cloutier & Tom McEvoy*. This is the bible of winning pot-limit and no-limit hold'em tournaments. You'll get all the answers here— no holds barred—to your most important questions: How do you get inside your opponents' heads and learn how to beat them at their own game? How can you tell how much to bet, raise, and reraise in no-limit hold'em? When can you bluff? How do you set up your opponents in pot-limit hold'em so that you can win a monster pot? What are the best strategies for winning no-limit and pot-limit tournaments, satellites, and supersatellites? Rock-solid and inspired advice you can bank on from two of the most recognizable figures in poker. 304 pages, $29.95.

CHAMPIONSHIP HOLD'EM *by T. J. Cloutier & Tom McEvoy*. Hard-hitting hold'em the way it's played *today* in both limit cash games and tournaments. Get killer advice on how to win more money in rammin'-jammin' games, kill-pot, jackpot, shorthanded, and full table cash games. You'll learn the thinking process before the flop, and on the flop, turn, and river with specific suggestions for what to do when good or bad things happen. Plus 20 illustrated hands with play-by-play analyses, specific advice for rocks in tight games, weaklings in loose games, experts in solid games, how hand values change in jackpot games, when you should fold, check, raise, reraise, check-raise, slowplay, and bluff. Also tournament strategies for small buy-in, big buy-in, rebuy, add-on, satellite and big-field major tournaments. Wow! If you want to win at limit hold'em, you need this book! 392 pages, $29.95.

CHAMPIONSHIP OMAHA (Omaha High-Low, Pot-limit Omaha, Limit High Omaha) *by Tom McEvoy & T. J. Cloutier*. Clearly-written strategies and powerful advice from Cloutier and McEvoy who have won four World Series of Poker Omaha titles. Powerful advice shows you how to win at low-limit and high-stakes games, how to play against loose and tight opponents, and the differing strategies for rebuy and freezeout tournaments. Learn the best starting hands, when slowplaying a big hand is dangerous, what danglers are and why winners don't play them, why pot-limit Omaha is the only poker game where you sometimes fold the nuts on the flop and are correct in doing so, and, overall, how you can win a lot of money at Omaha! 296 pages, illustrations, $29.95.

CHAMPIONSHIP TABLE (at the World Series of Poker) *by Dana Smith, Ralph Wheeler, & Tom McEvoy*. *Championship Table* celebrates three decades of poker greats who have competed to win poker's most coveted title. This book gives you the names and photographs of all the players who made the final table, pictures the last hand the champion played against the runner-up, how they played their cards, how much they won, plus fascinating interviews and conversations with the champions. This fascinating and invaluable resource book includes tons of vintage photographs. 208 pages, $19.95.

HOW TO WIN THE CHAMPIONSHIP: Hold'em Strategies for the Final Table, *by T. J. Cloutier*. If you're hungry to win a championship, this is the book that will pave the way to success! T. J. Cloutier, the greatest tournament poker player ever—he has won 59 major tournament titles and appeared at 39 final tables at the WSOP, both more than any other player in the history of poker—shows how to get to the final table where the big money is made and then how to win it all. You'll learn how to build up enough chips to make it through the early and middle rounds and then how to employ T. J.'s own strategies to outmaneuver opponents at the final table and win championships. T. J. shows you how to adjust your play depending upon stack sizes, antes and blinds, table position, opponents' styles, and chip counts. You'll also learn the specific strategies needed for full tables and for six-handed, three-handed, and heads-up play. 288 pages, $29.95.

GREAT CARDOZA POKER BOOKS
ADD THESE TO YOUR LIBRARY - ORDER NOW!

CRASH COURSE IN BEATING TEXAS HOLD'EM *by Avery Cardoza.* Perfect for beginning and somewhat experienced players who want to jump right into the action and play cash games, local tournaments, online poker, and the big televised tournaments where millions of dollars can be made. Both limit and no-limit hold'em games are covered, along with the essential strategies needed to play profitably on the pre-flop, flop, turn, and river. The good news is that you don't need to memorize hands or be burdened by math to be a winner—just play by the no-nonsense basic principles outlined in this book. There's a lot of money to be made and Cardoza shows you how to go and get it. 208 pages, $14.95

WINNER'S GUIDE TO TEXAS HOLD'EM POKER *by Ken Warren.* You'll learn how to play every hand from every position with every type of flop. Learn the 14 categories of starting hands, the 10 most common hold'em tells, how to evaluate a game for profit, the value of deception, the art of bluffing, eight secrets to winning, starting hand categories, position, and more! Includes detailed analysis of the top 40 hands and the most complete chapter on hold'em odds in print. Over 400,000 copies sold! 224 pages, $16.95.

HOW TO PLAY WINNING POKER *by Avery Cardoza.* New and completely updated, this classic has sold more than 250,000 copies. Includes major new coverage on playing and winning tournaments, online poker, limit and no-limit hold'em, Omaha games, seven-card stud, and draw poker (including triple draw). Includes 21 essential winning concepts of poker, 15 concepts of bluffing, how to use psychology and body language to get an extra edge, plus information on playing online poker. 256 pages, $14.95.

KEN WARREN TEACHES TEXAS HOLD'EM *by Ken Warren.* This is a step-by-step comprehensive manual for making money at hold'em poker. 42 powerful chapters teach you one lesson at a time. Great practical advice and concepts with examples from actual games and how to apply them to your own play. Lessons include: starting cards, playing position, raising, check-raising, tells, game/seat selection, dominated hands, odds, and much more. This book is already a huge fan favorite and best-seller! 416 pages, $26.95.

OMAHA HIGH-LOW: Play to Win with the Odds *by Bill Boston.* Selecting the right hands to play is the most important decision you'll make in Omaha high-low. More than any other poker game, Omaha is driven by hand value. This is the *only* book that shows you the chances that every one of the 5,278 Omaha high-low hands has of winning the high end of the pot, the low end of it, and how often it is expected to scoop all the chips. You get all the vital tools needed to make critical preflop decisions based on the results of more than 500 million computerized hand simulations. You'll learn the 100 most profitable Omaha high-low starting cards, trap hands to avoid, 49 worst hands, 30 ace-less hands that can be played for profit, and the three bandit cards you must know to avoid unnecessarily losing hands. 248 pages, $19.95.

POKER TALK: Learn How to Talk Poker Like a Pro *by Avery Cardoza.* This fascinating and fabulous collection of colorful poker words, phrases, and poker-speak features more than 2,000 definitions. No longer is it enough to know how to walk the walk in poker, you need to know how to talk the talk! Learn what it means to go all in on a rainbow flop with pocket rockets and get it cracked by cowboys, put a bad beat on a calling station, and go over the top of a producer fishing for a gutshot to win a big dime. You'll soon have those railbirds wondering what *you* are talking about. 304 pages, $9.95.

HOW TO WIN AT OMAHA HIGH-LOW POKER *by Mike Cappelletti.* Clearly written strategies and powerful advice shows the essential winning strategies for beating Omaha high-low poker! This money-making guide includes more than 60 hard-hitting sections on Omaha. Players learn the rules of play, best starting hands, strategies for the flop, turn, and river, how to read the board for both high and low, dangerous draws, and how to beat low-limit tournaments. Includes odds charts, glossary and low-limit tips. 304 pgs, $19.95.

THE CHAMPIONSHIP SERIES
POWERFUL BOOKS YOU MUST HAVE

CHAMPIONSHIP HOLD'EM TOURNAMENT HANDS by T. J. Cloutier & Tom McEvoy. An absolute must for hold'em tournament players. Two legends show you how to become a winning tournament player at both limit and no-limit hold'em games. Get inside their heads as they think their way through the correct strategy at 57 limit and no-limit starting hands. Cloutier and McEvoy show you how to use skill and intuition to play strategic hands for maximum profit in real tournament scenarios and how 45 key hands were played by champions in turnaround situations at the WSOP. Gain tremendous insights into how tournament poker is played at the highest levels. 368 pages, $29.95.

CHAMPIONSHIP HOLD'EM SATELLITE STRATEGY by Brad Daugherty & Tom McEvoy. Every year satellite players win their way into the $10,000 WSOP buy-in event and emerge as millionaires or champions. You can too! Learn from two world champions, the specific, proven strategies for winning almost any satellite. Covers the 10 ways to win a seat at the WSOP, how to win limit hold'em and no-limit hold'em satellites, one-table satellites, online satellites, and the final table of super satellites. Includes a special chapter on no-limit hold'em satellites! 320 pages, $29.95.

CHAMPIONSHIP TOURNAMENT POKER by Tom McEvoy. Enthusiastically endorsed by more than five world champions, this is a *must* for every player's library. McEvoy lets you in on the secrets he has used to win millions of dollars in tournaments and the insights he has learned competing against the best players in the world. Packed solid with winning strategies for 11 games with extensive discussions of 7-card stud, limit hold'em, pot and no-limit hold'em, Omaha high-low, re-buy, half-and-half tournaments, satellites, and includes strategies for each stage of tournaments. 416 pages, $29.95.

HOW TO WIN NO-LIMIT HOLD'EM TOURNAMENTS by Tom McEvoy & Don Vines. Learn the basic concepts of tournament strategy and how to win big by playing small buy-in events, graduate to medium and big buy-in tournaments, adjust for short fields, huge fields, and slow and fast-action events. Plus how to win online no-limit tournaments. You'll also learn how to manage a tournament bankroll and get tips on table demeanor for televised tournaments. See actual hands played by finalists at WSOP and WPT championship tables with card pictures, analysis and useful lessons from the play. 376 pages, $29.95.

POKER TOURNAMENT TIPS FROM THE PROS by Shane Smith. Essential advice from poker theorists, authors, and tournament winners on the best strategies for winning the big prizes at low-limit rebuy tournaments. Learn the best strategies for each of the four stages of play—opening, middle, late and final—how to avoid 26 potential traps, advice on rebuys, aggressive play, clock-watching, inside moves, top 20 tips for winning tournaments, and more. Advice from McEvoy, Caro, Malmuth, Ciaffone, others. 160 pages, $19.95.

NO-LIMIT TEXAS HOLD'EM: The New Player's Guide to Winning Poker's Biggest Game by Brad Daugherty & Tom McEvoy. For experienced limit players who want to play no-limit or rookies who have never played before, two world champions give readers a crash course in how to join the elite ranks of million-dollar, no-limit hold'em tournament winners and cash game players. You'll learn the four essential winning skills: how to evaluate the strength of a hand, how to determine the amount to bet, how to understand opponents' play, and how to bluff and when to do it. 74 game scenarios and two unique betting charts for tournament play and sections on essential principles and strategies, show you how to get to the winners circle. Special section on beating online tournaments. 288 pages, $24.95.

CARO'S PRO POKER TELLS
$59.95 Two-Video VHS Set
$49.95 DVD
This video is a powerful scientific course on how to use your opponents' gestures, words and body language to read their hands and win all their money. These carefully guarded poker secrets, filmed with 63 poker notables, will bring your game to the next level. It reveals when opponents are bluffing, when they aren't, and why. Knowing what your opponent's gestures mean, and protecting them from knowing yours, gives you a huge winning edge. Says two-time World Champion Doyle Brunson: "Mike Caro's research will revolutionize poker!" Prepare to be astonished!

CARO'S POWER POKER SEMINAR
$39.95 VHS 62 Minutes
This powerful video shows you how to win big money using the little-known concepts of world champion players. This advice will be worth thousands of dollars to you every year, and even more if you're a big money player! After 15 years of refusing to allow his seminars to be filmed, Caro presents entertaining but serious coverage of his long-guarded secrets. The most profitable poker advice ever put on video.

CARO'S MAJOR POKER SEMINAR
$24.95 VHS 60 Minutes
Caro's poker advice in VHS format. Based on the inaugural class at Mike Caro University of Poker, Gaming and Life strategy. The material given on this tape is based on many fundamentals introduced in Caro's works and is prepared in such a way that reinforces concepts old and new. Caro's style is easy-going but intense with key concepts stressed and repeated. This tape will improve your play.

CARO'S PROFESSIONAL POKER REPORTS
Mike Caro, the foremost authority on poker strategy, psychology, and statistics, has put together three powerful insider poker reports. Each report is centered around a daily mission, with you, the reader, concentrating on adding one weapon per day to your arsenal. These highly focused reports are designed to take you to a new level at the tables. Theoretical concepts and practical situations are mixed together for fast in-depth learning in these concise courses. *Caro's Professional Reports* are very popular among good players.

11 Days to 7-Stud Success. Bluffing, playing and defending pairs, different strategies for the different streets, analyzing situations—lots of information within. One advantage is gained each day. A quick and powerful method to 7-stud winnings. Essential. Signed, numbered. $19.95.

12 Days to Hold'Em Success. Positional thinking, playing and defending against mistakes, small pairs, flop situations, playing the river, are just some sample lessons. Guaranteed to make you a better player. Very popular. Signed, numbered. $19.95.

Professional 7-Stud Report. When to call, pass, and raise, playing starting hands, aggressive play, 4th and 5th street concepts, lots more. Tells how to read an opponent's starting hand, plus sophisticated advanced strategies. Important revision for serious players. Signed, numbered. $19.95.

POWERFUL POKER SIMULATIONS
A MUST FOR SERIOUS PLAYERS WITH A COMPUTER!
IBM compatible CD ROM Win 95, 98, 2000, NT, ME, XP

These incredible full color poker simulations are the best method to improve your game. Computer opponents play like real players. All games let you set the limits and rake and have fully programmable players, plus stat tracking, and Hand Analyzer for starting hands. MIke Caro, the world's foremost poker theoretician says, "Amazing... a steal for under $500... get it, it's great." Includes free phone support. "Smart Advisor" gives expert advice for every play!

1. TURBO TEXAS HOLD'EM FOR WINDOWS - $59.95. Choose which players, and how many (2-10) you want to play, create loose/tight games, and control check-raising, bluffing, position, sensitivity to pot odds, and more! Also, instant replay, pop-up odds, Professional Advisor keeps track of play statistics. Free bonus: Hold'em Hand Analyzer analyzes all 169 pocket hands in detail and their win rates under any conditions you set. Caro says this "hold'em software is the most powerful ever created." Great product!

2. TURBO SEVEN-CARD STUD FOR WINDOWS - $59.95. Create any conditions of play; choose number of players (2-8), bet amounts, fixed or spread limit, bring-in method, tight/loose conditions, position, reaction to board, number of dead cards, and stack deck to create special conditions. Features instant replay. Terrific stat reporting includes analysis of starting cards, 3-D bar charts, and graphs. Play interactively and run high speed simulation to test strategies. Hand Analyzer analyzes starting hands in detail. Wow!

3. TURBO OMAHA HIGH-LOW SPLIT FOR WINDOWS - $59.95. Specify any playing conditions, including betting limits, number of raises, blind structures, button position, aggressiveness/passiveness of opponents, number of players (2-10), types of hands dealt, blinds, position, board reaction, and specify flop, turn, and river cards! Choose opponents and use provided point count or create your own. Statistical reporting, instant replay, pop-up odds high speed simulation to test strategies, amazing Hand Analyzer, and much more!

4. TURBO OMAHA HIGH FOR WINDOWS - $59.95. Same features as above, but tailored for Omaha High only. Caro says program is "an electrifying research tool...it can clearly be worth thousands of dollars to any serious player. A must for Omaha High players."

5. TURBO 7 STUD 8 OR BETTER - $59.95. Brand new with all the features you expect from the Wilson Turbo products: the latest artificial intelligence, instant advice and exact odds, play versus 2-7 opponents, enhanced data charts that can be exported or printed, the ability to fold out of turn and immediately go to the next hand, ability to peek at opponent's hand, optional warning mode that warns you if a play disagrees with the advisor, and automatic mode that runs up to 50 tests unattended. Tough computer players vary their styles for a great game.

6. TOURNAMENT TEXAS HOLD'EM - $39.95

Set-up for tournament practice and play, this realistic simulation pits you against celebrity look-alikes. Tons of options let you control tournament size with 10 to 300 entrants, select limits, ante, rake, blind structures, freezeouts, number of rebuys, and competition level of opponents. Pop-up status report shows how you're doing vs. the competition. Save tournaments in progress to play again later. Additional feature allows quick folds on finished hands.

Order Toll-Free 1-800-577-WINS or www.cardozapub.com